Three Hundred Zeroes

Lessons of the heart on the Appalachian Trail

By Dennis R. Blanchard
(Also Known As "K-One")

Three Hundred Zeroes

Lessons of the heart on the Appalachian Trail

Dennis R. Blanchard

For information address inquiries to:

Three Hundred Zeroes
PO Box 18364
Sarasota, Florida 34276

Unless noted otherwise, all artwork and photography was created by the author.

Published in Sarasota, Florida

Email Contact:
Dennis@threehundredzeroes.com

Visit our website at: threehundredzeroes.com
Or the blog at: blog.threehundredzeroes.com

ISBN-10   1450557465
ISBN-13/EAN-13   9781450557467

First Edition V1.0.h
February 2010

To Tom, I miss you brother.

Disclaimer

This is a true account of the author's two-year venture along the Appalachian Trail. Some of the names and places, and the details of their encounters have been changed to protect their privacy.

Part I

Chapter 1 - Florida

In the Beginning

Have you ever dreamt about doing something totally foolish, something so absurd that perhaps you were afraid to tell anyone except possibly those closest to you? I harbored such a secret for most of my adult life — I secretly wanted to hike the Appalachian Trail [A.T.] from Georgia to Maine.

Then one Sunday morning, Jane, my wife and long-suffering confidant of 32 years said, "Honey, look here in the paper, there's an invitation to a local Appalachian Trail Club [A.T.C.] meeting. I know you've always wanted to hike the Trail; why don't you look into it?" I wondered, "Is she trying to get rid of me?" Besides, I had an uncle go out for a walk in the nineteen-thirties and he never came back. It might not be wise to tempt family history.

The Appalachian Trail has always fascinated me. In the mid-sixties my brother Tom and I were in awe of a woman by the name of "Grandma Gatewood." She completed the Trail in 1955, 1960, and 1963. She was 67 years old on her first hike and 75 on her last! I suspect she may still be the oldest female thru-hiker. In contrast to today's hikers, she wore common Keds sneakers, carried an army blanket to sleep in, a plastic shower curtain for a tent, and an old raincoat bundled in a laundry bag slung over her shoulder. I'm certain today she would have been considered a homeless person, but she was actually an early Trail pioneer.

Stories of her epic hike on television and radio were especially notable, since Davy Crockett and Daniel Boone were popular Disney themes at that time. She brought to life a real connection with the Appalachian

Mountain region; she was living history. My brother and I found the concept of an adventure hike from Georgia to Maine irresistible.

However, the realities of life have a way of interfering with such plans. The Vietnam War, or "police action" as it was referred to at the time, was coming to a boil and my brother Tom and I were both caught up in it. I joined the Air Force in 1966; my brother, the Marines in 1968. We promised each other that after we completed our military duty we'd go off on a cross-country jaunt on our motorcycles and then hike the Appalachian Trail.

It was not to be. A few months after Tom joined the Marine Corps, he was killed in action in Vietnam. Our family was devastated. My other brother, Ernie, was seven years younger than I and it was almost more than he could bear. Like so many others that have lost loved ones in war, our lives would never be the same.

Even without Tom, the A.T. still haunted me. In 1973 I did ride my motorcycle coast-to-coast, but never attempted to hike the Trail. Now, 33 years later, Jane was laying the opportunity at my feet. I contemplated attending the meeting and finally convinced myself that it might be interesting. We had only lived in Sarasota, Florida for about a year, and even though I was already involved with several other organizations, there was room in my schedule for another activity. Newly retired, and new to the area, I figured if nothing else, it would be a great way to make new friends with like interests.

Oddly, I couldn't find much information on the Internet about the Club, so a few days before the meeting, I called the phone number listed in the paper and talked with a very pleasant-sounding woman, Grace, who invited me to attend and filled me in on the particulars of the meeting.

A.T.C.F.

The Appalachian Trail Club of Florida [A.T.C.F.] meeting is held in an old mansion at a park not far from where I live. The meetings are simple: bring a potluck dish to share, dinner, a short five-minute business meeting, and then end with a presentation by a speaker or some Club group activity.

I arrived with a sweet potato dish and was immediately taken aback by the appearance of the club members: they were all *old*. I thought to myself, "How could this be? Surely they don't hike!" I was 58 at the time and hadn't yet realized that I was just as *old*. There was a flurry of activity: people were setting up chairs and tables, and arranging food. I stood there for a few moments, feeling quite lost, and then out of nowhere Grace appeared, greeted me, took my dish, and made me feel very welcome.

She gave me a name sticker to wear and invited me to join her at her table. Without any discernable command, a line formed. As we worked our way through the assorted dishes on the tables, I quickly realized that this was actually an *eating* club that occasionally went out for a walk. More than a few were carrying some extra weight and I wondered what I was getting into.

I had somehow envisioned a group more like Sir Hillary returning from Everest, all buff and tanned, mumbling about some expedition to some place I couldn't pronounce. The room would smell of old leather, frayed ropes and sun-dried vegetation. I imagined a few old gents sitting around smoking pipes with a few stuffed animal heads on the wall and old maps laid out on a table. Instead, I was in the midst of a feeding frenzy! This group was seriously hungry. I noted at the end of the allotted hour there were merely a few crumbs left on the serving tables. Thus far nobody had even mentioned "hiking," just recipes and lots and lots of food.

Simultaneously, with military precision, everyone finished eating and started putting things away. Tables were folded up, the chairs were rearranged, and in a few short moments the room was transformed from a dining hall into a lecture hall.

Following a short business meeting, the evening's presentation began. I don't recall the speaker, but it was a computerized presentation and featured scenery from a hike in some impressive snow-covered mountains, perhaps in a foreign country. It was all a blur. I recall being so impressed with the audience participation, quick-witted humor, and a really friendly atmosphere. This was a fun bunch of people. I knew I would be back next month; by then maybe I would have worked off the five pounds I had gained that evening.

Over the subsequent months I became actively involved with the club. The club was very supportive and really did encourage the members to get out and hike the Appalachian Trail and support its maintenance. This was the club for me. I made the mistake of asking why they didn't have a website; the next thing I knew, I was their web master.

Gearing Up

In early 2006, with Jane's encouragement, I decided to celebrate turning sixty with a thru-hike (an end-to-end hike) of the Appalachian Trail in 2007. The first step was to purchase up-to-date equipment. Most of my hiking gear dated back to the '60s and '70s, the Paleozoic Era in terms of equipment advances. I had never really done an extended hike of more than a few weeks. That spring I had an opportunity to travel to New England, so I went to L.L. Bean in Freeport, Maine. Like a kid in a candy store, I scurried around, quickly picking up most of the items on my shopping list. Fortunately, when I was stuck making a decision, the knowledgeable staff reliably guided me to the most expensive equipment. For some odd reason most of the smaller equipment was priced at $49.95. It didn't seem to matter what it was. A stove, long underwear, a package of socks, water filters, hats, etc.: they all came in at $49.95. I fantasized that the U.S. Mint was printing $49.95 bills and that was the only currency the store would accept. If I picked up, say, a penknife that was $17.95, the clerk would squint at it as if it were a lizard that had crawled into the rack by mistake. It was obvious *that* knife was for the tourists. I was, after all, a thru-hiker; a $49.95 knife was the only knife for someone of my stature.

The big-ticket items, the backpack for example, could cost hundreds of dollars (or many $49.95 bills). A staff member assured me that the more expensive packs would last the entire hike. Prior to this visit it had never occurred to me that a pack might not last the entire hike. I began to ponder: if the backpack may not last the duration of the hike, what about me? Why would a backpack not last that long? After all, it merely had to hang off my back all day long; *I* was doing all the work. I could see where shoes might show some wear, but the backpack? How much would *it* wear out? How much would *I* wear out?

I returned to Florida, inspired and pompous; I was a going to be a thru-hiker. In addition to what I had purchased at L.L. Bean, I had ordered a Hennessy™ Hammock. This was a gamble. There was considerable buzz in the hiker Blogs about using hammocks as opposed to tents. The modern camping hammock is quite an innovation. Like a standard hammock, it hangs between two points of attachment (trees, rock, posts, etc.) but it comes with a mosquito net sewn over the top of it and has a tent-like entrance at one end. It reminded me of those large Air Force cargo planes where the end opens and they drive vehicles in. With the hammock, you "back" into it, sit down, and then pull your feet up and slide in. It sounds technical, but it turns out to be rather pleasant, and is mastered readily.

The hammock comes with a fly (or tarp) that covers it to keep rain out. In all, it is quite a departure from standard tents and I felt a bit of a risk-taker deciding on it without ever sleeping in one, or even seeing one for that matter. On a trail such as the A.T. there are an infinite number of places to hang hammocks: not only trees, but also rocks, roots and poles. Finding good, flat, dry ground to put up a tent can often be challenging. Hammocks are also lighter than most tents, have no poles to break, and hang quickly. Once I was on the trail, there were a number of occasions where the other hikers expressed serious hammock envy.

The hammock also eliminated the need to carry a sleeping pad, reducing overall weight and bulk. Most hikers carry a sleeping pad to increase sleeping comfort on hard, rocky ground. The pads are either inflatable or compressible foam. They are bulky but not very heavy and most folks carry them outside their packs. They also use the same pad when sleeping in the numerous shelters along the A.T. The majority of the shelters have a flat, wooden floor for sleeping, and the pad really increases the comfort level. I chose not to carry the pad and save some weight, knowing that I might experience a few uncomfortable nights in shelters where I would be forced to stay in them.

So I had all of this impressive equipment, some of it quite high-tech and leaving me a bit puzzled as to how to use it. Being a guy, and not wanting to embarrass myself by asking questions, I opted for reading the user's manuals. Unfortunately, the majority of the equipment is made in China. Some things get lost in the translation such as the statement: "When using a hooker, be careful." Certainly seemed like good advice, whether on the trail or not, something my mother probably would have warned me about.

Not-So-Dry Run

It became obvious that it would be wise to try all this new equipment out on a trial run. I decided to return to New Hampshire later that summer and hike in the Pemigewasset Wilderness. This 71 square mile (184 km²) wilderness area is surrounded by the White Mountains, and is truly remote: no roads and *very* isolated. I promised myself that I would spend five days in the wilderness and test all these expensive newfangled gadgets and equipment.

After a short visit with my daughter, Áine, in Massachusetts, I drove north to the Kancamagus Highway in New Hampshire. I parked the van, loaded up all my gear, and took a deep breath. The day before my departure, my cousin Joyce had emailed me a photograph of four very large, hungry-looking black bears walking down a road and the caption said, "New Hampshire Street Gang." Now I was bravely going alone into that very same bear-infested territory with questionable ability, and a plethora of new and confusing modern technology — it was a bit unnerving.

I set out north on the trail towards the double peaks of Mt. Hancock. I was starting late in the day, but it was a fine day and I was in elevated spirits, because I was now actually going into the Great North woods for the first time in a very long time. I came to the intersection for the loop trail to the peaks and proceeded east. It was an enjoyable climb, but the sky was clouding over. I ascended the two peaks and started down the north peak. By now it was dusk, and as I neared the junction of the trail again, I encountered a young moose. We were both quite startled and it charged off into the woods with considerable bluster.

The wilderness area has a rule: no camping within 200 feet (61 m) of the trails. I had mixed emotions about this; the intent of the rule is to reduce environmental damage near the trails by spreading the damage over a wider area so the environment will recover quickly. However, what if I had some mishap or medical difficulty during the night? How quickly would I recover, provided anyone even knew I was in trouble?

Objection duly noted, I trudged off into the woods for the prescribed distance and selected a spot to set up camp for the night. It was now drizzling lightly and getting dark. Imprudently, I had never set up my hammock before, but in spite of that, it went up quickly and seemed an agreeable place to spend the evening. I cooked a meal on my new stove while sitting on a rock underneath the hammock to keep dry. The ground beneath the hammock was wet and swampy, with protruding rocks; but I was feeling quite smug about having a hammock, as opposed to a tent.

Figure 1: The first night sleeping in a hammock.

The rain began to fall in earnest, so there was little else to do but go to bed. I climbed into my *new* sleeping bag, in my *new* hammock, made a few notes in my *new* journal, and extinguished my *new* headlamp. The headlamp is extremely bright, like a battery- powered thermonuclear weapon; its brilliance is impressive! It was $69 so I knew it was something special, being more than the $49.95.

I now realized just how far I was removed from civilization. Without the light, it was dark, inky dark. I held my hand up in front of my face and could not see it at all. I took off my headlamp and hung it over a rope that runs the length of the hammock. The lamp has an intentionally cumbersome switch to turn it on and off, so that it doesn't accidentally get turned on while in the pack, draining the batteries. It draped over the rope in a position that I knew would allow me to quickly grab it in an emergency. I had already encountered the young moose earlier, so another encounter with a moose or something much worse was certainly a possibility. My plan was to shine the lamp and yell at the top of my lungs if an errant moose, bear or madman in a hockey mask showed up.

After making a few notes in my journal and getting comfortable, I dozed off into a very contented sleep listening to the rhythmic beat of the rain on the hammock. Being out in the deep woods was not so bad after all.

Long-distance hiking is often described as long periods of complete boredom, interrupted by moments of sheer terror. *Crash! Snap! Thump! Crunch!* About midnight I was shocked awake by the terrifying sounds of an extremely large animal charging through the underbrush. My sleepy mind was barely functioning; in milliseconds I realized that whatever it was, it was coming directly at me. Was it a moose? Bear? Tyrannosaurus Rex? I had no idea. I instinctively grabbed the hanging headlamp and executed my plan to shine it out into the wilderness, scream at the top of my lungs and hope that whatever it was would stop or change direction. If not, we'd be sharing a hammock. Trembling, I fumbled with the light switch, holding the light right next to my head. Finally the light flashed on. I screamed bloody murder — not to scare off the animal, as planned, but because the light was backwards and shining directly into my eyes, instead of out into the woods. It was like a million suns burning my eyeballs; I couldn't see a thing, and it hurt. I may have even worked on my tan as well.

Fortunately, my defensive maneuver, although awkwardly executed, did have the desired effect: the animal screeched to a halt. After a few moments it charged off to my left and went splashing through the nearby river. I'm certain it was a moose; I suspected that when it got to the other riverbank, it had a hearty laugh with its moose buddies about the screaming-glowing cocoon it had just seen hanging in the trees.

My heart raced. After significant time, I calmed down and took stock of the situation. The animal had turned aside. Thank goodness, I pictured myself being scooped up into its antlers like one of those personnel retrieval systems the Air Force uses where an individual on the ground is swooped up into a passing airplane overhead. I could potentially be hanging between its antlers for months, like some well-lit "Carmen Miranda" moose headpiece.

It was still very dark and my mind started to play games with me. I thought, "Wait a minute, if that moose was charging through the woods scared out of its wits, what was it running from?" I hardly slept the rest of the night, listening to every little "pop" and "snap" in the darkness. Fortunately, subsequent nights were much more peaceful.

I completed five and a half days in the wilderness area and became quite comfortable with being back in the woods again. The area was so remote that I had not encountered another human being. It rained all five days, which was actually a good thing; everything stayed dry. I came to trust my equipment in adverse weather and was satisfied that all worked as planned. In fact, during the last night on the trail, the region had a record-setting thunderstorm roll through and there was considerable damage. I came through shaken, but unscathed. I was now ready to tackle the Appalachian Trail!

Final Planning

The Trail is 2,176 miles (3502 km) in length, starting at Springer Mountain in Georgia and ending at Mount Katahdin in Maine. Most thru-hikers leave from Georgia in late winter, because for average hikers, this means walking for up to six months to arrive in Maine before the onset of severe winter conditions and the official October closing of Mt. Katahdin to hiking.

Initially I planned to set out in early March of 2007 from Springer Mountain in Georgia, but the more I researched options, the more I felt it would serve me better to do the right thing environmentally. Each year about three thousand enthusiasts set out to do a thru-hike from Georgia starting in late February through early May. They're known as "Northbounders," often abbreviated as "NOBO's." There are a few radicals that work outside of that time frame, but they are either very crazy, freezing in those mountains in the dead of winter, or very fast, attempting to finish the whole hike in the three summer months. Many of the college-age hikers take this high-speed approach. There's a much smaller number of hikers, known as "Southbounders," or "SOBO's," who start in Maine and head south, usually a few hundred a year, but that didn't appeal to me.

Since the main body of hikers shows up at Springer Mountain over a span of a few weeks in late winter, the Trail, campsites and shelters become extremely burdened. It is not unusual for fifteen or twenty people to start out on the same day. As they progress, they tend to camp in the same camping spots and shelters. Most campsites and shelters are not designed for that capacity. The Trail turns to the consistency of thick oatmeal with so many pounding feet. The shelters become exceedingly crowded, to overflowing; and vacant tent sites can be at a premium. Add to this equation the often dreadful weather of late winter, and the conditions can become formidable.

I decided that to ease this burden on the Trail (and myself); I would either Flip-Flop or Leapfrog hike. The Flip-Flop is becoming quite popular. A Flip-Flop hiker sets out from Georgia later, perhaps mid-April to mid-May, hikes to an intermediate point on the Trail, possibly Harpers Ferry, West Virginia, and then "flips" up to Mt. Katahdin in Maine, and hikes back to the "flipping point," thus covering the entire Trail in one year. This offers the hiker reasonable weather for most of the journey, but a disadvantage is leaving all of your new acquaintances made on the Trail since Georgia.

A Leap-Frog hiker, on the other hand, sets out from Georgia in April or May, hikes to perhaps Harpers Ferry, then jumps up to Southern Connecticut, hikes to Mt. Katahdin, then returns to fill in the missing piece between Connecticut and Harpers Ferry. The big advantage to this hike is that one can expect exceptionally nice weather for the entire hike. Of course the same friendship breakups exist for this method as well, and is exacerbated by leaving two groups of friends.

Camaraderie on the trail is significant. Bonding is serious amongst hikers, not unlike that of a military organization. You spend your day-to-day life together at mealtime, hitching rides, solving problems, sleeping, encountering animals, and sharing equipment. It's only natural that strong friendships form under these conditions.

Farewells

In March of 2007 my family and friends gave me a going-away party. I had the feeling they mostly wanted to get one last look at me, so they could remember what

I looked like before I disappeared forever. More than a few looked at me as if I was losing my mind.

Sarasota has a sizeable elderly population; a friend refers to Sarasota as "Geri-assic Park," or "God's waiting room." In Sarasota, most of the folks my age consider eighteen holes of golf a long walk, and that's using a golf cart; a short walk is to the bathroom. I suspect those that know me consider me an oddity because I rarely drive a vehicle and prefer to travel by bicycle whenever possible. It is not uncommon for me to ride 20-50 miles (30-80 km) a day running errands. Now I was going to do something even more primitive...walk. It wouldn't surprise me if there were bets on how many days or miles I would complete, or if my photo would end up on a milk carton.

Food, drink, and good conversation made for a wonderful party. I brought my backpack and did a public inventory of what was in it and how things worked. I had a set of ten-pound barbells in the bottom of the pack, and when I brought them out I explained that I was concerned that I would build up my legs on the hike and wanted to ensure that my arms wouldn't be neglected. Then I confessed, and explained that they were in there to simulate what the food and water would weigh. All told, the pack weighed 37 pounds.

After my presentation, my friend Dave got up and roasted me with a funny and creative speech about how my wife, Jane, might be feeling:

"As some of you may know, there is a help column in the local newspaper, the Herald-Tribune *called ANNIE'S MAILBOX. I recently saw a letter from a distraught wife about her husband. The situation sounds awfully familiar to me. I quote:*

"Dear Annie:

I really don't know what to do. I am hoping you can help me with my jerk of a husband who has decided to go off on a crazy six-month hike in the mountains. I will be stuck taking care of the house, paying the bills and looking after his damn motorcycle. He's always after me at home, if you know what I mean, so on top of everything else, I am concerned about what he will be like after spending all those months with deer. Some of them are awfully cute. What can I do?

Abandoned in Sarasota

Dear Abandoned:

My suggestion is to sell the house, sell the motorcycle, take all the money, and leave the bills for that jerk. I can only imagine what he has come in contact with after spending six months in the woods with deer! I would get as far away as you can, Dearie, and look for someone who likes to cuddle up, talk politics and breaks out in a sweat at the thought of hiking or riding a motorcycle!

Annie"

Following Dave, another friend, "Meigs," a skilled Toastmaster, did an impromptu speech about my hike. She observed that I did in fact ride my bicycle everywhere, and on occasion drove, but she had "never seen me walking anywhere, not a step!" I didn't let on at the moment, but I began thinking that she was right, I really didn't walk that much; maybe she was onto something. Suppose I *did* need to walk more to build up for the hike? What if the bike riding merely built muscles but didn't build them in a fashion that would prove useful? This question would haunt me until I actually got on the Trail and realized it is impossible to train for such a hike.

Not So Fast

I settled on a starting date of May 16, 2007. However, my hike nearly ended even before I had put one step on the Trail! A month before my planned start date, I worked several days laying ceramic tiles in our home. I spent many hours on rubber kneepads. I wore short pants and the rubber straps on the pads would "creep" up my leg and tighten, dangerously cutting off circulation to my lower legs. By the time the job was completed my ankles were starting to turn odd colors and went numb. The next day my doctor examined me and concluded I had done something similar to what drunks occasionally experience. The medical nickname for it is "Saturday Night Palsy." A drunk may fall asleep in a hard-backed chair with an arm slung over the back of the chair. When he awakens, after many hours, the nerve in his arm has been pinched and he loses control of his hand for some period, in severe cases, permanently. Both of my feet had experienced a similar symptom, particularly the left one. The doc prescribed a medication for it and the prognosis was that I would recover, but he said it may take some time, and some of the damage could be permanent. Great, I was going off on a hiking adventure and my feet were numb!

Gradually, over the subsequent weeks, the right foot did improve dramatically; however, I had lost about 20 percent of the control of the left foot. I ended up with something called "drop foot." It would "drop" when I walked because I had lost some control of it.

One side effect of the medicine the doctor prescribed for the swelling was possible "angina-like events." Sure enough, after a few days taking the medication, the swelling did go down, but for three days in a row I had "angina events." This in turn led to a series of heart stress tests. Nothing was found, and so I was given a clean bill of health and told I could go on my walk. I was ecstatic! Undaunted, I was going on my hike anyway, damn the torpedoes.

Chapter 2 - Georgia

Good-bye Sweetheart

A fellow hiker, Nancy, from our Trail club was driving to Pennsylvania for some hiking and agreed to drive me to Dahlonega, Georgia, near Springer Mountain on her way north. We both planned to stay the night at the Hiker Hostel, in Dahlonega, and the next day she'd continue on and I would at last be on the Trail. Before going to work, Jane drove me to the gas station where Nancy and I agreed to meet. I wasn't certain if Jane was having second thoughts about suggesting that I go hike the Trail; if she was, she didn't show it.

There were quick good-byes and then I piled into Nancy's Scion and off we drove. We had an uneventful trip to Dahlonega and arrived there shortly before dark. The road leading to the hostel was very serpentine and climbed to a dizzying altitude. Living in Florida, anything taller than our local landfill seems like the Alps. It felt great to arrive at the Hiker Hostel and know that the adventure was close at hand.

We settled in and shortly Joshua, one of the owners, arrived with another hiker, Bill who he had picked up at the Atlanta airport. Ironically, Bill lives only a few miles from my home in Sarasota and belongs to the same A.T. club that I do, though I couldn't recall previously meeting him. Bill was doing a long section hike, from Springer Mountain to Fontana Dam, North Carolina. I'm a retired electrical engineer, he is a retired engineer from another discipline, and shares many of the same interests I do. He told me that he likes to get out every year and do a portion of the Appalachian Trail, his long-term goal being to eventually hike the whole thing, a section at a time. We would end up hiking together for many miles.

The Hiker Hostel is a perfect jumping off point. Situated in the foothills near Springer Mountain, it had the feel of outdoor adventure. Joshua and Leigh, the hostel hosts, knew what a newbie or experienced hiker needed, and made us feel quite at home. They offer a very nice bunk, breakfast, Internet service, and a spacious sitting room for a very reasonable price.

Leigh was off on a business trip so Joshua was running things. Bill and I sat and talked with him at length about hiking the Trail and he graciously answered any questions we had. Joshua convinced Bill and me to avoid hiking up the access Trail that goes through Amicalola State Park. It is a 7-mile (11 km) climb that is challenging and doesn't count as part of the Appalachian Trail. We agreed to a shuttle the next morning; we were both anxious to get onto the Trail.

As I sat on the porch at the hostel that evening, I couldn't help thinking how much my brother would have loved this. In his honor I was carrying his Purple Heart Medal with me. As I held it in my hand I promised myself that I would do this in his memory. I wrapped the medal in a sturdy plastic bag to protect it and tucked it into my belly bag. Then my mind wandered—should I really be leaving my wonderful wife alone for such a long time? Is this really the right thing to do, or is this something that should be left to more youthful folks? Would I become romantically involved with a deer, as Dave insinuated in his Dear Annie letter?

Starting Line

Early the next morning, in an old beat-up Suburban, we snaked our way up the winding dirt road to the parking lot near the summit of Springer Mountain. The lot was empty. We exited the vehicle and Bill and I stood together while Joshua took our photos. I was feeling quite the hiker until Joshua deflated my balloon. Looking at my pack, he kindly and gently asked if I would appreciate help adjusting the straps. Even though I considered myself an experienced hiker, my equipment knowledge was very outdated. The last pack I owned before purchasing this one for the A.T. was bought during the Nixon Administration.

My new pack is an internal frame design as opposed to the external frame packs I was familiar with. With the old external-frame packs most of the weight bearing is on the shoulder straps; the newer internal-frame models have a wide padded belt that actually supports the weight on the hips. Of course, I had the straps all wrong, which was obvious to a truly experienced hiker such as Joshua. Meekly I succumbed to his adjustments. He tugged and pulled; I felt like one of those young ladies in the eighteen hundreds having a corset fitting. At least he didn't put his foot on my chest and pull the straps. Finally everything was adjusted properly. Thank goodness, or surely I would have had shoulder and back problems.

Joshua departed and the two of us stood there in solitude for a few moments. A few birds sang in the distance; everything was still. We were truly alone. This was it, no turning back now. Even if we did, it was a long walk home.

The parking lot is situated such that hikers have to backtrack on the A.T. for 0.9 miles (1.4 km) to the summit of Springer. We ambled up to the summit under gray skies.

The Appalachian Trail is easy to follow, it is marked with a white "blaze" every few hundred feet. The blaze is a two-inch by six-inch white rectangle. Connecting trails use a blue blaze and other major trails use an assortment of other colors.

We found the rock outcropping with the bronze plate that designates the spot as the beginning of the Appalachian Trail. After taking each other's pictures, we found the storage drawer on the side of the rock that contains the sign-in register and signed in. We were *now* officially Thru-hikers!

Figure 2: Springer Mountain, Day 1.

Trail Names

Hikers usually go by some moniker or trail name, instead of using their actual name. Bill told me his trail name is "Blitz" and then explained that it was meant to be humorous, because he is anything but fast on the trail. I told him my chosen trail name is "K1YPP," which is a ham radio call letter that was issued to me by the

Federal Communications Commission [FCC] back in 1962. Over time the other hikers shortened that to "K1," or "K-One."

Trail names serve an important purpose for there may be 10 "Bills" or "Jennifers" hiking the Trail in any given year, but rarely will there be more than one "Aardvark" or "Swooping Gull." The moniker individualizes the identity of a hiker and readily identifies him or her to all the other hikers without explanation. A few names I heard were light and whimsical: "Happy Feet," "Splendora," "Sunshine," and "Blissful;" others were very descriptive: "Old Buzzard," "AquaMaria," "Thinker," and "Persistent." Some of the more comical ones bring some interesting mental images: "Dances With Beers," "Barking Spider," and "Drunken Dragon." More than a few are on the dark side and made me wonder what they were thinking: "C4" (a military plastic explosive), "Captain Blood," "Cowboy Killer," "Serial Killer," "Drifter," "Pond Scum," "Alabama Outlaw," "357 Magnum," and "Thought Criminal." I was beginning to think I might be walking through an Agatha Christie mystery.

Blitz and I are the same age and both love the outdoors. As we hiked along we talked about many things and found we had much in common. The terrain was reasonably easy and we made decent time getting to the first shelter, the Stover Creek Shelter. We stopped for a brief break, since it was only two miles from the start and too early in the day to make camp. At 7.6 miles (12 km) we came to the Hawk Mountain Shelter. Our neophyte bodies were tiring and ready to stop for the night. The air was cooling and the shelter was inviting. There were even a few bags of unopened hiker food there and some reading material. There was also a brand new Bible on the shelf; oddly, at the next shelter we would see *two* new Bibles.

Figure 3: Gooch Mountain Shelter, typical of southern shelters.

Blitz was hiking without a tent, something I found curious. He planned to stay in shelters all the way to Fontana Dam. If it had been earlier in the year, when most of the thru-hikers start, he may have had trouble. Consequently, we were starting in mid-May and the traffic was light so it wasn't a problem. Since we were the only ones there, I figured, just to be sociable, I would stay in the shelter as well, even though I didn't have a sleeping mat. I still had plenty of body fat and it provided adequate cushioning. We cooked our evening meal and laid out our sleeping gear for the night.

As I did throughout the trip, I kept my hiking pole very near me. The pole isn't exactly a weapon but I figured it would be all I would have to defend myself against an angry bear or chipmunk. I took care to hang my backpack on a sidewall inside the shelter. Many of the later shelters had strings suspended from the rafters with old tuna cans attached to provide a "block" so that the mice couldn't climb down and get into the packs. The string usually had a piece of stick at the bottom to loop the pack handle over. It was very effective; I never had damage from mice anywhere on the hike, but I did see plenty of damage to those that didn't exercise caution. On this night, since there were no stringed hangers I left all the zippers and pockets open to allow mice access to the bag. I had heard that if I didn't do this they would just chew their way in. Additionally, to protect my food from the mice and bears, I used the steel bear cables in the trees outside to hang the food.

About midnight I was awakened to the sound of squealing mice. I shined my headlamp around the shelter; there were at least 30 mice visible, as well as the two or three in my backpack that were fighting over something and making all the noise. There were so many mice it looked like a scene from a Disney movie! I grabbed my hiking pole and, quite un-Disney- like, gave the pack a few whacks. The mice abandoned their squabble and I went back to sleep for a while. This scenario repeated itself several times. In the morning I asked Bill if all the noise bothered him and he asked, "*What* noise?"

After such a disturbing night I decided I would prefer sleeping in my hammock and for the rest of the hike did so. Only on a few rare occasions, when I was either very tired or the weather was just terrible, did I sleep in shelters. The mice rule the shelters, and if there are no mice, that's because there are lots of snakes eating the mice...take your pick.

Hamming it up

I've been an amateur radio operator since I was fourteen years old. Radio technology has shrunk to where it is feasible to carry electronic communications on the hike, as is evidenced by all the cell phones and Ipods that hikers carry. Amateur radio, or ham radio as it is more commonly known, is well-suited to hiking. The ham radio short-wave frequencies tend to travel over and around mountains and through trees; while cell phone frequencies act much like a beam of light and don't penetrate trees well or go over obstacles. Cell phone towers are placed where it is economically feasible: near population centers and highways. Areas with very sparse population have little cell phone coverage. Practically every town and county nationwide has an active amateur radio population so there is usually someone available to help with an emergency. On those great spans of the Trail where there is no cell phone service, an amateur can always rely on ham radio communications.

I was carrying two radios; one was a walkie-talkie that communicates on VHF and has a typical range of 20-50 miles (30-80 km) depending on terrain and location. Physically, it resembles a cell phone. The other was a homemade radio that operates Morse code on the short-wave bands. I learned Morse code when I was only thirteen. Short-wave signals can quite literally travel around the world even at low power levels, which in this case was about 1 Watt, less than used by many flashlights.

I spent considerable time designing and building the radio for the trip. Even though there is commercially available equipment, I took making a radio just for the A.T. as a personal challenge. My goal was to build a radio that weighed less than three pounds. The complete radio ended up just over three pounds, and that was without batteries. Since it required an external antenna, I built an antenna that consisted of two lengths of wire thirty-three feet long, one to throw up into a tree, and the other to lay out as a "ground wire."

My goal was to make contacts with other radio amateurs from each of the fourteen states the A.T. traverses. This didn't seem especially challenging; after all, I would be out there for many months, how hard could it be?

My first attempt to make contacts was at Neels Gap on the fourth day of the hike. Gaps are relatively low spots in the mountains where trails or roads pass through. In the North they are referred to as *notches* and sometimes *passes*. Neels Gap has the distinction of being the only place where the Trail actually goes through a building. The Gap also has an outfitter (merchant selling outdoors equipment), a restaurant, and a hikers' hostel. Blitz and I were staying at the hostel and we arrived early enough in the day so that I was able to get on the air.

Figure 4: Neels Gap. The trail actually passes through the building, note the white blaze.

In mid-afternoon I set up the station on a picnic table behind the main building, threw the antenna wire into a tree, and had the radio on in no time. I tuned around the forty-meter shortwave band and found it alive with signals from all over the country and Europe. However, as often as I called to various stations, no one would reply. For some inexplicable reason they weren't hearing me. My location was excellent, high altitude can really add to a radio's effectiveness, and everything seemed to be in good working order. I tried for two hours without success.

All excited, Blitz came out looking for me. A troop of Boy Scouts was due to arrive shortly and would completely fill the hostel, destroying any peace and quiet for us. The Neels Gap management had graciously offered to shuttle us to an off-site cabin they have for employees. There were two other hikers, Dave and Bob, that had arrived and they were going to the cabin as well. We scrambled to gather up our gear and get out to the van.

The four of us hit it off right away. Dave and Bob were also retired engineers and the same age as we. The two of them were real characters! They had been section hiking the A.T. for 41 years and in just a few days they planned to hike southbound to Springer Mountain and finish the Trail. One of them joked that they might get to the parking lot just before the finish and leave that 0.9-mile (1.4 km) section to the summit for next year.

All of our conversations had an engineering hue, regardless the topic. I brought up the matter of seeing new Bibles in the shelters and Dave and Bob confirmed they had seen many Bibles as well. The conversation evolved into a fairly novel number-series concept.

In the world of mathematics and engineering there are number sequences that prove useful and interesting for solving things, such as the simple series 2, 4, 8, 16... (It doubles each increment) and the Fibonacci series: 0, 1, 1, 2, 3, 5, 8, 13... where each number in the series is the sum of the two previous numbers, out to infinity. The Fibonacci sequence occurs in nature everywhere, from the number of petals in flowers, to seashell development. Dave and Bob theorized that there is an A.T. series: a young man sets out to hike a section of the A.T. with fifty Bibles. His goal is to leave one at each shelter he passes. The weather is hot; the pack is heavy with fifty Bibles, causing him to struggle up the hills. At the first shelter he leaves a Bible, wipes his brow, and continues on to the second shelter. To reduce the weight, he leaves two Bibles, realizing that his goal is harder to achieve than he ever imagined. It is so difficult that by the third shelter he leaves all 47 remaining Bibles; hence 1, 2, 47, the A.T. number series!

Be Prepared

The next morning a Neels Gap staff member transported us back to the hostel and we rejoined the Trail. The Scout troop was still there in force, but they didn't seem a very merry bunch. Some of the boys truly did not seem to enjoy each other's company, and to make things worse, neither did some of the adult leaders. Two of the adults were confidentially overheard saying, "If we walk quickly we'll leave that old buzzard and his kid behind; they'll find their way back here anyway and we can get on with the hike." So much for "Be prepared" and "Teamwork." It turns out their plan was to hike quickly and leave a whole chunk of the troop behind so they could "enjoy" their hike. Blitz and I were glad we didn't stay in the hostel that night; they did not seem a cheery group. Additionally, their packs were huge and the room would have been very crowded.

I encountered this oversized-scout-pack phenomenon throughout the Trail. Scout troops tend to carry enough equipment to support an infantry regiment for months even though they typically hike for a long weekend or at most a week. Weight is the single most important factor to consider on a long-distance hike. Agility, endurance, comfort and overall well-being depend on having as light a pack as is reasonable. This is especially true in the most southerly and northerly sections of the A.T., which are the most mountainous. I recall meeting up with three young Scouts that had somehow separated from their main troop and were lost. As we had lunch with them at a shelter I was looking over their packs. I was amazed to observe complete cooking kits that included several pots, iron frying pans and dishes, a knife-fork-and-spoon, military entrenching tools (folding shovels that can also be used as a pick), fold-up chairs, propane stoves (such as those used at a family outing), and many changes of clothing, most of it way warmer than needed.

While these Scouts were perhaps 14 and weighed around 110 pounds, their packs weighed around 70 pounds. As a rule of thumb, the pack should weigh about twenty percent of one's body weight, yet these young men's burdens were about sixty-five percent!

Consequently they looked like they were in "hiker hell". It appeared that the only thing this hiking experience taught these Scouts was that hiking was way too much work! No wonder the ones we saw at Neels Gap were so cranky. After lunch two adult leaders showed up looking for the lost lads. I noticed that the leaders had left their packs somewhere to pursue the search; I can only imagine how heavy *their* packs were. I wondered if either of them was carrying fifty Bibles.

Neels Gap Outfitters offers a free service to hikers: pack inspections. They are uniquely situated several days from the start of the Trail, just far enough for those with a pack that is too heavy to really appreciate how overweight it is. The experienced staff goes through the pack with each hiker, making suggestions on ways to reduce overall weight. According to their website, each year they inspect upwards of 500 packs, shipping home as much as 9,000 pounds of equipment that hikers just don't need. Additionally, they pick up some business replacing iron frying pans with titanium pans, but the reality is that these hikers would never make it to Mt. Katahdin in Maine with these massive packs.

A few days beyond Neels Gap I met a thru-hiker named "First Timer." He was a cavalier mid-twenty year old. First Timer was strongly built, talkative and seemed to be totally enjoying himself. His trail name was well chosen, he'd done no research before his hike; he just packed up and left. First Timer confessed to a group of us at the shelter that at Neels Gap he'd shed 38 pounds of pack weight. After removing three pairs of long pants, sweatshirts, books, 47 ballpoint pens, and Lord knows what else, his pack was down to a still-heavy, 42 pounds from over 70+ originally.

I asked him why so many pens. First Timer said that he'd started out with 50 pens his Mom gave him and used one to write with and gave two away before they convinced him to dump the rest at Neels Gap. I was hysterical, for he was actual living proof of the A.T. series: 1, 2, 47...! Dave and Bob would have been thrilled to know their A.T. series theory was proven correct.

Bears

About a mile before we arrived at the Low Gap Shelter, Blitz and I had our first bear encounter. It was a yearling, near the Trail, but when it saw us it charged up a very steep hill and stopped to spy on us. We had been seeing bear scat along the Trail but this was our first actual bear contact.

That night I hung my hammock very near the shelter, just off to one side. Several others decided to "cowboy camp" without a tent and just sleep on the ground with a ground cover and sleeping bag. It was a beautiful night to do so, cool and clear. About 3 a.m. there was a banjo-like, "BOOOIIIING" as something tripped over one of the support strings that keep the hammock steady. The moon was brilliant that evening and as I peered out through the mosquito net I could see the distinct form of a young black bear; I'm fairly certain it was the same one we had encountered earlier. He had tripped and tumbled and was recovering from the fall when I spotted him. He then continued on around the camp sniffing and looking for any food remains. He walked right by my sleeping friends, not aware they were being studied by a black bear. Finding nothing of interest, he left the camp. In the morning no one believed me when I told them about our intruder.

The next day Blitz and I made it to the Tray Mountain Shelter in good time and decided that it was too nice a day to stop so early, so we continued on another four miles and decided to cowboy camp at Sassafras Gap. It was a nice spot for a camp, the water source was just to the east about a quarter mile and there were a few areas just off the Trail where it was obvious others had camped before us. The campsites were surrounded by tall growths of blackberry bushes giving a sense of being secluded from the Trail. Two young college students were already there, local Georgia boys, Alan and John Scott. We had been playing leapfrog with them for a few days. Blitz and I hung our bear bags over the Trail using his rope. The boys hung theirs at another spot also near the Trail but south of ours. We all cowboy camped and hit the hay early, being tired from the day's walk.

At midnight, much like in my trial hike in New Hampshire, I was shocked awake by a large *CRASH!* Blitz was also wide-awake. We lit our headlamps and couldn't see what caused the noise but the calamitous nature of it convinced us it was a bear. With a trembling voice Blitz suggested that we try barking like dogs, since they hunt bears in the South using dogs. We barked. The bear charged through the underbrush with a tremendous amount of crashing and crunching, and disappeared to the west. Blitz went right back to sleep; I was still too shaken after that close encounter. It was obvious that the bear had been only a few feet away and we were unable to see it. I lay there listening to every little crack and pop in the dark of the night. About 2 a.m. I heard another crashing and crunching coming from the water source trail and this time the animal sounded considerably larger. I couldn't see it at first. It was moving big, heavy logs looking for grubs and anything else that might live in the dead logs. It was like a scene from Jurassic Park, the taller bushes and blackberry bushes were tossing about and the smaller trees were trembling. All the while Blitz and the two young guys never stirred. I didn't dare make a sound, but finally couldn't take it any longer and put on my headlamp. I could just make out the outline of the bear; it was huge! I used my better judgment and decided against barking; imagining this bear might have dog tags in its scat. Unwavering, it worked its way up to the Trail, sniffed around where the boys hung their bear bags, then reversed direction and headed back down the same trail it had come up.

Then, about 3 a.m., I heard another bear coming from the west. I concluded that this was the same one we had barked at earlier because it passed around us in a large swath, avoiding where we were, and headed east. I couldn't sleep the rest of the night. It was amazing that as I lay there I observed all sorts of small animals traveling through where we were camped. They seemed to know we were sleeping and disregarded us. I saw fox, raccoon, rats, mice (of course), and a few animals that I couldn't quite make out in the dark. It was a veritable animal highway and we were sleeping right in the middle of it. I couldn't have been more astonished if a rhino had sauntered through.

In the morning I mentioned the bear encounters the night before to Alan and John Scott and they said that they had not heard a thing all night. I'm a sound sleeper, but not that sound. I went down the access Trail about thirty feet and found where the first bear had created such a ruckus; an old dead tree stump about eight feet high had come all apart. Apparently the young bear had climbed up the rotted tree and it collapsed under its weight, and the whole thing had come crashing down.

Out of Gas

Mistakenly I had started the hike with a canister of stove fuel that was partially used on my earlier hike in New Hampshire. I had assumed, incorrectly, that I could easily replace it along the way. Neels Gap had plenty of canisters, but it didn't occur to me to replace it there. Sixty-seven miles from the start we arrived at Hiawassee, Georgia, and I went in search of a fuel canister. As accommodating as the hiker hotel was, they didn't have replacements. I walked around for a good part of the afternoon checking every hardware and department store. I even found an outfitter. Unfortunately, "outfitter" means different things to different people. The outfitter in Hiawassee is merely a sporting goods store for fishing and hunting. They had every conceivable fishing pole and gun imaginable, but no hiker-sized fuel canisters. They did have the large Coleman canisters, which weigh several pounds and are fine for home cookouts, blowtorches or automobile campsites, but not hiking.

Senior Moment

To lighten the pack, I routinely tore out the completed sections of the guidebook printed by The Appalachian Long Distance Hikers' Association. Somehow, in Hiawassee I erroneously managed to throw away the upcoming section while keeping the Georgia section I had already hiked. The hotel had four maps someone had left of the southern area of the Trail. I took them but again managed to send home the maps for the area I was about to hike and kept the maps for the area I had already covered; at least I was consistent. Senior moment? Fortunately the Trail is reasonably well-marked, and in the South one can hike without carrying much information. I did miss having the guidebook pages to help locate water, especially in the drought conditions I was hiking in.

It may seem silly to rip out pages of a book to save weight, but every ounce counts. Some take it to the extreme. I know one couple that even goes through all their clothing to remove the tags and extra buttons. At one shelter someone had left a paperback novel and all the margins surrounding the print had been removed. In Pennsylvania I ran into a fellow that was carrying a deck of playing cards that he had resized to just the corner of the card that showed the suit and number, creating a card deck that was about one inch by one inch. For those serious in cutting down the load, there are no limits.

Pains

The morning we left Hiawassee the hotel owner gave us a shuttle ride back to the trailhead. It was a beautiful morning and a great day for hiking. Going north, the Trail immediately starts to climb. As a rule I was a tad faster than Blitz, but that morning as we started the climb I was having angina pains similar to the ones I had in Florida. This couldn't be: they had checked me out and found nothing. I told him to go on ahead, I just hadn't warmed up enough and would see him shortly. I didn't say anything about the pain and after about fifteen minutes things cleared up and I was on my way.

Communications

I was nearing the North Carolina border and had not yet made my radio contacts from Georgia. As I hiked along from Neels Gap I rationalized that something must have come loose in the radio, because it functioned well before leaving Florida. At Low Gap Shelter I unpacked the radio and looked it over carefully. There is an adjustment knob that I built into it so that I could independently tune the receiver separately from the transmitter. Sometimes a radio station can be off-frequency from the desired transmitting frequency and require the operator to compensate for this difference. Somehow during the hike, the knob had dramatically slipped from where it was supposed to be, causing the radio to be off-frequency. Apparently that afternoon at Neels Gap was unsuccessful because I wasn't listening to where I was transmitting; if people were replying to me, I couldn't hear them.

After I readjusted the knob on the shaft to where I thought it belonged, I made contact with a station in Tennessee, Jim, W2VEC. His signal was weak, but at least things were working. I then had a contact with Rich, WA1SKQ, in Rhode Island. His signal was much stronger and we had a nice chat in Morse code. I was thrilled. I was communicating with a radio that I had conceived, built and was now carrying up the East Coast of the United States. Since only an engineer could really appreciate the significance of this, I didn't share my joy with the other hikers. I think most of them figured me to be a fringe lunatic that threw wires into trees and spent precious hiking time beating on a Morse code key.

North of the Border

Early on day ten, Blitz and I crossed our first state border, from Georgia to North Carolina. Make that one state down and thirteen more to go. The border is only 75 miles (120 km) from the start but it is a psychological victory that is difficult to describe. I believe it was the longest contiguous hike I had ever done, as it probably is for the majority of first-time thru-hikers. For me, there was no turning back now. In the Georgia section many hikers drop out, some even on the very first day. Many hikers come to the Trail with a romantic notion that this is merely a walk in the woods; no consideration is given to the difficulty, weather or other hardships that are encountered on such a hike. For this reason, this first state border crossing is so significant a personal victory.

Figure 5: Crossing the North Carolina/Georgia border.

Chapter 3 - North Carolina

New Friends

Often, when the Trail crosses state borders, coincidentally the terrain changes. Georgia-North Carolina was no exception. Just after the border crossing there is a substantial hill climb. It goes through boreal forest, yet the ground is covered in tall, thick grass, unlike anything Blitz and I had seen thus far. Thousands of grasshoppers were jumping everywhere; I felt like I was walking through popping popcorn. These critters made me conscious of my surroundings, since many snakes eat grasshoppers. When it comes to rattlesnakes and copperheads, the locals there have a saying that the "Third person gets bit." The theory is: the first person gets the snake's attention, the second person gets the snake aggravated, and the third person gets bit. There were only two of us, but I didn't feel like testing the theory.

At the top of the climb I came to a well-known landmark, the Gnarled Oak. This majestic tree is mostly in a prone position lying along the ground for maybe 30 feet and then swinging upward for about an equal distance, taking on the appearance of a contorted dragon's body, guarding the trail from intruders. The trunk is in an advanced stage of rot, and I suspect it will be gone in the not-too-distant future, but I was intrigued by its beauty and notoriety.

It was here that I hooked up with two other hikers: "Oorah" and "Promise Keeper." Oorah was an ex-Marine and since Marines are always chanting "Oo-rah, Oo-rah" during exercise he took that trail name. Promise Keeper confided that she was so named because she promised to

go on the hike. Promise Keeper is a registered nurse, so
with my chest pain incident, I thought it wise to not get
too far from her. Though they were closer to my age,
they had done like many of the younger hikers: sold
their farm, put everything in storage, and hit the trail.

Promise Keeper proved to me that women are tougher
than men. On several occasions I had seen her tending
to a serious blister on the back of Oorah's heel. He had
been complaining about it for some time. While hikers
often develop blisters early in the hike, their feet
typically toughen up and blisters become less of a
problem. For some hikers, blisters never cease. One
afternoon at the Blue Mountain Shelter, Promise Keeper
was sitting there in her bare feet, which were a mass of
blisters, perhaps a dozen, many quite serious. I was in
awe; never once did she complain. All the men sitting
around her were in a constant torrent of complaints.
Even though she had more serious blisters than they, I
never heard her whine. I came to realize that many of
the women on the Trail are very tough and most
complained very little.

On day eleven we arrived at the Big Spring shelter. Since
I had been unsuccessful in finding a propane fuel
canister in Hiawassee, I was cooking with Sterno,
fortunately having found a Sterno canister in the
Hiawassee hotel hiker box. Many of the hotels and
hostels along the Trail have "hiker boxes" where hikers
dump equipment and supplies they don't need so others
can pick them up. Sterno cooks much slower than a
pressurized propane canister, but it gets the job done. As
I was cooking, First Timer showed up. He noticed I was
using Sterno and asked why I wasn't using the canister
stove as he had seen me do in the past. I explained my
unsuccessful search in Hiawassee. He told me not to
worry; he had a spare and proceeded to unload his pack.
Even after disposing of almost 40 pounds of extra

weight at Neels Gap, he produced not only one spare canister, but five! These canisters weigh 12 ounces each, for a total combined weight of nearly four pounds. I asked him if he was planning on opening a trailside welding shop to repair broken backpack frames.

First Timer could sure get dirty. He would put on a clean T- shirt; sit down, not move and within five minutes the shirt would look like a child's finger paint project. He would do this time and again. I likened him to the Charlie Brown comic character "Pig Pen." I'd swear he had a constant cloud hovering over him waiting for the next clean apparel to appear. This isn't to say that any of us was overwhelmingly tidy. Living out in the woods, sweating all-day and sleeping on the ground is not conducive to impeccable clothing or hygiene. It was only May and over the summer, as our clothing and gear started to wear out and the stains and dirt wouldn't wash out, we gradually took on the appearance of homeless people. First Timer was merely at the head of the class in that department.

First Timer brings about another interesting demographic about many thru-hikers: he quit his job as a chef to go hike the Trail. Scores of hikers *are* in a sense like homeless people with credit cards. Many young hikers admitted to me that before leaving for the hike they had sold their car, gotten out of apartment leases, quit jobs and a whole host of other daring and bold life changes. A few had lost jobs or their homes in what turned out to be the 2008-'09 mortgage crisis before anyone actually realized it was coming. Several were realtors, and since business had gotten so bad they simply decided to take some time off. They were the precursors of the economic collapse, hoping that over the ensuing months the world would change and when they returned to it, it would be a different, more accommodating place; for many, it changed, but not for the better. The Trail became a "canary cage" of the economy and there were certainly more than a few canaries that appeared to be falling off their perch.

Many of these hikers were actually looking for a new place to live. They confided in me that they were going to hike the A.T. and look for an area that suited their lifestyle and then settle there. If these people had lived 150 years ago they would have probably been on Conestoga wagons heading west. They were cut from the same material as those early pioneers; many shared that sense of having to see what was over the next hill. I felt almost out of place with this rugged bunch. After all, I had a home, a family, stability, and food in the refrigerator that I was returning to once I finished hiking the Trail.

Strong friendships were forming after a few weeks on the Trail. There are groups of hikers that seem to maintain a similar progression rate and end up camped at the same locations each evening. They don't all necessarily hike at the same rate: some go very quickly but stop to take lots of pictures, smoke, or just smell the roses. Others can be quite slow, but like the hare and the tortoise, they manage to get to the same destination every day. I was somewhere in between the hare and tortoise. Starting at my late date, I found myself with many that were intent on flip-flopping. Some college students were flying by and I only spent one or two evenings with them before they left us slower hikers behind.

Up until North Carolina, the hike consisted mostly of walking a well-defined trail. Now I needed to use my arms as well as my legs to climb up and over obstacles and at times I wondered if I was still on the Trail. Climbing a stiff ascent up to a fire tower at the top of Albert Mountain provided a fabulous vista. Oorah, Promise Keeper, Blitz and a host of others were there for the photo ops. We took each other's pictures and met some other day hikers. It was pleasurable to stop and schmooze and socialize after spending so much time in the solitude of the woods. It seemed like I had been on the Trail for months. Then the realization struck me: I hadn't yet done 100 miles (161 km) and had been out for a mere 11 days!

At Albert Mountain, doing a long section hike, I met a couple that was from French-speaking Quebec. Frederick and Chauteley were on the A.T. for the first time. Initially they were quiet and seemingly withdrawn; I suspect they felt their English wasn't good enough, but it turned out to be excellent.

At the Big Spring Shelter I went up to where they were camped and asked them to join us. They did and in no time at all they appeared to relax and fit right in. Chauteley was very pleasant to listen to since she had a wonderful French accent, and reminded me of my wife, Jane. Chauteley would have the distinction of having two rattlesnake confrontations in two days. She had never seen a snake before and was quite shocked by the experience. Fortunately she was unharmed in both incidents, although both snakes did coil up and rattle.

Bald

The next day at the Winding Stair Gap road crossing, many of my new friends decided to shuttle into Franklin, North Carolina and spend the night at a hostel. I decided to continue on. Late in the day I came upon Siler Bald, one of a number of balds I would see in the South. "Balds" are grassy flat-topped peaks that have no trees on them. There are several theories as to how they came about, Native American farming or religious activity being the most predominant. In any case, Siler's is the first one on the A.T. There are several Siler's Balds, as there are several Sassafras Gaps, Low Gaps and so on. I was amazed at how many times the same name is used on the Trail; it can be frustratingly confusing.

Siler Bald has a spectacular view. It was a stunning revelation of just how many mountains I had crossed thus far and how many more were to come. In a grassy field below the bald, I ran into a man that was looking for his college-student son, George, who had left Springer Mountain on Monday, only five days earlier. Since it had taken me twelve days to get here from Springer Mountain, this kid must have been flying. I told the father I would watch for George. We parted and he headed down the mountain to the trailhead where he was parked.

It was Saturday afternoon and I had cell service, so before descending I called ahead to the Nantahala Outdoor Center [NOC] and made reservations for Monday night. Since it was Memorial Day weekend, I feared there would be no room at their hiker hostel. The NOC was still 24 miles (39 km) away, but I figured I would make that distance easily.

I was at least a day ahead of Blitz now and figured I would take my first "zero" day of the hike at the NOC. A zero day is a day of no hiking, or zero miles. A near-zero, or "Near-oh," day is where you might hike a few miles into or out of town, but spend a good portion of the day in town.

While descending Siler Bald I ran into George ascending the bald. He and his friends seemed to be doing well so far. I gave him the message about his Dad and continued on, figuring I would never see George again, unless he flew by me in his rush north.

Somehow I managed to miss the Siler Bald Shelter and by the time I realized it, I decided to continue on to a campground I knew to be near the highway NC 1310. I managed to get there just before dusk. It was more of a parking area than a campground, but it did have water and picnic tables, so it was home for the night. There were a few other section hikers there and I talked with them before going off to my hammock for the night.

Sometimes I could sleep through the loudest noises and yet if it were really quiet, a twig cracking or a thump would awaken me — I can't explain it. On this night I was sleeping soundly and about 3 a.m. I awoke with a start. I could detect the heavy footsteps of an animal going down the trail at a fairly good rate. My hammock was hanging in some heavy underbrush right next to the trail, so I peeked out and saw a bear go right by in a real hurry, as if he were a thru-hiker headed for free pizza down at the road crossing. He was massive, maybe 500 - 600 pounds, every bit as big as the one I had seen that night at Sassafras Gap. Thank goodness he was intent on his destination.

Double-Dare

Sometimes two people will share a trail name; Sunny and Larry are just such a case. With their dog "Chloe," they were hiking the Trail in two long sections, some in 2007, some in 2008. Sunny had done a thru-hike some years before and now she was doing it with Larry. Since they were doing it in two years, in two sections, they called themselves "Double-Dare." They were at the Cold Springs Shelter when I arrived. At first it was just the three of us, then little by little more and more hikers showed up. Frederick and Chauteley, a large family of perhaps seven or eight people, First Timer, and a few others were all there. Chauteley reported another rattlesnake encounter, and the large family and Double-Dare had a rattlesnake confrontation as well. Strangely, those that were ahead of me, and those that followed saw the rattlesnake, yet when I passed, I didn't. The drought seemed to really be bringing the rattlesnakes out. Later that day First Timer stepped over a rattlesnake on his way to the privy.

The immediate Cold Springs shelter area was not very inviting. The shelter was old and looked the sort of place snakes and mice would inhabit, so I continued up the trail a few hundred feet and found a blue-blazed trail that went up a rise and offered a splendid view of the valley below.

Many of the shelters in the South have bear cables. The cables are thick steel cables suspended between two trees, about fifteen feet high. Another cable runs up to a pulley on the suspended cable and a food bag (bear bag) can be attached and pulled up, safely out of reach of the bears. The other end of the cable is then clipped to a ring at ground level. Big bears are so strong that they can pull at the cables so much that something eventually snaps or breaks, rendering the cable useless. Bears had destroyed the bear cables at the Cold Springs shelter, so I hung my bear bag in a tree with great care. I set up the hammock and had the most wonderful sleep thus far.

NOC

In early afternoon I arrived at the NOC (Nantahala Outdoor Center). The trail runs right through the center. Here there is canoeing, kayaking, river rafting, mountain biking, and of course... hiking. What's really exciting for a thru-hiker, however, are several eating establishments on the grounds. Since my hiker appetite had kicked in, I looked forward to a day off from hiking and a day of eating.

I found my bunkroom and cleaned up. This was the first time I had really seen myself in a mirror—I was shocked! I had only been on the Trail for two weeks and I was already emaciated looking; my face was gaunt and I thought I was looking even older than I was. My once red beard was now very white and my upper body was thinning. I realized I needed to increase my caloric intake, if that was even possible.

I went to an NOC outdoor café and ordered a burger and worked on my journal and took in the atmosphere. It was quite relaxing and I wasted several hours just watching people going by in their kayaks and enjoying the river. The river is managed and has controlled releases of water from an upstream dam. A whistle blows before the release occurs and exciting white water flows through the center. While I was sitting there, George showed up. He and his father had linked up and George and his friends took a day with Dad to eat up and rest. Even with the time off, George had caught up to me. He was doing 25-30 miles (40-48 km) a day! George asked me if I could spare any cash, as he was broke. I was just about to offer him $5 when a voice behind us piped up and offered George $20. I was outbid; I didn't counter-offer. Had George been wise, he would have argued that he could have used both contributions, but he didn't, so I quietly put my wallet back.

Mr. High-bidder was a motorcyclist that was staying at the NOC for the night and was also an occasional hiker. It was a very nice act of generosity, my first real "trail angel" encounter. Trail angels are folks that all along the way help out hikers. Often they are previous thru-hikers, hiker family members or just decent people that like to help the hikers and would never consider hiking the Trail themselves. I was to learn about the basic goodness of American trail angels as my hike progressed.

Earlier I had left word at the NOC office that I needed a ride to town. While I was at the café with George an attractive young lady by the name of Julie came up to me, walking her dog. She told me that she was an NOC employee and she shuttled hikers. As we made our plans to meet the following night, I asked her how she found me and she bashfully admitted that the office had told her to look for a guy that looked like a "thin Santa Claus." After she left, George enthusiastically exclaimed, "She's hot!" George had a grasp of the obvious. He then started asking me about advice on women, a topic I never claimed to be an authority on. This would happen many more times on my hike along the A.T. I was beginning to think my senior citizen status automatically advertised, "Free relationship advice."

A true zero day means staying in the same place for two nights. The next morning I slept in until seven a.m., then went to the extravagant NOC hiker kitchen. The place is very modern and has two of everything: sinks, refrigerators, ovens, microwave ovens and stoves. They had several hiker boxes there. I scrounged through them and discovered a sack of buckwheat pancake mix and pancake syrup. There were also some beer brat sausages in the freezer. I cooked and ate until I was ready to burst; it was nirvana. I decided since I had little to do that day I would clean the kitchen. I swept everything, washed all the stoves and sinks and then attacked the refrigerators. They showed signs of decent upkeep but needed organizing and throwing out of old food and frozen goods, some of which looked like it may have been there since the last Ice Age.

Hikers leave stuff supposing that someone will be interested in it. However, more often than not, the "stuff" will be in an unmarked plastic bag, contents unidentifiable. I did find plenty of things that were still quite usable, labeled them with a grease pencil, arranged things nicely and was quite proud of my work. I then applied the same technique to the hiker boxes.

One of my favorite gripes about hiker boxes is that one will usually find, at minimum, six clear plastic bags with white powder in them. There is no date, no identification and no instructions. The white powder could be laundry soap, flour, starch, pancake batter, powdered sugar, powdered milk, foot powder, make-up, pixie dust, cocaine or any other of thousands of things. I'm certain the donor feels they have accomplished two things by donating it to the box: they have done the Christian thing and contributed something that someone can use, and they have lightened their load (the real reason they dumped it in the first place). White powder, you'll find it in every hiker box.

Later, around 5 p.m., as promised, Julie showed up to drive me to town. She was quite pleasant and on the way there we had a nice discussion about the NOC. She'd been working there for some months and was living in her tent with her large dog. She loved the region and was roughing it just to be able to live and work there. I told her about what George had said about her being "hot." She gave a sweet chuckle and commented that she thought he was hot too. Too bad, I suspect George was another thirty miles down the Trail by that point; so much for my advice. In town I hit the local drug store to burn a CDROM of my photos to mail home so I could empty the digital camera, and then picked up a few supplies. The outfitter at the NOC had very little hiker stock left since it was getting late in the season for thru-hikers and they have a much larger market to cater to: the automobile tourists of mid-summer.

When I returned, Blitz was there, as well as Double Dare, First Timer and a bunch of others. The first night I had the room to myself, not so the second night.

Blitz had sent himself a supply package from home the previous year. He had intended on getting to the NOC the year before, but never made it. He went to check at the office and they still had the package. He brought it to the bunk area and opened it. It was like giving a Christmas present to himself; he couldn't recall what he had sent. It was loaded with energy bars, pounds of powdered milk and way more supplies than anyone could reasonably use. He gave me as much as I dared carry and then gave away the rest. We had a good laugh about just how much stuff he had sent versus what he really needed. I wondered how much of the powdered milk was going to end up in a hiker box.

After rifling through Blitz's bonanza, Blitz went off to the kitchen to make himself an evening meal. I contented myself with preparing my pack for leaving the next morning. Blitz was taking a zero day the next day so we would be parting ways once again. He returned from his meal looking a bit puzzled. While he was in the kitchen eating, two people came in. They were quite overweight, on the scale of sumo wrestlers, and seemed to know their way around the kitchen quite well. Blitz didn't pay them much mind and figured they were staff in there to clean up the place, which I had already done.

Suddenly, they were gone. He hadn't been paying all that much attention, but they just disappeared out the door, carrying several boxes. After they were gone he realized that these two had come in, gone through both fridges, cabinets and hiker boxes, helped themselves to anything that looked edible or useful (my labeling that morning made that task a cinch), loaded it all into the hiker boxes and walked off with it! They no doubt were passing through, knew the goods were there and hauled them off to their RV. I wouldn't be surprised if they do this every summer vacation. I really hope they find a good use for the white powder.

Celibate

Later that evening most of us gathered at the Paddler's Pub for a beer. It is a nice place located above a restaurant. We were all quite jovial about having made it to the NOC; it is a major milestone. For me it was day 14 and 134 miles (216 km). When we all had a brew I lifted my glass and exclaimed in a rather boisterous voice, "Tonight I am here to congratulate all of you for making it this far and enjoy my celibate mood." Jaws dropped and I had a moment of very strange looks, then laughter broke out. I mentally re-ran what I had just proclaimed and realized I meant to say "celebratory mood." For weeks afterwards strangers, upon hearing my trail name, would ask if I was still celibate.

Back to Work

It was time to hit the Trail again. I left the NOC at a reasonably early hour. Blitz was already up and we said our good-byes. Since we hike at similar rates, he would stay a day behind me. It was only a few more days to Fontana Dam, his destination. I was going to miss him; we hiked well together.

The climb out of the NOC is quite robust. It is steep and long, and after lying around for a day my body was protesting. Though my drop foot was healing, the sensory feedback was not that accurate and I had to use care on stumps and rocks. I hiked sixteen miles to the Brown Fork Shelter. It was a nice day and I met a few new hikers along the way, "Poke" and "Slow-Poke." These two fellows were in my age bracket and had a subtle sense of humor. They had a continuous friendly argument about which one was "Slow-Poke" and they had lots of interesting theories about why the world was going to hell in a handbag.

What really got my attention at the Brown Fork Shelter was the privy. It was a sight to behold. It seemed that ever so gradually the hiking accommodations going north were deteriorating; this privy was the last word in privies. It was obviously quite old and at one time did have a building standing around it. Weather and years of exposure gradually wore away the building and now all that was left standing was one wall, and that wall had every other board missing; I don't know how it continued to stand. It was basically a toilet seat sitting in the forest with remnants of one wall remaining. Shutting the door wasn't a concern — there wasn't one.

Figure 6: Going north the privy accommodations were becoming more primitive.

Many of the hiking clubs maintaining the shelters don't have much for financial resources and it was starting to show.

Most of the privies along the Trail are of the "moldering" type. A moldering privy combines the solid human waste with added forest debris, and over time decomposes the waste matter. Urine upsets this process, so a procedure must be followed. There is usually a sign instructing the user to:

- Pee in the Woods.

- Take out your trash.

- Follow with a small handful of wood chips or leaves.

- Close the lid after use.

At first this is challenging. Peeing in one place and then doing #2 in another is a bodily trial; it's just not something that comes naturally (try it). After months of perfecting this drill I was concerned I would go home and pee on the lawn and then go into the bathroom.

Code Red

I spent a night at the Fontana Dam Shelter, nicknamed the "Fontana Hilton." The shelter is relatively new and spacious and has nearby hot showers and indoor plumbing. Oorah and Promise Keeper were there and we caught up on the most recent gossip. We were all excited about crossing the dam and getting into the Smokies and Tennessee.

In the morning Oorah and Promise Keeper left about a half-hour before I did. There was a warning sign at the store that indicated at least one shelter was temporarily closed due to bear encounters and that the bears have been very active due to the drought. Bears have difficulty finding food when the vegetation dies off and the water holes dry up, so they roam further and more often. A few hikers complained of the bears stealing their water bottles; I wondered how the bears did it?

I started across the dam and about halfway across there were two Park Service trucks parked on the road. As I started to pass I said, "Mornin' " to one of the park employees on the truck and he replied, "I reckon you might want to hang here a bit." Confused, I asked, "Why, has Homeland Security declared a Code Red?" Homeland Security has jurisdiction over dam security and the threat of terrorists attempting to blow up such facilities is something of a concern. Code Red is the highest level of alert. The employee responded, "Well, for you it could be; ya see there's a big ole black bear down there at the end o' the dam and it could get nasty if y'all get down there." Just then I saw the bear come out from behind the concrete barrier at the end of the dam. He roamed over to the picnic area, looked around for a while, then went back and forth across the road a few times, then returned back to the picnic area just to double-check and make certain nothing new had magically appeared in his absence. Finally after about a half hour he disappeared up into the woods in the direction I wanted to go. Of course the federal employees in the trucks loved it. The park rules specifically prohibit them from disturbing the animal life so they just sat with their binoculars and morning coffee and enjoyed the show with the clock running.

Figure 7: Fontana Dam and the start of the Great Smokey Mountains National Park.

Great, another bear to hike with, what a wonderful way to start off the day! Amazingly, Oorah and Promise Keeper must have just missed the bear; their timing was perfect. The picnic area the bear was scampering around in is the official start of the Great Smoky Mountains National Park. This park is reputed to be home to more 1500 black bears, and I had already met one.

I went about eight miles into the park and stopped to cook up some lunch. Eventually I would eliminate cooking in mid-day and would eat cold lunches but I was still enamored with the luxury of a hot lunch. As I ate, I noticed a bear was watching me. It appeared to be a female and she would slowly make a large circle around me, never getting closer than perhaps 100 feet. Bears can cover that distance very quickly, perhaps a few seconds, so it was an uncomfortable position to be in. I finished quickly, didn't bother to clean things, just shoved them in my pack and scurried off up the trail.

In addition to the bear concerns, I was hearing increasingly loud rumblings of thunder. I'm rather nervous about lightning. In 1980, only twenty miles from where I ate lunch, lightning killed two hikers in the Double Springs Shelter. The log shelters are really no protection at all from lightning, but there is a certain psychological comfort to being there anyway. I hoofed up the two miles to the top of the mountain in under a half-hour. It was a steep hike and I really pushed. The Mollie Ridge Shelter is located at the top and it was comforting to make it there before the storm broke. It also meant staying dry from the ensuing monsoon-like rains that come with big summer thunderstorms.

There was a good-sized gathering of hikers already at the shelter as well as "Ridge Runner" Carl and his wife Shirley. Ridge Runners are personnel that are hired by park services to cover sections of the trails during the heavy-use periods in the summer. They do minor maintenance and also watch for infractions of laws, injuries and any illegal activities that might occur. They are not armed and have limited jurisdiction but really are an asset to keeping the parks safe and orderly.

Even though it wasn't that late in the day, I decided to stay at the shelter, having expended a lot of energy running up the mountain with a heavy pack on my back. I climbed down to the spring to refill my water bottles and found the "spring" to be just a drip. It took about a half-hour to get enough water for the evening; this drought was really drying up the water sources. The climb back up to the shelter was steep and I knew I would have to repeat this ritual again in the morning; I didn't have enough water for tomorrow's hike and I had forgotten to bring my water sack down to the spring.

It rained off-and-on all night and I awoke early. I trudged back down to the spring; it was as dismal as the night before and took even longer to fill my water bottles. I wasn't feeling quite right and after starting back up the climb to the shelter I had the chest pains again. I stopped for while and just relaxed and the pains subsided, but didn't totally vanish. Foolishly I decided to ignore this event and figured if it became a regular event I would get it checked out.

A Paper Trail

The entire length of the A.T. has approximately 250 shelters; the Great Smoky Mountains National Park has 12 of them. The Federal Government, in its infinite wisdom, has decided that in the Smokies it's best to have people go out into the woods and defecate around the shelters rather than build privies. This seems somehow more "natural" and pleasing. The reality is: it stinks and it's a mess. Logically, people are not going to walk into thick brush, off cliffs or anywhere that is impassible. So they end up walking on familiar footpaths a short distance from the shelter (particularly in the dark, in bear country) and do their business nearby. At night, especially in bad weather, inexperienced weekend hikers may or may not remember to bring something with them to bury their "business." What happens over time is the entire area around a federal shelter becomes a virtual surface septic tank. In some places the rotting toilet paper looks like late spring snow. It is truly a tribute to Washington and their outstanding decision-making process. I'm certain the wildlife appreciates it too. I'm convinced that this technique should be employed at the Washington Mall as well, since it is such a resounding success. At least there they could hawk little souvenir plastic shovels that the tourists could take back to China with them; thru-hikers have their own digging implements.

Reverse Zoo

I headed north once again and around noon stopped for lunch at Dicks Knob Shelter. The shelter had Anchor Iron fence across the front of it with a gate to allow access. It was one of the few remaining shelters in the Smokies that still had the fence to keep bears out. The fence was a failed experiment at keeping humans and bears from direct contact. The theory was the humans would spend the night in the shelter and the bears would stay outside and have their own picnic. The reality was quite different; the park visitors would be inside the shelter pushing bits of food through the fence to the "cute" bears. I might note that these were not serious outdoors individuals; anyone that spends extensive time in the woods with bears knows to keep the food well away from them. The Smokies, however, have lots of inexperienced weekend visitors that pass through and therein lay the problem. On more than one occasion the fed bears would hang around waiting for more food. An animal that weighs many hundreds of pounds eats lots of food every day. A few snacks through the wire are just teasers; they're going to patiently wait for the main course.

This situation creates the "Reverse Zoo" situation: the people are in the cage, and the animals are looking in. I've heard stories of individuals spending considerable time in the shelter because they couldn't leave and I don't doubt this to be true. Bears are voracious eaters and human food is quite attractive. They're very patient and will wait around a very long time for a free meal. A large male can consume 25,000 calories a day and food is the driving force behind almost all their activity.

The good news is: bears are not really aggressive. They don't go around looking for humans to consume; they're looking for human food and humans have a nasty habit of occasionally getting in the way. The National Park Service finally realized that as foolish as it may sound, removing the fences at the shelters actually reduced bear-human conflict. Neither party enjoys the other's company, the fence created a false sense of security for both the bears and the humans. Removing the fence made humans more cautious.

Opera

Climbing a hill I encountered another hiker going southbound. For some strange reason I was in a very mischievous mood. We stopped to exchange pleasantries. I noticed he had earphones on and was listening to something; I asked what. He replied, "Opera." I was a bit taken aback, "Opera?" Opera is just not something that has ever held any fascination for me. Without thinking (a strength that I exhibit often) I piped up: "I listen to the opera all around me," meaning the forest sounds about me. He took it to mean I also listened to opera, but since he couldn't see any music device or headphones, in a lowered voice, while looking around, he asked, "Do you have some sort of digital device implanted?" I had mentioned that I am an electrical engineer and I suspect he thought I had something surgically implanted. I alluded to the fact that I was field-testing something and he wasn't to tell anyone; he was stunned.

I asked which opera he was listening to. He answered with something that sounded to me like "Rigatoni-Lasagna in the Third Hiccup," I couldn't contain myself and exclaimed "Oh, that was my mother's favorite!" Truth is, she hated opera. We parted ways; he was thrilled to have met another enlightened mind on the trail. Me, I was amused and hardly able to contain myself. I don't know what possessed me; perhaps it was the long hours alone.

Figure 8: Near Clingman's Dome, in the rain. I made a wrong turn and a passing family re-directed me and took my photo.

The next day, while still in the Smokies, I was gaining altitude and approaching the highest peak on the entire A.T., Clingman's Dome. Clingman's, like so many points of prominence along the Trail, has a road to the top and a parking area. Near the parking lot I encountered Oorah and Promise Keeper. It was a cold, wet reunion, but it was great to see them again. I started down the mountain with them but since I was considerably faster downhill than they, we parted ways. Subsequently I took a zero day and I would not see them again; they would always be a day or so ahead of me.

The north slope of Clingman's Dome had recently been devastated by a serious windstorm. Thousands of very large trees were uprooted and strewn about like so many toothpicks that had been tossed from a table. There was considerable trail re-routing to work around the fallen trees and it was obvious it would be a long time before this forest recovered. About halfway down the mountain I stopped to make lunch. As I ate lunch I appreciated the fact that I wasn't camped there when this storm roared through.

Eight miles from the summit of Clingman's the Trail crosses US 441 at Newfound Gap. The gap has a parking area and the place was alive with tourists. As I crossed the road a man named Travis approached me from the parking lot and asked if I was "K1." I affirmed that I was and he told me he had driven up to the summit earlier and had offered Oorah and Promise Keeper a ride into Gatlinburg, Tennessee. They weren't interested but told him that I might be. Travis drove down to the parking lot and waited three hours for me to show up! I asked how he recognized me. You guessed it; he looked for the guy that looked like a thin Santa. At least he didn't look for the "celibate Santa."

Travis had his SUV there and his wife and daughter were in their car. They split up and Travis took me to a hotel right at the edge of Gatlinburg. Travis had done a thru-hike of the A.T. previously and was well aware of how appreciated he was. He filled me in on the best places to eat and how to find my way around. He asked if there was anything else he could do. Imagine that, these folks had wasted half their day waiting on me and wanted to do more if they could. I couldn't believe it. I had truly found the real Americans, the ones that don't show up on the front page of the paper every day, but the ones that I could really be proud of.

Glitterburg

Gatlinburg, Tennessee should be more appropriately called "Glitter-burg." It and nearby Dollywood (Dolly Parton's personal fun-town) are truly an anomaly. Gatlinburg is nestled in the foothills around the north side of the Great Smoky Mountains National Park and completely contrasts with the park. Its bright lights, gaudy sideshows, and hawkers of every sort is replete with every factory outlet store imaginable. Why someone would drive to Gatlinburg to buy dishes or clothes at exorbitant prices is beyond my comprehension, but they do.

I stood in the doorway of a Kilwin's Ice Cream shop and realized I was looking across the street at a Ben and Jerry's and a Baskin-Robbins Ice Cream shop, all three upscale vendors of calories. By this time I had already lost ten pounds hiking the A.T. and was underweight so had no guilt in indulging, but looking at the tourists around me reminded me that there is no shortage of calories in this country's diet.

I guiltily admit enjoying my stay in Gatlinburg. I took a zero day, did laundry, rested, swam in the hotel pool, caught up on sleep and re-charged my battery. The town has a very nice trolley system; I highly recommend taking the Red Trolley up to the Hilton Hotel. It isn't billed as a thrill ride, but it should be. The curves and switchbacks would be challenging for a racing motorcycle, much less a trolley.

The hiking outfitter was a short walk from the hotel. I browsed around there and picked up a few things. The outfitter had a hiker box, yep, with plenty of white powder for the taking. Another thing that caught my eye was a ten-pound bag of dried black beans. Ten pounds! I can't imagine the hiker that was carrying these beans. First of all, dried beans need to be soaked for many hours before cooking, and then take some serious cooking time to soften them. This wouldn't be the last time I would see this.

The owner of the outfitter and I discussed snakes and he told me that a child in Texas had been bitten by a rattlesnake that week. The outfitter himself had been bitten twice the previous year by a copperhead. I hadn't given much thought to copperheads; rattlesnakes get all the attention. However, copperheads are just as poisonous and give no warning. This added something else to my mental list of things to watch for.

Gatlinburg gave me an opportunity to assess my situation regarding my chest pains. I wrote in my journal, 4 June 2007:

"The last few days, in the early morning I have had some concern about my cardiac condition. In the morning, when starting out my lungs feel odd, almost hurt. Not sure if it is just the 6000' altitude or something going on to be concerned about? On Friday afternoon I stopped to have a late lunch and after lunch I could hear an approaching thunderstorm so packed everything in a hurry and did the 2 miles up the mountain to Mollie Ridge Shelter in 35 minutes! That was about 17 minutes per mile and climbing maybe 1500'!!! I think I may have overdone it; the next morning I had the pains.

Anyway, yesterday morning I went down for water at the Siler Bald Shelter and the climb back to the shelter gave me pains again. When I arrived back at the shelter I took a 300 mg aspirin, chewed it and swallowed it with some water. In about 7 minutes the pain subsided.

So, what to do? If I check with a doctor, they'll tell me to stop the hike. At this point I just can't do that, I'm too much in love with it. If it gets worse, I won't have any choice. I suppose I'll just have to see what happens. This must be what the old timers referred to as "angina." Seems to occur in the morning for some reason. I may be nuts, but I really want to continue. As much as I love Jane and the kids and would somehow cheat them if I kicked off early, I must continue. The good news is, I have lived the most wonderful life any man could live.

I have few regrets, millions of wonderful memories and experiences and couldn't be happier. I really believe that there are very few men that have had the good fortune to have met, much less marry the wonderful bride that is mine. I think of her constantly throughout the day, what a fortunate man am I."

Boot Camp

I was concerned that I would have difficulty finding a hitch back to Newfound Gap from Gatlinburg, but once again trail angels came to the rescue. I had no difficulty getting a ride up the road a few miles from someone going to work on some trails in the Smokies and then another young fellow picked me up and even though Newfound Gap was five miles beyond where he was going, he took me to the gap. People never failed to amaze me.

After about eleven miles of hiking I came upon a woman and her son that were quite startled to see me. They hadn't seen another soul all day. Somehow they had become separated from their family and seemed totally confused as to where they were going. She looked quite bedraggled; her son looked exhausted. She told me that they had made a wrong turn on the trail and had walked an extra 11 miles (18 km) before getting back to the A.T. I asked if they were okay and she claimed they were. I pushed on ahead of them, but I was concerned, they didn't seem comfortable with their situation. At the intersection for Pecks Corner Shelter I decided to stop and cook lunch. The break would be a good excuse to wait for them and see if they were okay. After an hour or so they slowly approached, looking the worse for wear. It was five more miles to the next shelter and I really didn't think they had it in them, particularly since it was getting late in the day. The Pecks Corner Shelter was down a side trail about a half-mile.

Certain they needed help, I offered to stay with them at the Pecks Corner Shelter (even though I had not planned to do so) or they could go to the Pecks Corner Shelter and I would continue on the five miles to the Tri Corner Shelter and let the rest of their party know where they were. I think the woman felt a bit odd about staying with a strange man at a shelter alone, particularly one that looked like a skinny version of "Grizzly Adams," so she opted for me to continue on to the next shelter and let her family know where she was. I asked about her camping gear and she responded that she did have sleeping gear and food, but nothing to cook in, but would figure something out. She promised they would stay there for the night and I promised to make certain someone would be waiting for them tomorrow, even if it was just me.

We split off and I hiked to the next shelter. About a mile from the Tri Corner Shelter I ran into a couple going the other way and told them about the woman and son and asked them to let her know they saw me.

It was very late in the day when I arrived at the Tri Corner Shelter. As I approached the shelter I could hear a heated debate about which was better: the F-111 or the F-14 fighter jet. There were perhaps six or seven adult men and a number of teenagers. It seemed everyone was outfitted in surplus military equipment, even the teens. There were military sleeping bags, cookware, packs, canteens, etc. This stuff is heavy and not the norm for hikers. They struck me as an odd lot. The shelter was very crowded and I was glad I had the hammock.

The debate about the fighter jets was so heated that I decided not to interrupt with questions about the woman and son back on the Trail. Nobody inquired about them; even though it was obvious I had come from that direction. Finally, after a considerable time, one of the men turned to me and asked if I had been in the military, I affirmed that I had; in the Air Force. I refused to get involved and changed the subject to the woman and boy I had seen earlier and asked if anyone knew them? One older fellow said yep, he was the woman's father and another answered that he was her husband. Puzzled, I filled them in on their whereabouts and status. There didn't appear to be any concern and the only reply I got from the father was that they were a couple of "wimps" and the husband seemed to agree. I didn't bother to broach the topic again and nobody asked any further questions. As darkness fell, the kids were ordered to bed and all fell quiet. I went off to my hammock fearing there would be a bugle for reveille in the morning.

I was up early and noticed that all the teens were made to rise immediately and pack away their things, much as would occur in a military organization. One lad was given very specific instructions on just how to roll up the bed roll, it had to be just "so." This was spooky; hiking is supposed to be fun, not boot camp.

As I packed up my things and finished breakfast, I overheard the father and husband in a discussion, the father finally relented and said he would stay and wait for the "wimps." I was both relieved and yet sad to see such a family relationship, especially when I felt so fortunate in mine. It would weigh heavily on my mind for some time: how do folks get into such relationships? The F14 vs. F-111 debate started again and I left.

Figure 9: Charlie's Bunion, Great Smokey Mountains National Park.

Green Corners

I made good time getting to the Standing Bear Hostel at Green Corners. It's a rustic, backwoods Tennessee setting for a hostel. The buildings looked like something that may have served as a home base for either the Hatfields or the McCoys, only with running water. The place runs on the honor system. There is a building where there are supplies, a bunkhouse and a kitchen shed. From a hiker's perspective it was perfect. I settled in and had an enjoyable evening meeting some new thru-hikers and section hikers. The owner was away in

Oregon and a young woman, Elizabeth, was running the place.

In the morning I was in the kitchen building with two hikers about my age. We were having breakfast and the hostel's cat was attempting to be everyone's friend. She was so friendly that we finally had to put her outside because we couldn't eat without her sticking her nose in our breakfast.

There was a pot of water boiling on the gas stove and it was making substantial noise. The guy sitting next to the pot was hard of hearing and with the additional noise of the stove; he wasn't hearing our conversation well at all. I asked the fellow near me if he knew where Elizabeth was, that I wanted to settle up my bill and get going. He didn't know where she was, but thought she was still asleep. I asked where she slept. Before he could answer, the one hard-of-hearing chimed in, "I think she sleeps under the house, or maybe in the shed. Then again, I've seen her hanging around up by the privy quite a bit. I'm sure when it gets cold out she goes up to the bunkhouse and climbs into a sleeping bag with one of the men." We were stunned until we realized he thought we were talking about the cat and not Elizabeth. This wouldn't be the last time that hearing would be an issue on the Trail.

Roaring Forks

Just before climbing Max Patch, a spectacular Southern bald, I had my first encounter with a Southern black snake. It was huge and curled up in the middle of the Trail. Even though these snakes can bite, they are not poisonous, and I kept my distance. This reptile was about eight feet long, certainly longer than I. It hissed at me and simulated the noise of a rattlesnake by shaking its tail in the leaves. Finally, after a little coaxing, it decided to leave the trail. Much to my astonishment it climbed quickly up some bushes and was soon about ten feet off the ground! I wasn't aware these snakes could do this; now I had something else to think about when hanging in my hammock at night. A half mile later I spooked a mom turkey and her three poults. Now a turkey isn't a particularly awesome opponent, but when they rush up into the air they make a fantastic amount of noise and at close range it can cause the heart to pound. After all, I wasn't yet fully calmed from the black snake.

It was a glorious June afternoon when I hiked over Max Patch and found my way down to the Roaring Forks Shelter. Several of the members of my A.T. club in Florida are part of a group known as the "Mountain Marching Mommas," six women that got together many years ago to hike the A.T. in its entirety; they succeeded after twenty years of effort. They became involved in sponsoring and building a shelter called the Roaring Forks Shelter, which is located just after Max Patch Bald. One of the Mountain Marching Mommas, Grace, (the same Grace that greeted me my first night at the Florida A.T.C.), filled me in on the shelter's history, so I was looking forward to seeing it.

The shelter was in very good repair and had a nice bronze plaque on the wall dedicated to the Mommas. The shelter was really dark inside. "It could use some light panels in the ceiling," I thought. I built a fire in the fireplace and hung my hammock. It was a nice evening and I had the place to myself. It would be the first of perhaps three times on the entire hike that I would be alone at a shelter.

Figure 10: Plaques in Roaring Fork Shelter, a tribute to those generous volunteers that make shelters possible.

Hot Springs

I was nearing Hot Springs, North Carolina. This town is a hiker's Mecca. It has hostels, outfitters, and a friendly attitude toward hikers; I couldn't wait to get there. On the way to Hot Springs, I passed the Walnut Creek Shelter. The register was loaded with accounts of bears getting food bags and packs; it didn't sound like a place I wanted to stay. The day was stifling and I was low on water and couldn't find the water source. Sometimes I would leave my pack at a shelter when I would search for water, but wisely decided not to here. Subsequently I would hear much about this infamous shelter and the bear activity from many other hikers along the trail.

A few miles before Hot Springs I stopped at the Deer Park Shelter for lunch. I was starving, even though I had eaten just a short while before; my appetite was really flourishing. I ate quickly, and could hear another thunderstorm approaching. I scurried down the mountain in a real hurry, doing the 3.5 miles (5.6 km) in about an hour. I have never climbed up so much to get down to something. This section of trail would go down for maybe 200 feet, and then climb back up steeply for perhaps 150 feet. It seemed I would never get to town and alas, I was caught in the storm for the last half-mile or so. It was a torrential downpour and I was soaked. More frightening though was the lightning, which was popping all around me.

When I finally arrived in town I could not find the Sunshine Bank Inn, better known as "Elmer's" (the owner). After asking directions several times I realized I had passed it a number of times; it was an old Victorian-style building that actually looked too classy for hikers; it threw me off.

The building is old but enchanting. Much of its furniture is antique. When I arrived, the storm had already blown through and the area had lost power. Elmer invited me in, explaining that they were already full but they could accommodate me by putting something together for me in the tool shed. I agreed, and they set up a bed in the shed. The shed was a solarium attached to the building where they stored things. I was about to sleep in a "glass house," since all the walls were glass. I didn't care, it was dry, warm, and I was in Hot Springs.

I wasn't aware of it, but apparently the other guests were fascinated by the fact that I was sleeping in the shed. Traditionally there is a big breakfast at the Inn, and next morning I was the last to arrive. Breakfast is served at a long table with all the guests crowded in to eat. When I sat down Elmer inquired as to how I had slept, I replied,

"Elmer, I couldn't have slept any better if twelve concubines had fanned me with feather fans all night long." There was a big round of laughter at that and then Elmer suggested that "you may not have slept all that well if there *were* concubines" which brought on more laughter.

I spent the day doing the routine things a hiker does while in town: re-supply, laundry, and eating. In mid-morning I packed my ham radio and lunch and went back up the trail several miles to Tennessee/North Carolina border and made a few contacts with amateurs in Indiana and Michigan. That afternoon I went to a bluegrass festival in town and thoroughly enjoyed myself, soaking in the sounds, smells and foods of the region.

Figure 11: Hot Springs, NC, is a really hiker-friendly town, the A.T. runs right down Main St.

After a really relaxing day, I returned to the Inn. I went out on the porch and sat in one of the inviting rocking chairs to do some hand sewing. It was a wonderful summer evening, filled with the music of singing insects and soft breezes and I was quite content. Two women that were staying at the Inn came over and joined me. They had some wine and offered to share it, but I'm not much of wine drinker and declined. They were moderately younger than I and attractive. After some time I caught one of them glancing at the other as if to agree upon something, then she said, "You know, we saw some feathers hanging around inside the inn. We could get those feathers and help you stay cool tonight, and you wouldn't have stay out in that nasty old shed." Flummoxed, I didn't know quite how to respond! I decided it would be best to stay celibate and excused myself and disappeared into my tool shed.

It was time to get to Tennessee!

Figure 12: The south is replete with unusual tree formations. The Gnarled Oak is top-right.

Chapter 4 - Tennessee

Altered States?

Most states along the A.T. have some sort of greeting that welcomes you to the state. Some are quite elaborate; others are just a board on a tree with the border drawn on it and the state abbreviation, but at least something. It was difficult to discern when I was in Tennessee. The A.T. does a serpentine dance along the North Carolina-Tennessee border and it would be difficult to keep putting signs at every crossing, but I think it would be nice to at least acknowledge *somewhere* that the A.T. does in fact run through Tennessee. I did see signs at a few road crossings that informed automobile drivers *they* were in Tennessee. The only time I was positive *I* was in Tennessee was when I hitched a ride into town and there was a city limit sign telling me so.

Strike One

Not long after leaving Hot Springs, North Carolina, the Trail crosses over the U.S. 25 & 70 overpass. It then re-enters the woods and climbs up some log stairs. I had just hoofed up the steps and was wandering along, lost in thought, when suddenly there a very loud "rattling" sound by my left foot. Instinctively I leaped up and away — backwards. Simultaneously, a rattlesnake struck out and hit my hiking pole, nearly knocking it from my hand. It all happened so quickly I was never really conscious of my Pavlovian response. I now had some distance between the snake and me. Regaining my composure, I took out the camera and took a few photos. It was a very perturbed Timber Rattler. Eventually it tired of rattling at me and slithered off the Trail and hid in some bushes about ten feet away. I waited around because I had only recently passed Double-Dare and their dog Chloe and wanted to warn them about the snake, the dog was so quiet and meek I was afraid it might walk right into the venomous foe. They arrived shortly and everyone was relieved to get past it safely.

What really impressed me about the incident was how quickly the snake was able to recoil and ready itself for another strike. It was a large snake, about as fat as my pre-hike thigh, and quite agile. Reptiles are very active when warm, and this guy was at full operating temperature. It had been sunning itself on the trailside and even though I am usually observant of such things, I had let my guard down for just a moment. The encounter left me with at an elevated level of vigilance for some time to come.

Thelma and Louise

Finding water was starting to be a problem. There was a serious drought in the region and water sources that were traditionally iffy were going dry. Usually the first topic of discussion with hikers going in the opposite direction was about water availability.

Seven miles before Big Bald, TN I stopped at a spring to refill my water bottles. My routine was always the same: remove the water pump/filter from the bottom pocket of my pack, fill up the containers, replace the filter into its zippered bag, then place the bag back in the backpack and close the zippered pocket. I'm an engineer, and I'm into an orderly world. Pleased at finding water, I moved on toward Big Bald. About a mile before the bald I encountered a southbound section hiker by the name of "Spook" and we swapped trail gossip for a few minutes. As he was leaving, he asked if I knew the bottom pocket on my pack was open. This is the hiking equivalent of leaving your purse or briefcase on the car roof and driving off. I put my pack down on the side of the trail and started to backtrack with Spook, figuring I had hiked at least five miles from the spring. As luck would have it, about three hundred feet down the Trail we found my pump. That lower zippered pocket carried my hammock, pump, rain poncho, and spare fuel canister. Nothing else was missing from the pack.

It seemed on more than one occasion that timing on the trail worked in my favor. In this instance I had lost my pump, but had the good fortune of running into Spook and fortuitously found the pump nearby. It always seemed that when I needed a solution to a problem, within short order a solution would arise.

Spook hinted that I might meet two women hikers up on top of the bald. He said that they were hiking with their two daughters and were a joy to talk to. As he predicted, they were still on the bald having lunch, only there were three daughters. I told them that Spook had told me they only had two *lovely* daughters, so the daughters would have to argue over which one wasn't the lovely one. The Moms gave me a stern look as if to say, "Don't you dare; they'll be arguing for the next week!"

I too decided this was a fabulous place for lunch, and joined them. They told me that each year they took a few weeks to hike the Trail to get away from it all and have some quality time with their daughters. I can't think of a better way for family members to bond (or develop an inclination to kill each other) than to do a long section on the Trail. It brings everyone back to some primitive level of life and eliminates, for a time anyway, the complications of everyday living.

I asked if they had trail names and the Moms said they were "Thelma and Louise," although they weren't certain as to who was which. I assured them that I didn't want a ride in their convertible when I left the Trail. Ours was one of the many chance encounters along the Trail that remains etched into the mind. One of their daughters offered me a piece of gum, a flavor I had never had before or since; it was delicious and I can still taste it just thinking about our get-together on Big Bald.

Spivey Gap

Thelma and Louise and all three of their lovely daughters left before I did. A couple who were also there with their very young daughter had done a day hike up to Big Bald and offered to take all of our trash down when they left. This may seem insignificant, but trash disposal is important to thru-hikers. There is a very strict mentality regarding carry-in/carry-out among serious hikers and it isn't always easy to find somewhere appropriate to unload trash. Carrying empty containers, bags and wrappers is extra dead weight. Additionally, trash smells of food and can be very attractive to rodents and bears. The trail angels who hauled our trash out were doing us more of a service than they realized.

I continued north from Big Bald and was racing ahead of a thunderstorm. Thelma and Louise and daughters had pulled off the trail and decided to camp at Whistling Gap so they would have shelter from the storm. I offered them help setting up, but they didn't need it, so I continued on and managed to reach Spivey Gap and set up camp before the storm broke.

Three other trekkers arrived and set up camp nearby. The father, Bob, was an Army doctor on leave from Iraq, and was spending two weeks with his sons, Patrick and Ross, doing a long-distance section of the Trail. We had been leapfrogging each other for several days. They planned on arriving at their destination, Erwin,

Tennessee, the next day. They intended to spend a few days in Erwin, whitewater rafting and relaxing. I planned on taking a zero day in Erwin myself so that was the central topic of discussion that evening.

Close Encounters

Morning dawned overcast. I set out early and once again played "leap-frog" with Bob, Patrick and Ross. Around noontime I was walking along, whistling "Zip-a-dee-doo-dah," and lost in thought. I came around an outcropping of rock on the Trail and encountered my three friends with an extreme look of terror in their eyes. They had just stopped for lunch, their last lunch on the trail, about a mile from Erwin. Dad had poured the juice from a can of salmon on the ground. A nutrition-starved thru-hiker would have drunk the juice, but this thought never occurred to these less-starved section hikers. The smell of the juice had attracted a huge male bear. We later learned that this bear has had a history of harassing hikers, stealing backpacks and being a general nuisance in his quest for human food.

The three of them had quickly grabbed all of their belongings up in their arms and ran up the trail about seventy feet and stopped to watch the bear investigate the juice on the ground. This was their second serious error. Bears are very food-aggressive and do not like to be watched eating, thinking that the watcher might try to take their food away. Black bears are known to bluff an attack and will charge the watcher in an attempt to scare them away. This bear did exactly that. Fortunately father and sons stood their ground and didn't run; running is a certain cause for the bear to give chase and can end badly. The bear skidded to stop a few feet from them.

Just at that moment I arrived. Not being aware of what was going on, and shocked to see a huge bear charging this family, I yelled out. At that point the bear, confused by another hiker on the scene, decided to scamper down the hill into the woods. The father and sons repacked their stuff and asked me what I thought they should do. I figured the best thing to do would be to leave the area and to impress the bear with our collective numbers. So we marched down the Trail four abreast, making noise and safely made our escape.

They credited me with saving them from the bear but the reality was that I merely happened upon the scene and, not having the eye-to-eye with the bear, I was a bit more cavalier.

Erwin, TN

In Erwin, Tennessee, I stayed at Johnnie's Hostel. Johnnie offers a shuttle service into the town center and a bunch of us went to town on the first evening there. We descended on the local Mexican Restaurant and devoured our meals. My appetite was insatiable. I asked the waiter for a taco salad, which was a chimichanga bowl filled with salad, guacamole, and cheese, a meal in itself for most non-hikers, and then asked him to bring me the largest meal on the menu. He looked a bit puzzled and brought me something that was for two people, which I finished with gusto. After eating dessert, I was still hungry, so I went across the street to a Hardee's and scarfed down a large burger meal. From there, I went into the grocery mart and picked up my re-supply for the hike, plus a few goodies for the next day, which I planned as a zero day. I finished a tube of fig bars while waiting for the shuttle. On the way back to the hostel, the shuttle stopped at a Walgreen's because the store was having a buy-one-get-one-free special on Ben and Jerry's ice cream pints. Since our appetites knew no limits at this point, we all chipped in and had a pint of ice cream each.

The next morning, since Johnnie's had bikes on hand for hiker residents, I rode a bicycle into town. I went to a local breakfast restaurant and ran into Bob, Patrick and Ross again and had breakfast with them. We couldn't seem to lose each other.

The next day, at a road crossing, seven miles from Erwin, I stopped to sit and eat an energy bar. While munching on the bar I noticed a female bear watching me from across the road. There was an approaching thunderstorm and I was trying to decide if I should try to hide somewhere from the storm or push on; the bear was complicating the decision-making process.

A pickup truck came up the hill and it was Bob and his boys again. They pulled over and we had a laugh about not being able to lose each other. There were a few close lightning strikes, so much so that we ducked. They offered for me to take refuge in the truck until it blew over, but then, as quickly as it started, it ended. They drove off and I hurried off down the trail, wanting to put some distance between the bear and myself. I didn't have the heart to tell my friends about the bear; they had enough of that a few days before.

Cherry Gap

After a zero day at Erwin, it was time to get back to work. It was mid-June, thunderstorm season, and there were storms all about. As a rule I was able to avoid most of the storms by controlling my hiking speed. I would either accelerate to get down the trail before a storm, or slow down and let it pass ahead of me. On this day I managed to avoid three storms with this technique. I arrived at the Cherry Gap Shelter before sundown and cooked dinner. As darkness settled in it appeared there would be no other hikers there that evening, so I decided to hang my hammock inside the shelter, a sleeping arrangement I had not previously tried.

I picked out some sturdy logs to wrap the hangers around and hung the hammock so there would be room should some late arrivals show up. About 10 p.m. an angry thunderstorm blew through with plenty of lightning and hail. Following the storm, the air cooled and it turned out to be a rather pleasant evening. I nodded off into a very comfortable sleep.

About 4:30 a.m. I awoke to hear some distant thunder, and could detect some flashes of light; unconcerned, I went back to sleep. At 5:30 I was awakened by an extremely close lightning strike and the accompanying crack of thunder.

The lighting I was experiencing now was all cracks, not rumbles, meaning it was very close and it was striking about every five seconds. The bolts were huge; two struck about one hundred feet in front of the shelter and one bolt traveled horizontally across in front of the shelter, right over the picnic table, maybe ten feet from where I was hanging in the hammock. This was one of the few times on the entire hike that I felt there was a chance that I might not survive; this was an extreme storm. Hail was piling up, making it look like a snowstorm had passed.

When there is a direct lightning strike on a tree, the heat generated inside the tree is so intense that the sap literally boils, and instantly turns to steam. The steam cannot escape the internals of the tree and the tree spontaneously explodes. It's extremely impressive. A bolt struck a tree just outside the shelter and the tree exploded with ear-splitting fury. All I could do was cower in my hammock and hope for the best.

Thank goodness the storm didn't last long. After it subsided, I went out to survey the damage. The exploded tree was in a million pieces. The top of the tree, which must have been up at seventy or eighty feet previously, had fallen intact, minus its bark, and was captured some forty feet up in the top of two other trees. It formed a football goal post configuration, the top caught horizontally in the "Y's" of the two trees supporting it.

There were leaves everywhere, torn off with the hail and wind, and small branches scattered about. Nature's fury was awesome to behold; I felt lucky to survive and witness it. Up until that point, it was easily the most powerful and dangerous storm of my hike.

Maytag Moment

The day was stunning. The passing storm had cooled things down and there was bright sunshine. I hiked along feeling fortunate to be alive. About mid-day I came to a side trail that had a note tacked to a tree to indicate there was some sort of supply and hostel about a half-mile off the Trail. I really didn't need re-supply, but visions of ice cream and cakes were my siren call to check it out.

The side trail turned into an old dirt road and it was starting to feel like I had walked much more than a half-mile when I spotted some old buildings. The yard off to the left had three ferocious dogs that were going berserk at my passing. Fortunately there was an anchor iron fence between us. The yard off to the right had several out buildings and an old mountain home. One of the out buildings appeared to be a barn that had been modified as a bunkhouse, although the door was boarded up. I went around to the house and knocked on the door. It was Saturday and nobody responded. I peered through the window on the door and knocked again. Nothing. I knocked one more time and was just turning to leave when some motion inside the building caught my eye. It was a dog and cat. The dog didn't bark but just looked up at me. Then a woman appeared and looked a bit startled to see me. She came to the door and inspected me through the window and then, seeing my backpack, realized I was a hiker. She cracked the door and explained that the hostel was technically closed for the season but she did have some food items left and offered to let me have a look. I agreed and she let me into the entry room, which had a freezer, fridge and some shelves stocked with various items that hikers thrive on: energy bars, rice cakes, etc. The freezer had ice cream, and the fridge had soft drinks.

I grabbed a cola and some snacks and she invited me into the dining room table to sit down and eat like a civilized human being, something I was becoming unaccustomed to. She was very pleasant, attractive and introduced herself as "She-Bee." We talked about the previous night's storm and she feared she had lost all of her electronics to a lightning blast: the TV, VCR, radio, clocks and perhaps the computer. As bad as that was, she was lamenting the loss of her washing machine. It seems that many weeks previously the washing machine had died. She told me that it had died in the same manner a few years before and that her ex-husband had ordered the parts and repaired it. She figured that if she ordered the same parts (she had the original slip) she could get it running again. However, having tried to work on the machine she realized that she could not figure out how to open it up.

I offered to have a look at it, having no clue if I could actually fix the thing, but I've never let a lack of knowledge get in the way. She pondered this but was conflicted; she had recently converted to Judaism and Saturday is the Sabbath, a day when work is not allowed.

After a few moments thought she rationalized that it would be okay for she had just converted from being a Baptist and therefore she was technically a Baptist-Jew.

I finished my snack and looked the machine over. It seemed to be a rather well-designed unit but, as She-Bee had already discovered, access to the internals was a mystery. Taking considerable time to look things over, I finally found hidden latches and releases and eventually had the cover off the machine. Then, crawling around on the floor, I was able to get a look at the inner workings. Sure enough, the transmission linkage to the motor was broken and she did indeed have the correct replacement parts. Unfortunately, she didn't have the correct tools; the machine was American standard sizes and her tools were metric, but after a laborious and judicious use of pliers and hammers, I was able to repair the machine.

All the while I was working we carried on a very friendly conversation. It was wonderful to have someone to talk with and I think she felt the same way. It had been many days since the last hiker had passed through and she lived out in a very lonely area. She told me that she worried that her very odd neighbor would scare away hikers, which were her livelihood at that time of year. About every hour he would mount up his riding lawn mower bedecked with Confederate flags and ride down the driveway, firing fireworks and in general making a scene and then go back into seclusion until the next hourly go-round. He wasn't very sociable so her life was isolated in the hiker off-season.

All told I had spent about five hours working on the washing machine. It was getting late in the day and I had several miles to go to the next shelter. She-Bee was obviously disappointed that I was departing. She looked at me a bit exasperated and then suggested that since that shelter was some distance away; perhaps I would be interested in staying there for the night. I could sleep in a big bed and not have to be in a cold drafty shelter full of mice. Recalling all of the destroyed electronics in the place I had visions of work for the next month.

Not to be rude, I picked up my pack and explained that I really wanted to get a move on. Disheartened, she followed me outside. As I turned to say good-bye she became teary-eyed and asked: "Could I give you a hug?" I said "Sure." She wrapped her arms around me and hugged me so hard that I suspect if it had lasted a minute longer, I'd have had to explain to Jane why I had gone to Argentina[1] instead of hiking the Appalachian Trail! As soon as I could break free I headed for the trail, relieved that I once again escaped...celibate.

Laurel Fork Falls

I didn't know what to expect at Laurel Fork Falls. It was listed in the *Thru-Hiker's Companion*, but there was no description. The manual briefly described the nearby shelter as, "Laurel Fork Shelter (1977) Sleeps eight. No Privy. Constructed from native rocks, this shelter is located on the blue-blazed high-water route above Laurel Fork. Water source is a stream 50 yards behind the shelter." I didn't expect much with this mundane description.

As I followed the trail to the falls, it became obvious that a long time ago someone had carved a route through miles of solid rock to provide a flat trail. I was walking along, inspecting the work, and as I rounded a corner I heard a muffled grunt and realized I had almost stepped on two people sitting right on the trail. A rather rotund

---

[1] In the summer of 2009, Governor Mark Sanford of South Carolina made the news when he claimed that he was going off to hike the Appalachian Trail, when in reality he was caught off on a love tryst in Argentina.

man, with what appeared to be two black eyes and a dark-haired woman I assumed to be his wife were startled by my approach. They confessed they thought I was a bear; their eyes were still wild with fear. I greeted them and after a few moments they calmed down and we struck up a conversation. It was obvious they were not serious hikers, because they had no packs, just belly bags and were carrying a six-pack of cola, not the best thing to be drinking on a hike.

After a time the gentleman lowered his voice and almost whispered, "You want to know a secret about this place?" Never one to pass up a good secret, I replied, "Sure!" He continued, "Not many people know that this area around the falls is loaded with meteorite. I have a theory that at one time a giant meteor impacted here and formed this canyon, and I have the proof: meteor material." Before I could respond, he reached into his belly bag and took out a sample, offering it to me for inspection. As soon as he handed it to me I was impressed with the extreme dark color and the lightness of the material. It truly did appear to be foreign to the area since everything around us was a pale gray tone and looked to be granite. He continued, "And better yet, I've discovered — and this is just between us— " he looked around to make certain nobody was eavesdropping, "this stuff has mystical properties." Now I was hooked — mystical properties! I was finally getting to the *real* secret. I gazed at the material, as one would inspect the freshly removed head of an alien. I was very puzzled. I'm an amateur astronomer, no expert, but I do know that meteorites are composed mostly of iron. The only reason meteorites are found on this planet is because during entry into our atmosphere some quantity of the iron does not burn up and impacts the earth but most ends up burning as a dust trail that is visible in the sky for a short time.

What this man had handed me was extremely light and felt as if it might disintegrate if squeezed. I asked, "Have you ever put this stuff into water to see if it would float?" Bubbling over with enthusiasm that someone was actually showing interest, he replied, "No, but I have ground it up and put the powder in water and some of that floats. I've discovered that if I rub it on my face it gives me a funny sensation, it tingles, a mystical tingle and I can't seem to get enough of the stuff." His wife nodded in agreement, obviously very proud of his genius. I had noticed earlier that his face, predominantly around his eyes and ears, was covered with something black, like the eye black you see under a football player's eyes.

I carefully handed back his precious sample. He handled it as if it were an unstable explosive and placed it back in his belly bag. He cautioned, that if I kept my eyes opened, I might be lucky enough to find some as well. At that point we parted ways.

As I walked along I did indeed find some samples, small bits of it were everywhere. As I picked up a piece, it disintegrated in my hand, and looking at it closely I realized it was coal, bituminous coal. It then hit me: of *course* it was bituminous coal. Back in the 1930's when the CCC or the WPA or whomever cut their way through these rocks, they needed jackhammers to do the cutting. In those days a steam-powered jackhammer was fed steam from a boiler that used coal to heat the water. The coal I was finding was from those long-ago workers.

There is a dandruff shampoo on the market that has coal tar in it. When I use it to control dandruff, it "tingles." My friend has been rubbing coal on his face and experiencing this tingle and somehow construed it to be the mystical properties of meteors. What possessed him to rub it on his face in the first place had me baffled. Then I thought how fortunate his wife was: supposing he was into studying bear scat, would he have rubbed that on his face as well? "Hey honey, check out *this* mystical property!"

Laurel Fork Falls were impressive, but after my encounter with mystical properties I was tingling way too much to pay it any mind. The shelter proved as unimpressive as the description.

Figure 13: Laurel Falls in the midst of a drought.

Mama and the Three Bears

The trail experience tends to unfold in a series of separate events. The hike is obviously one long, continuous trek, but some parts tend to fade from memory while others stand out, and are a source of continual mental reruns. For me, the Watauga Lake area is more memorable than Fontana Dam because the lake is much more visible. The trail follows the lake for a long way along a high ridge. Even though there are many trees obscuring the actual lake, there were enough short glimpses through the branches for me to enjoy views of the lake and provide a measure of progress. Walking in the woods without landmarks makes it difficult to ascertain your progress. One tree looks just like the last fifty.

I stopped at the Vandeventer Shelter at the north end of the lake. It was a warm afternoon and it felt great to stretch out and have a snack. I had the place to myself. I had not seen another hiker all day, just increasingly more deer. They were becoming so commonplace that I promised myself no more photographs of deer unless they were doing something more interesting, like maybe playing poker. Alas, I would break my promise many times; they were just such icons of the forest that I couldn't help myself.

I left the shelter lost in thought. I was nearing Virginia and excited about entering another state and taking a zero day. Time and again other hikers had told me that Virginia was so flat that a hiker could do 25-mile (40 km) days there — I was ready! I trudged along, looking at the ground, hardly noticing where I was going; hiking was becoming so automatic. As I strained up a small, steep section of the trail I was shocked awake by a dreadfully loud, "AAWWWEEERRRRGGG!" Twenty-five feet in front of me was a large female bear standing directly in the path. I then realized that there were three little black teddy bears with her — cubs! Nothing strikes more fear in the hearts of hikers, hunters or Lewis and Clark than a Mama bear and her cubs. I practically walked into her kindergarten session totally unaware.

I immediately froze. Regaining a modicum of equanimity, I softly started to talk to her and walk tenderly backwards. She seemed pleased with that and when I was about fifty feet away she hopped off into some bushes to the right of the trail and instantly became invisible. The cubs hadn't immediately noticed her departure and when they did, they started to run around in small circles whimpering and carrying on like the Three Stooges. "Great," I thought, "whimpering cubs; that should make Mama really happy." They were tripping over each other and pushing and shoving. Finally one of them noticed me and immediately flew up a tall oak next to the trail, way faster than any squirrel could have done. Soon the second cub spotted me and followed the first. The third cub was now in panic mode: no Mom and no siblings. It really started to whimper and then stopped dead, spotted me, and joined the others way up in the oak. What impressed me enormously was the effortless speed with which they accelerated up the oak. I judge it was nearly as fast as running on flat ground, and a healthy bear can cover ground at about 35 miles per hour (56 km/h). Their climbing speed was astonishing!

Now I had a real dilemma. Mama was hiding right on the side of the trail, her cubs were posted up about seventy feet in a tree about three feet on the other side of the trail. This was a bruin landmine that I wasn't going to attempt to get through. I knew Mama bear would wait all night if necessary, so I had to convince her that I was gone. I started to bushwhack off-trail and work my way around the bears. The brush was very thick and was mostly nettles (which itch) and poison ivy (fortunately, I'm not allergic to it) and thick blackberry bushes (loaded with thorns). I was bushwhacking through a virtual jungle.

It was demanding work and my progress was glacial. All the time I kept talking to Mama Bear as if I were in a group of people so she would know exactly my whereabouts. After an interminable time I encountered an extremely large fallen tree that offered a natural bridge over approximately 150 feet of the brush. I hopped up on it, grateful for a wooden "sidewalk" and made great progress for about 80 feet, when suddenly, "CRASH," my boots caved right through the tree trunk and I sank up to my waist, feet inside the tree and very stuck. My pack was resting on the tree trunk and I just could not gain an advantage to extract myself. I was sweating bullets because rattlesnakes love to live inside dead, hollow trees. Here I was, an upset bear family nearby, my legs possibly in an Indiana Jones snake pit, and stuck in the rotten tree. All I needed now was army ants, or maybe a forest fire to make the day complete.

Finally, I unbuckled and removed my pack and extricated myself from the predicament and hurried north on the trail. The thought occurred to me that anyone northbound behind me would be walking right into the bear ambush, but I never heard anything more about them, thank goodness.

I was ready for a break in Virginia.

Chapter 5 - Virginia 2007

Five

State number five, Virginia, contains a quarter of the entire Trail within its borders, 525 miles (845 km). Hiking from Springer Mountain to the Virginia border is 460 miles (760 km) and took me 38 days to hike; it was obvious I was going to be in Virginia for a while. As was the case with the other states, there wasn't much fanfare noting the state line, just a small line of stones placed across the trail by a hiker, with a note tacked to a tree indicating the border.

Damascus, VA is not far from the state boundary. I arrived there in late morning and went to the Mt. Rogers Outfitter to check into their hiker hostel. It is, by hiker standards, plush: hot showers; dry sleeping accommodations, and comfortable places to sit. Promise Keeper and Oorah left me a message that they were jumping up to Harpers Ferry, West Virginia and would come back from Maine to finish the Virginia section later. I would miss them; I had hoped to catch up with them.

My roommate, Curtis, was from Germany, with a Doctorate in Electrical Engineering, and a fellow ham radio operator. He was attempting a thru-hike, but the company he works for had contacted him to go back to Illinois to solve an engineering emergency and it didn't look like he would be able to return in time to finish his thru-hike.

It was nice talking with Curtis; we had much in common. His English was impeccable. How is it so many foreigners acquire such a mastery of English and we struggle to learn their language? He turned out to be a very adept designer of homemade hiking equipment;

most of his gear, including his hiking boots, was homemade. He saw me sewing my canvas bag for the water pump/filter and enthusiastically offered to do it for me. His skill was incredible; the bag looked better than new when he was finished.

He made one comment that I just adored, explaining that he had such vivid dreams about food that he feared they'd attract bears. He accurately described the mental state of most hikers by the time they reach Virginia: food was becoming an obsession.

I spent most of that Saturday doing laundry, eating, sleeping and relaxing; it was a vacation from the vacation. Sunday morning I decided to go back up the trail and put my ham radio on the air for while. It was a glorious day, the weather was tempting and I was anxious to make radio contacts from Virginia. As I climbed back up the trail, I gained considerable altitude and once again experienced those pains in my chest.

I found a nice spot, threw a wire up into a tree and put the "peanut whistle" of a station on the air. Tuning in I discovered that there was an amateur radio contest known as "Field Day" going on; I had forgotten it is on the fourth weekend of every June. The object of this contest is to take the radio into the field, operate from emergency power (batteries, generator, solar, etc.) and talk to as many stations as possible within 24 hours. The ulterior motive of this contest is to train participants in providing communications under simulated emergency conditions away from the grid and comforts of home.

I wasn't planning on being competitive but I figured it would be fun to see just how well the radio that I designed and built would perform. In under an hour I made seven contacts, talking to folks from New Jersey to Illinois, and down to Mississippi. I was once again impressed with modern technology. The radio uses less power than a penlight flashlight and yet was capable of direct communications to all these places.

Figure 14: My amateur radio operation from Damascus, Virginia.

Back in town I re-supplied and went to bed early, anxious to get deeper into Virginia.

Lost Mountain

Why do they name places "lost?" If it's lost then how did I find it? If it is truly lost, how did *anyone* find it? It may have been "Lost Mountain Shelter" but I did manage to find some new friends there. "Speedy" and "Maria" were the only two there and we hit if off right away. Speedy, a young man from Switzerland, was doing a long section from Springer to central Virginia. Maria was a thru-hiker but her snail's pace was putting her further and further behind schedule. I had encountered Maria briefly back in a North Carolina hostel, but she was asleep for most of my time there so I never really "met" her. At this point her goal was to hike to a friend's wedding at Harpers Ferry at the beginning of July. It was evident even *that* was a stretch and she would have to hitch a ride to the wedding. The good news is Maria was hiking the Trail to lose weight so she would look her best at the wedding and she definitely was having success.

Wise Shelter

On the way to the Wise Shelter there is a gigantic fenced-off area known as the Grayson Highlands State Park. The 4,822 acre (19.51 km²) park is renowned for its herd of wild ponies. As soon as I entered through the gate I was greeted by a number of them. They were not at all shy and came looking for treats. I didn't have anything to give them (you're not supposed to feed them anyway), but they tried nibbling on my pack, so I decided to move along before one of them tore something. The terrain in the park is unlike anything I'd experienced previously along the trail. It is populated with large rock outcroppings and barren of trees; it closely resembled the high plains and foothills of the Rocky Mountains in Colorado.

Not far from the park's northern exit is the Wise Shelter. Approaching the shelter, I could hear voices up in the nearby woods and the breaking of dead trees and branches. Maria and a disabled ex-marine named Kevin were gathering firewood. Though Kevin suffers from severe Vietnam-era injuries, he manages to hike the Trail for most of the hiking season. Kevin didn't lose any limbs in the war, but he was shot up very badly and his body is a mass of healed wounds. He's very engaging and has many entertaining stories about the Trail and every tale is laced with plenty of expletives. Prior to my arrival, Kevin had found the shelter taken over by Boy Scouts and their leaders. Groups are not supposed to commandeer shelters, and are in fact required to leave open a few slots for thru-hikers. Not one to mince words, Kevin verbally attacked them so aggressively that they all packed up, and retreated down the hill to set up camp.

Kevin embarrassed them so badly that they returned later, and offered some free food as an apology for taking over the shelter. Kevin didn't need the food, but Maria was extremely low on food and they gave it to her. The trail and timing was again proving magical. With the Boy Scout supplies and some dehydrated scrambled eggs I gave Maria, she had barely enough provisions to make it to her next re-supply. Thru-hikers are so food-obsessed that everyone teased Maria that only she could get scrambled eggs from a thru-hiker.

While there, the Scout leaders asked if they could take a photograph of the shelter, we said, "sure." We wondered why they asked us since we didn't own the shelter. Even more mysteriously, they didn't photograph the shelter from the front, but went way off to the side and I could tell they were actually taking photographs of *us* and not the shelter. At the time I thought this odd — we all did — but it wouldn't hit me until much later, in Pennsylvania, as to why they might want photos of a bunch of scraggly hikers.

Aren't They Cute?

Over the next several days I hiked on and off with either Maria or Speedy. They were good hiking companions and even though we all came from very different backgrounds, we had many interesting conversations about life after the trail. Maria comes from the world of clothes design and expressed an interest in going into law. Speedy works in mechanical design and plans to work for a time and save enough to go off on other adventures. His visa did not allow enough time to finish the trail and he would be leaving for Canada a few days later.

Late one afternoon it started to get rainy — that misty, drippy sort of weather that doesn't seem to be able to decide what to do. The three of us ended up at the Chatfield Shelter in early evening. Working with our headlamps, we set up for dinner at the picnic table. There was a heavy mist in the air, but it was tolerable. The headlamps pierced the wet air like searchlights, highlighting the droplets of water seemingly suspended in the air. We had our pots and eating dishes all arranged on the table, the stoves hissing away as the water boiled for our meals. A mouse came out from the shelter, hopped down the stone steps, scurried over to the picnic table, climbed it quickly and started running from dish to dish to see if it could find anything edible. There wasn't any food on the table; we were all holding it, and the pots were too hot for the mouse to get near. Surprisingly, to me anyway, Maria said, "Oh, isn't it cute?" Speedy agreed that they were cute. When I offered to take my boot and flatten the little critter, they were aghast! "How could you do such a thing, they're so cute" protested Speedy. Grudgingly I backed off and the mouse, finding nothing, climbed down and went back to the shelter.

After the meal it started to pour. With nothing else to do, we all got into our sleeping bags. Maria and Speed lay at opposite ends of the shelter, and I was in the middle. We extinguished our lamps and quieted down to sleep. After a few moments I heard Speedy shout, "Hey! Get away, go away!" Mice were crawling around on his sleeping bag. He shooed them away and a minute or two later they returned. After several iterations of this routine I heard him searching for his headlamp. Turning on his headlamp, he exclaimed in impeccable English, "Hey, the little bastards shit right on my camera!" I couldn't help myself and replied, "Aw, Speedy, but they're *soooo* cute." I could hear Maria giggling. In spite of that remark, Speedy and I did remain friends.

Nutt

One afternoon as I was walking along, I heard a woman scream just up ahead on the Trail. She sounded terrified, so I sprinted as hard as I could up the hill in the direction of the scream. As I accelerated I could feel something snap in my right lower leg, but adrenaline allowed me to ignore it. I had visions of a bear attack, but as I rounded the corner I spied Maria jumping up and down, yelling at the top of her lungs. I ran up to her and asked what the problem was; I couldn't see anything wrong. She pointed up into a tree where there were a few clear plastic bags hanging from a limb, with a rope tied to them. A trail angel had hung supplies in the tree for hikers. There were juice drinks, treats, toilet paper and other hiker-useful items. Maria was so excited because she was still low on supplies. I was happy for her; however, for me her euphoric cry and the ensuing sprint resulted in a painful leg and I feared I might have actually broken something. As I walked along, the leg became more painful and slowed me down.

My goal the next day was the Knot Maul Branch Shelter. Normally I would have arrived there in late afternoon, but because of the extreme pain and resulting slower pace, I didn't get there until 10 p.m. The shelter was full of hikers I had never met. It was dark, raining, and I was in no mood to put up the hammock. In spite of being wet and arriving after everyone had already gone to sleep, they all graciously and cheerfully made room for me and

I settled in. My new friends, "Boots," "Little Engine," "Caboose," and I talked for a few minutes once I was settled in and just as sleep was starting to overcome us, another headlamp appeared in the mist; it was Maria. As crowded as things were, everyone adjusted so Maria could climb in as well. It was one of the few nights I didn't hang my bear bag, not that anyone else did either, so everything was hanging from the shelter rafters: bear bags, wet clothes and packs. It was like sleeping on the floor in a department store under the merchandise racks. Boots thought the arrangement looked like "Bear Piñatas." Fortunately there were no prowling bears that evening and all went well.

I left early next morning, barely able to walk. It took me most of the day to cover five miles to U.S. Forest Service [USFS] road 222. The Forest Service roads are primarily access roads for the USFS, so many don't allow public travel, but some allow public access. I had no idea as to the status of this road crossing but I was convinced I was going to get to it and stay there until a vehicle would pass and see if I could hitch a ride.

When I came to the road there was a pickup truck parked at the parking area and the driver was sitting in the truck. I was hungry and sat down to cook up something and we struck up a conversation. His name was Tim and he told me he was waiting for his wife "Hiker Nutt," who was doing the A.T. in sections. He would drop her off at the start of the section and pick her up at a road crossing when she finished. Tim offered me a ride to town when she arrived. I couldn't believe my good fortune. Once again it seemed that when something was needed on the trail, it would somehow happen.

Hiker Nutt arrived and we crowded into their truck. Tim planned to get me to Bland, the nearest town that purported having a medical clinic. After a seven-mile drive to Bland and disappointedly finding that there was no clinic, they decided to take me to Wytheville, about eleven more miles away. In pain, I really didn't have the heart to resist and I suspect they would have ignored the protest anyway.

Wytheville had a full-blown hospital and emergency room. Tim and Hiker Nutt dropped me off and told me they would be back later to check on me. I told them not to bother, but they insisted.

The staff at Wytheville inspected my leg, took X-rays, and concluded that nothing was broken, but I did have a badly pulled ligament or tendon. The prescription was to stay off the leg and take Advil. Advil seems to be the pain killer of choice for hikers. Up until this point I hadn't taken anything other than aspirin to ward off my angina pains. I doubted that Advil would perform any special magic, but planned to follow the doctor's orders.

Tim and Hiker Nutt returned as promised. They had rented a room at a motel and insisted that I was to stay with them that night and they wouldn't have it any other way. Since they wouldn't let me pay my share of the room, I agreed to stay with them only if I could buy them dinner. I couldn't believe how kind and generous these folks were.

When my new friends brought me back to the trail the next morning, Hiker Nutt left on her hike and I limped along to the Chestnut Knob Shelter. My plan was to hike up to Chestnut Knob Shelter and "zero" there for a few days. Amazingly, hiking uphill did not hurt much, but downhill was sheer agony. Fortunately the walk up to Chestnut Knob was mostly uphill.

The shelter was fabulous; it was the first one that actually has a door and windows. This stone structure was a former fire warden's cabin. It was situated up on a high ridge with excellent views in many directions. This was going to be a marvelous spot to zero. The shelter actually has bunk platforms so I picked out one, cooked a lunch and took a nap — life was good.

Later in the afternoon I went out to find water. The *Hiker's Companion* guidebook states, "No water is available at this shelter, but is sometimes found 0.2 miles south on the A.T." I went back down the trail looking for water, but with the drought, found none. If I couldn't find water, I wouldn't be able to stay. I hunted around in the woods and not far from the shelter I did find a "pond." It was perhaps fifty feet across and smelly and murky. There were signs of life in the water; something was jumping and splashing about — I thought perhaps it might be a mutated ten-pound E. coli bacterium.

Dirty, or not, I needed water. I put my water filter hose into the "murk" and started pumping. Gradually the pumping became more difficult, the pump was sucking up so much mud that the filter was clogging. I pushed harder on the pump handle and suddenly there was a "*pop*" and the bottom of the pump blew out! Great, now I couldn't get any more water. I did carry water purification tablets for backup but, even if I used them, the water would still be mud pudding. I had pumped enough water before it broke, but I wouldn't be able to stay more than the one night.

Later that day a few others showed up. One fellow, "Clark," was hiking with his dog, Petey. Clark and Petey were doing the Trail in sections. There's mixed emotions about dogs on the Trail. Well-behaved dogs, like Petey, are nice to be around but there are some that have no social skills and a wet, muddy dog jumping around in a shelter, shaking off and lying on a sleeping bag, can really taint one's view of dogs.

Most thru-hiking dogs fit right in, but many weekend and section hikers fail to realize the ramifications of their dogs' behavior when in the hiking environment. They're out for a weekend or perhaps a few days and haven't fully considered that the trail can be a crowded place at times. This is no different than any neighborhood, really; some neighbors do a marvelous job of keeping their dogs in control and others just don't bother. I've lived with dogs for most of my life and love them, but in close-quarter living, dogs barking all night or stealing food from plates can lead to serious tensions. In that respect the trail is really no different from anywhere else.

Figure 15: Chestnut Knob Shelter, one of my favorite shelters; it actually had a door.

The next morning I struck out for Bland, VA. I figured it would be a good place to zero for a day or two and let my leg rest. Clark indicated he would be interested in sharing a room at the motel; the next day he was getting a shuttle back to Damascus to pick up his car, having completed his section hike for the year. We made it to the road leading into Bland and after perhaps half an hour managed to hitch a ride from a woman driving to work in her Jeep. She drove like a NASCAR contender and dropped us right at the motel. Across the street from the motel there was a truck stop with a Dairy Queen and burger shop. I have a weakness for Dairy Queen, so this was my idea of paradise. Pets were accepted at the motel, so Clark, Petey and I settled in. I offered to split the cost of the shuttle with Clark and ride back to Damascus with him the next day if he would drop me back at the motel, which was on his way home anyway. This would be an opportunity to fix or replace my water filter/pump at the outfitter in Damascus and do some laundry.

The next morning the shuttle picked us up and brought us the eighty miles back to Damascus. When Clark attempted to start his car, the battery was dead. He told me to go ahead and do laundry and go to the outfitters; in the meantime he would call for assistance to get the car started.

I walked the mile to the Laundromat and on the way there I had a serious chest pain, so much so that I had to sit on a park bench for while. This was my worst angina incident to date and it was nearer to noon, not the usual early-morning variety. Unfortunately, I had forgotten my aspirins; they were back at the motel. I gradually recovered and did my laundry. I stopped at a convenience store to look for aspirin but they didn't have any. When I told Clark what happened he panicked and drove around to find me some; I guess he didn't want a dead stiff riding around in his car.

Our ride back to the motel was uneventful. He explained to me how as a Spanish teacher he had the good fortune of being able to visit Cuba as part of his teaching experience. We took the scenic route back to the motel, rather than the highway. It was a nice way to kill the day and take in some of the local scenery. Clark dropped me at the motel and we parted ways; I was alone again.

I was also alone again with my thoughts. Was it time to think about getting this heart situation checked out? I couldn't really decide. Was I playing with the dice of life? Was it something else and not the heart? Was I being foolish? I concluded that if it happened again I would get off the Trail at Pearisburg, VA and head back to Sarasota to have it checked. Pearisburg would have many opportunities for transportation; there wasn't much in Bland.

I spent a quiet evening at the motel. I went outside, sat in a lounge chair, and talked on my ham radio walkie-talkie for while with some local hams from the Virginia Appalachian Wireless Association and then went to bed.

Happy Birthday

It was the 5th of July; I called Jane to wish her a happy birthday. It was wonderful to hear her voice; communications in this region was iffy at best and cell connections were rare. My leg was doing much better. To my amazement, the Advil and rest worked just as the doctor said it would.

I hiked all the next day in relative comfort. That evening, on the way to Jenny's Knob Shelter, I stepped right over a copperhead snake as it wriggled between my feet. I never saw it coming. It stopped at the trailside and I managed to take a few photos of it. Copperheads are just as dangerous as rattlesnakes and give no warning. I'm told they have an odor like cucumbers, but I didn't smell anything.

When I got to the intersection for the blue trail to the shelter, there was a handwritten note posted that said there was no water at the shelter. I figured that I had enough to hold me for the night and went to the shelter. As I ate dinner I noticed two deer walking by at a distance. I quietly followed them, figuring they never get too far from water. Sure enough, about four hundred feet from the shelter they stopped and drank from a small pool of water. There was enough flow to easily refill my water bottles. The next morning I left a note that there was water and drew a map for those that would follow.

Wapiti Shelter

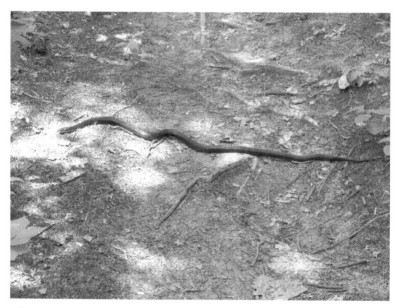

Figure 16: A typical Southern Black Snake.

On the way to the Wapiti Shelter, in the span of about two hundred feet, I managed to spook a large female bear, encountered a large Southern black snake, and spied on a doe and her twin fawns standing in the Dismal Creek drinking. This was a great photo opportunity had I not had been singing loudly to let the bear know where I was, so the deer bolted off at the sound of my crooning. My singing seems to have that same effect on my human audiences.

That evening at the shelter was one of the most peaceful moments I think I have experienced in my life. I built a fire. As I was appreciating the beautiful sunset, a deer walked around the campsite, ignoring me. It was moments like this that made me really treasure being alone in the wilderness. I didn't realize it at the time, but 15 years previously two thru-hikers were murdered not far from this shelter. The shelter register showed that the previous night the shelter was so crowded that people had to put up tents, and here I was serene and alone.

I slept well in my hammock until about 1 a.m. A bear awakened me trying to get at my food bag hanging in a tree. It struggled for about an hour and was making so much noise that I couldn't sleep. Finally I barked like a dog and the bear took off. I went back to sleep and wasn't bothered the rest of the night.

Leaving the next morning I had severe angina pains and that was it, I decided that I would go back home to get it checked out; it wasn't going away, regardless of how much I wished it would. The last thing that I wanted was for some poor hiker to have to load me onto their backpack and carry out my body. It was time.

Pearisburg

Originally I intended to stay in a motel in the center of town at Pearisburg, but it was crowded with tourists and didn't appear inviting. I continued two more miles across town (after stopping at the Dairy Queen of course) and stayed at the hiker hostel at the Catholic Church. This hostel is *top shelf*! It has bunk spaces, a reading room, kitchen, porches, and a gazebo. They ask for a contribution, but there is no specific charge. Hopefully they get sufficient funds to keep it running, because it really is awesome.

Boots, Engine and Caboose, my friends from Knot Maul Shelter, were there. Engine and Caboose were getting off the trail for a few days to go to a family function and were getting a shuttle the next day to Virginia Tech [VT], so I asked if I could tag along. From VT I would be able to take the Smart Bus for just three dollars, a low-cost regional transit, to Roanoke Airport. That evening several of us walked down to the local shopping plaza, ate at a nice Italian Restaurant, and returned to bed early.

The next day everything went like clockwork. Our shuttle driver, Brenda, from the local hotel, arrived and drove us to Virginia Tech. We laughed for most of the trip as she related a story about her son and my hiking friend Maria. It didn't sound like Maria was going to make it much further up the trail. From VT we caught the Smart Bus and arrived at the airport as planned. Since I couldn't find a reasonably priced airfare on short notice, I rented a car and drove home. I was in Sarasota by midnight on the 8th of July, 2007. Now I faced the biggest challenge of my hike.

Part II

Chapter 6 - 300 Zeros

Fixing the pump

Jane was thrilled to see me again, as I was to see her; we had never been apart so long. I took a few days to get caught up on sleep, eat, and line up appointments with doctors.

Once again I passed the various stress tests, EKG's and medical inspections. The cardiologist then scheduled me for a catheterization. During this procedure, a small tube is inserted into a vein in the thigh and pushed up into the arteries around the heart to inspect them. In some cases, if a blockage is found, an angioplasty is performed. Here a balloon-like device is inflated in the blood vessel to break up cholesterol blockages.

On July 19th I went in for my catheterization. I dressed minimally, knowing I would have to wear one of those open-backed medical robes. Why don't they just give us a short-pant version of "Dr. Denton's," the ones with the little flip-down door in the back? At least that would be more civil. This procedure didn't even need a door; they were going in through my thigh.

The original plan was for Jane to pick me up after the procedure. Much to our surprise, as soon as I was lucid, the cardiologist explained that I was in serious danger of dying and ordered me to get to the Sarasota Memorial Hospital immediately to have a heart bypass operation. The cardiologist didn't even want me to take time to return home to get my glasses; he felt my condition was way too urgent for such trivial things. This was getting scary.

We arrived at the hospital, only a few minutes from the outpatient office, and Jane scolded me for attempting to walk from the van to the door. She *ordered* me sit in a wheelchair while she parked the van. I felt a bit foolish, having just walked 622 miles (1001 km) on the Appalachian Trail; surely I could walk into the hospital. She rolled me into admissions and in no time at all I was off for my heart surgery.

You're Getting Sleepy

In pre-op a fellow named Joseph came to shave the hair off of my chest. He was very pleasant and had a great sense of humor. Why wouldn't he; I was the one getting cut open like a rib roast? We joked around and I was actually enjoying everything. I wasn't feeling any pain and didn't really think I was that serious. I asked Joseph, and I wanted an honest answer, what my odds were to make it through this surgery? He didn't know and went to ask; I figured if I'm going into this, I might as well know. Joseph came back and told me my odds "are about 1 out of 99 for not making it." That was a bit sobering; if that was odds in a lottery, there'd be a good chance of walking away with some money, but in surgery there was a sizeable chance of not walking away at all.

They rolled me into the operating room and I was rather surprised by the layout; it was a large room, bordering on vast. I had pictured something like the TV operating rooms where they all seemed crowded into a hospital closet. But then again on some of those TV hospital shows a lot more goes on in the closet than the operating rooms. They gave me a preliminary sedative and told me that I might start feeling sleepy an..d...th...e..n...

Six?

I could hear a woman's voice, it seemed very far away, "Try not to cough, Mr. Blanchard, we have a tube down your throat and I will remove it shortly." As I regained consciousness, I slowly became aware of my surroundings.

I was in an Intensive Care Cardiac Unit [ICCU]. Michelle, a nurse with a wonderful Irish brogue was assigned to me, one-on-one. She explained that I had a six-artery heart bypass (I didn't know there were that many). She explained that there are six pairs of arteries, six bringing blood into the heart muscles to run them, and six others taking away the depleted blood to recharge it with oxygen. I had one artery in each pair that was shutting down.

As it was explained to me, I was suffering from a genetic failure, as opposed to the more common cholesterol blockage. My arteries would collapse when I relaxed, such as sleeping at night. Subsequently, upon becoming active (climbing the hill after getting water in the morning came to mind), the arteries were unable to keep up with the demand and would cause the angina pains. After a short period of time, the arteries would "pump up" and I would be fine. The danger was, if they didn't pump up I could have a heart attack. The heart attack is much more severe than angina because heart cells can actually die during a heart attack and most often cannot be repaired. I hadn't had a heart attack but certainly would have, had I not left the Trail and returned for medical attention.

My first reaction in the ICCU was hunger. My hiker body was starved. Michelle asked if I would care for some breakfast. "Would I? Of course!" I replied enthusiastically. Since I had no food restrictions, she brought scrambled eggs, yogurt, toast, cereal, fruit, tea, and milk. I devoured it. I noticed other nurses stopping by with a puzzled look on their face. My nurse explained that the word had gotten around that I was eating like a horse. Usually after artery surgery patients are not interested in eating; they might nibble on Jell-O or something, but I was eating like a lumberjack.

An hour later it was lunchtime and the nurse asked if I would care for lunch, having just had breakfast, I said, "Sure!" Lunch was meatloaf, mashed potatoes, gravy, peas, drinks and dessert, a feast fit for a king. Once again I had nurses peering in disbelief. The Sarasota Memorial Hospital has some of the best food I have ever had anywhere and that only made my appetite more ravenous. They're lucky I wasn't stealing food from the other patients. I was starting to think like a bear; maybe I had been out in the woods too long. At least the other patients hadn't started hanging their food in bear bags yet. My appetite never did subside while I was in the hospital.

After a day or so they moved me to a regular cardiac ward where I was to start my actual therapy and learn how to work toward a complete recovery. It was surprising to me how quickly the medical professionals wanted the patient to get up and walk. During the surgery they cut open my chest, pushing the ribs aside like a folding door, and worked on the heart. The incision was about ten inches long, and as large as that sounds, I suspect it is cramped working quarters. The surgeons also removed a length of vein from my leg to use as material to repair the arteries. They turned the vein inside out and actually sewed it in as a bypass around the defective sections, not in place of the old material. The work was microscopic, intense and demanding; I have nothing but respect for the surgeons, nurses, and my cardiologist.

I was up and walking right away and welcomed it. My legs just didn't want to stay still. My lungs were doing well too. After artery bypass surgery, the lungs have to recover from the stress of the operation. Their capacity is diminished due to the stress and need to rehabilitate. One tool used to do this is the "incentive spirometer."

To use the spirometer one inhales and attempts to raise a gauge that indicates lung strength. Prior to the operation I impressed the nurse training me in its use by exceeding the device's 100% indicator. At sixty, my lungs were in good tune. Following the surgery I was remarkably back to full lung capacity, with effort, on the third day. Because I was doing so well with the incentive spirometer, and also lapping the nurses' station in unassisted walks, they decided it was time for me to go home, a day or two earlier than most. I suspect the real reason was I was breaking the budget for the kitchen.

Part of the discharge routine requires taking a chest X-ray to record the chest's condition upon leaving. The X-ray technician came into my room with a portable unit and took the X-ray. A little later someone came back to report on the X-ray; saying, "Mr. Blanchard, your X-ray indicates you only have one lung." Stunned, I argued, "That can't be, I know I have two, and I've been sending the spirometer through the ceiling." He replied, "I'm sorry, of course you have two. What I meant was that you have only one that is functioning, the left one is collapsed and the cavity around it is filled with liquid." I was told this is not uncommon after artery bypass surgery. After all the hiking and years of competitive biking, I was in really good physical condition with a lung capacity beyond what they normally see, especially for an old codger.

They rolled me to a lab to drain the liquid. This is a simple procedure: using a syringe that appeared the size of a soda straw they enter the cavity through the back and extract the liquid from around the lung so it can pop back into place. This procedure sounds dreadfully painful, but it was easy to ignore the pain, especially since I had several good-looking female doctors performing the procedure; they could have cut off a finger and I would not have noticed.

Returning me to the cardiac unit for a day's observation, I was told to expect some minor discomfort afterwards, but it shouldn't be anything to worry about. About half an hour after returning to the room, I did start to get uncomfortable and after another fifteen minutes or so I was hurting. I called my nurse, Margo.

After taking one look at me Margo hurried out to get another nurse and the head nurse. They conferred briefly and then called the surgeon who happened to be nearby; he in turn called in the cardiologist and another specialist. By this time I was in extreme pain. My chest felt ready to explode, my lower abdomen was wrenching, the muscles felt ready to tear apart and I was so stressed I lost the ability to talk; all I could do was nod my head yes or no. The huddle around my bed consisted of three doctors on one side and three nurses on the other side; I felt like a football on the line of scrimmage.

Now I was so stressed that my entire backside was off of the bed, my back bowed. I was supporting myself on just my heels and the back of my head — everyone could see that I was in agony. The doctors were at a loss. Margo, on the other hand, suggested that I was having a muscle spasm, not a problem with the heart, and that morphine should bring me back under control in five to seven minutes if a spasm was the problem. I thought if not, what then? The doctors, willing to take any suggestion, agreed to try it. Within five minutes of receiving the morphine I was comfortable enough to talk again. I was so impressed with Margo's coolness under fire that I told her I thought she should have been a fighter pilot.

This episode left me with torn stomach muscles and damage in my rib cage and possibly a few broken ribs.

These injuries hurt far more than the surgery did and lasted for about two months after I left the hospital.

Therapy

Five days after surgery, I went home. I was not allowed to lift anything heavier than five pounds—I was eating meals that weighed that much. I couldn't drive of course, and I had to attend physical therapy. Walking is considered really good therapy and I was encouraged to walk as much as possible and I was ready for that. The first full-day home I walked three miles and it was bliss. The next day I walked about five miles. On the third day I was intending to walk as much as seven to ten miles but I noticed my ankle was swelling where they harvested (that's what the medical folks call it) the vein from my leg to repair the heart.

I called the surgeon to find out if anything was amiss. He asked how much walking I had been doing. I replied, "Well, let's see, on the first day I did three, on the second day I did five and today I was planning on maybe seven to ten miles..." there was a long silence on the phone and then the doctor said, "Mr. Blanchard, they didn't write that therapy book for you. They're expecting you to do maybe five *minutes* the first day, seven to ten the second day and so on. *Minutes!* Perhaps you should cut back a bit." Once again, the medical profession expects the patient to be out of shape, to dislike exercise and to eat all the wrong things; they simply didn't have exit instructions for someone in good physical condition.

For the next few months I took things slowly. I attended therapy sessions three days a week and worked out on exercise bikes, treadmills and did some minor weight exercises. Gradually I was allowed to advance the exercise programs and, even though the therapy paled in comparison to my normal regimen, it felt good to be alive and regaining my strength.

I normally never watch television, maybe an hour or two a year at most. During this recovery period I couldn't do much, so I watched television and read. I especially enjoyed the Discovery Channel but after a few months I was starting to see re-runs. I voraciously read a number of books each week and eventually started to get back to my normal activities, including my beloved bicycling.

It was about five months before I could ride the bicycle again. The last thing I wanted to do was fall down on my chest. It felt terrific to be on the bike. I wasn't very aggressive and the rides were fairly leisurely, ten to twenty mile affairs, but I was outdoors and really appreciating life. My post-surgery biking was a long way from my favorite sport, mountain bike racing; five years prior, I had won the New England Mountain Bike Masters Division Championship. Now, in some ways, I was feeling quite the champion for having come through everything in such good condition.

There were a number of artery bypass patients in my therapy sessions at the gym who were depressed, unenthusiastic, and discouraged. The medical staff had warned me prior to going into the surgery that there was a high probability of depression afterwards. Some people, they said, only suffer a few hours depression; others can go for months, even years. Even though I had not experienced any depression, it was now all around me.

It seemed that I didn't suffer depression because I was still high from hiking the A.T. and I now realized that I was going to be healthy enough to finish the Trail. Furthermore, the surgery was a result of a genetic problem and I didn't have to make major changes in my lifestyle. For example; Jane and I tend to avoid eating large amounts of meat and favor a well-balanced diet from all the important food groups. We don't eat out that often; restaurant serving sizes are fine for hiking the A.T. but way too caloric for the average American's sedentary lifestyle. Even an active lifestyle can't handle that many calories!

My advice for those facing heart surgery and the impending depression is to get into shape, eat right, quit smoking and get involved in something active, be it golf, tennis, walking, biking, swimming, or rowing. I once suggested increased sex could work wonders, but I just got that "stare" from Jane. Get off the couch and get away from the television. Get outside, smell the roses, take a walk, ride a bike, or find a yoga class.

Above all else, take an interest in *something*. I had finishing the hike to look forward to; the desire to complete the hike drove me toward healing. Find something motivating to do, be it volunteer work, learning a new skill, such as how to play a piano or operate a computer. The point is, the mind needs a goal, something to shoot for and that target will pull you along and leave behind your pain and other post-surgical distractions. View the operation as a temporary situation that will improve; see it as a second life, a new opportunity.

One unfortunate woman in my therapy class kept bemoaning the fact that she had always eaten correctly, moderately exercised, kept her weight down, never smoked, and yet she had an artery bypass. Rather than accept the fact that these were the cards she was dealt, she fixated on the problem rather than the solution. I could see she was headed for a disappointing outcome. Don't look back, look forward; appreciate the gift of life and move on. Life is too short to squander lamenting the past. You cannot change your past, but you *can* change your future.

That is exactly what I did. After 300 days, 300 hundred "zero days," as I saw them, my cardiologist could no longer find excuses to keep me from returning to the Trail. On the 20th of May, 2008, that is exactly what I did.

Part III

Chapter 7 - Virginia 2008

Happy Trails Again

I had given a presentation about my hike at the local
A.T.C. club meeting, announcing that I was going back
to re-start the trail again at Pearisburg. A club member,
Brendan, asked if he could join me and hike from
Pearisburg, Virginia to Bear Mountain, NY. Brendan had
hiked everything south of Pearisburg, as well as some
north of it and wanted to knock off another large chunk
of the trail.

Brendan's wife Linda drove us to the St. Petersburg,
Florida airport for our flight to Roanoke, VA. After she
dropped us off we went through the usual gyrations
involving the Homeland Security shakedown. I had
checked my pack and Brendan had shipped his ahead, so
all we had were carry-on items. At the peek-a-boo bag
inspection machine they found that Brendan had a
serious terrorist weapon, a 20 oz. jar of unopened
peanut butter. This was serious cause for alarm and it
seemed that at any minute Brendan would be whisked
away to Guantanamo and I would never see him again.
As his accomplice, the staff took a dim view of me as
well. Even though the jar was sealed, and he offered to
open it and eat some, even share it with them if they
cared to, that jar of peanut butter was a security risk and
simply could *not* be taken on the plane. What was
almost comical was the fact that I was carrying my
hiking pole, a potential deadly weapon (I only use one,
just a personal preference; most carry two) and nobody
looked twice at it. Go figure.

After making a memorable scene about the peanut
butter, we went into the boarding area. As we were

waiting to depart, we were walking around chatting, not really watching where we were going. We walked through a small security gate and into a larger room, and then realized we had just exited the boarding area and were now back in the main lobby. Even though we were only about three feet past the gate, right next to the security guard, we couldn't re-enter without going through the peek-a-boo carry on bag inspection again. We went around to the entrance and some very puzzled looking Homeland Security types stared us up and down very suspiciously with that "What are these characters up to?" look. Once again we had to remove shoes, get inspected, detected, dissected, corrected and almost rejected before they let us back in. We weren't even near the trail and it was already an adventure!

Brendan had arranged with the owners of a motel in Pearisburg to give us a shuttle ride from Virginia Tech, so we caught the Smart Bus to the Tech. Brenda, from the motel, was there to meet us and it was like old times. I don't know how well she recalled me, but her son had become involved with my old hiking friend Maria, who never made it beyond Pearisburg.

Brenda informed us of an attempted murder the night before, up near the Wapiti Shelter, the last shelter I stayed in before going back to Florida. It appears a deranged ex-convict befriended two fishermen and they invited him to their camp; they even shared some of their catch with him and then he pulled a gun on them. When they ran, he shot one of them; the other made it to his pickup truck. The ex-con caught up with the truck owner and shot him in the head while he was attempting to start the truck. The ex-con then dumped him out of the truck and disappeared. Miraculously, both men survived, or at least had up to our arrival. So there was a manhunt on the trail around Pearisburg. This was just what I needed, some excitement to liven up the hike. We learned the next day that the ex-con died in a police chase. Later, down the trail, I would learn much more about this incident.

The next morning, at long last, I was hiking again. The trail is literally in front of the motel and it felt so "right" to be back out there; back into my adventure, one that for while I was certain was over.

We did the seven miles to Rice Field Shelter in short order and were there around noontime. It was 13 miles (21 km) to the next shelter so we called it a day, no use pushing when just starting out. I hung my hammock and it was like going home after being away for a long time; it seemed like I had just left the Trail.

Unlike the previous season, we were now hiking right in with the main wave of northbound thru-hikers. Most of them had started in the March timeframe in Georgia and were now just arriving in the Pearisburg region. Additionally, there is an annual event held in Damascus, Virginia known as "Trail Days" and the current crop of hikers, as well as many that have previously done a thru-hike, attend this three-day event. Hiking vendors hawk their wares and the town celebrates the A.T. with seminars, parades and eating opportunities, fulfilling it's reputation as one of the friendliest towns on the trail. I was a few days ahead of all the hikers that attended that event and I knew they would be coming up behind me.

Most importantly to me, my heart and chest felt fine.

Bonk

Mountain bike racers have a term for getting to the point the body is running low on fuel and can't keep up with the physical demands being imposed on it: "bonking out." On the second day out from Pearisburg I bonked. My body wasn't used to the physical demands of hiking, or feeding it properly so as not to run out of energy before day's end. I realized I would need to eat more in the morning and snack more during the day.

I took a break about a mile before the Pine Swamp Branch Shelter, ate a peanut butter sandwich, and then continued to the shelter. I was so exhausted I put up the hammock and took a two-hour nap. It was only a thirteen-mile day, but I just wasn't ready for that kind of aggressive hiking yet. I awoke, had dinner and was in bed by 6:15, well before sundown.

By the third day out I was already running low on food and looking forward to a zero day. As good fortune would have it, on day five, we hit the jackpot for trail magic. It was Memorial Day weekend and two long distance hikers, "Walrus" and "Root," were now trail angels. They had set up a picnic site at the VA621 road crossing. They served everything a hiker could wish for: salads, burgers, hot dogs, desserts, drinks and even had folding chairs. I spent about two hours there just eating. While talking with Walrus and Root, I learned that they were former members of the Florida A.T. club in Sarasota and knew many of the members I now knew. Small world!

Someone there asked Brendan what his trail name was, and he replied, "Pawn Power" because he is an avid chess player. Pawn Power has a Maryland "twang" and when he pronounced his trail name, it sounded more like "Porn Power." That brought a good laugh from all those gathered at the trail magic. Try as he might, Pawn Power couldn't throw the accent. He vowed at some point in the future to come up with another name, something that would work with his twang.

Figure 17: Memorial Day Trail Magic. Life is good.

A few of the hikers had been there all day, relaxing, eating and in general just taking it easy. It is difficult to relate how much a stop like that can mean to folks that have been walking all day, day in and day out, for months. For me it was sheer bliss. Upon leaving, our hosts packed a meal to take with us. I was extremely grateful for their kindness.

A few miles from the magic, after a considerable climb uphill, I came to the Audie Murphy Memorial, honoring the country's most decorated WW II soldier. After the war Murphy found his way to Hollywood and starred in some B Westerns but never found the acclaim he enjoyed during the war. In 1971, he was killed in a plane crash very near the location where the monument stands. It seemed so appropriate to be there on Memorial Day. It made me recall my brother and what our family had endured. As I gazed at the monument, lost in thought, I was snapped back to reality with the arrival of "Trout" and the "Three Chefs;" ("C.C. Rider," "Hare" and "Neon," but my trail name for them was the Three Chefs due to their cooking talents). The next day Trout was to meet her Dad and leave the trail. She was going back to the "real world" — and a job.

I joined this merry crew and that night the Three Chefs outdid themselves with their cooking at the Pickle Branch Shelter. I'm certain the smell of garlic and spices alerted every bear for twenty miles around.

The next day, at a road crossing, there was a going-away party for Trout with cake, beer and soft drinks. Even though I hardly knew them, I was brought into the circle of friends as if I had known them for years — such is the generosity of thru-hikers. People often ask, "Weren't you lonely on the trail, hiking by yourself?" The truth is you're never really alone and friendships come and go almost daily. It is almost impossible to be alone, unless you really want to be.

Dragon's Tooth

Since Georgia I had been hearing about the "Dragon's Tooth." There were stories of climbs, rocks and a descent that would challenge the best of thru-hikers. It seemed to strike fear in the hearts of many and I admit being a tad concerned. Of course those telling the stories had never actually seen that area, but they *knew* someone that had. It reminded me of the ancient sailors that lived in fear of sea monsters and falling off the edge of the flat earth. I decided to wait and see for myself.

I found the Dragon's Tooth to be eye candy, but the approach to it was not especially challenging. In several places trail maintainers had made the descent northbound easier by putting in rebar handgrips, but all in all, I didn't find it exceptionally difficult. I was learning not to respond to hearsay and to decide for myself how bad or good things really are; everyone seems to have dramatically different standards.

After leaving the Dragon's Tooth, a road crossing offers access to the Catawba Grocery on route VA311. Never one to miss an opportunity for food and refreshments; I found my way there. I waited for some time before Pawn Power showed up and I had eaten several burgers, soft drinks and milkshakes in the interim.

Pawn Power went on ahead, taking a shortcut, walking up the road rather than the Trail. He had previously hiked this section and just wanted to get to the next shelter. We were to meet at the Catawba Mountain Shelter, but when I arrived there he had left a note that he had pushed on to the Campbell Shelter. It was late in the day but I figured I could make the Campbell shelter by nightfall. Along the way I passed McAfee Knob. This is no doubt the most photographed precipice on the A.T. It is an overlooking cliff that is about 3,100 feet above sea level and over a thousand feet from the valley floor below. It offers spectacular views and, of course, I had to stop and have my picture taken on the edge. The Three Chefs were there cooking dinner; I could smell it even before I saw them. We chatted for a time and then C.C. Rider took my photo for me.

I bid them farewell and got down to the Campbell Shelter. It was very near dark when I arrived. Pawn Power was listening to a mother reading an adventure story to her two young hikers. Their Dad had a fire going but the smoke made it nearly impossible to sit at the picnic table. Suffering through the smoke, I made chow and listened to the story as well. While sitting there I could see headlamps coming down the trail from the direction I had just come. I figured it was the Three Chefs. Suddenly their lamps seemed to dance in every direction and didn't advance for a few minutes. I saw the flash of cameras and figured that they had found something interesting; they did indeed — a rattlesnake. The snake was laying on rocks right in the trail and they didn't see it until they almost stepped on it. It struck at them, but missed. They were pretty shaken and excited when they got to the shelter, but they did have good photographs of their encounter.

While we were reviewing their pictures on the camera, Pawn Power gave out a yell! He was in the shelter in his sleeping bag and a friendly, but harmless, corn snake slithered into the bag with him. He leaped out of the bag and got the snake out and put it outside the shelter. He calmed down and then finally got back into the bag, only to have the snake come right back and crawl in again. This snake was determined to stay warm for the night. He finally transported the snake far enough away so that it didn't come back; at least it wasn't a rattler. I tried to convince him that he should have kept the snake, then he wouldn't have to worry about mice bothering him, but he didn't see the humor in it.

Figure 18: The obligatory McAfee Knob picture that every thru-hiker has taken.

Lost

Early next morning Pawn Power and I headed north on the trail. It was a cool, crisp morning, the sun was shining and the world was alive with the sounds of the forest, birds, insects, water flowing and no sounds of civilization. Over the previous few days I had concluded that Pawn Power was hard of hearing, so I made certain to stay close in case I heard something interesting. He had been complaining that with all his years hiking he had never seen a bear in the wild; I assured him if he stuck with me that would change, since I was becoming something of a bear magnet.

We were only a few minutes from the shelter and I had fallen behind, perhaps 30 feet, when Pawn Power stopped to point to a box turtle right in the middle of the trail. At that very same moment I heard a huge amount of noise just over the other side of a rock outcropping next to where we were standing. There is only one animal that makes that much noise in the forest—a bear, a *big* bear. Pawn Power didn't notice the noise and thought my gestations of alarm resulted from excitement about the turtle. Not wanting to alert the bear to our presence, I did a pantomime routine: grimacing like a roaring bear showing its teeth and alternating between waving my arms as if to engulf him in my grip and moving my hands as if to click a camera. Only then did he understand my message.

Moving like a Laurel and Hardy re-enactment, more than a Lewis and Clark team, we climbed onto the rock wall and peered over. Sure enough, there was a massive male bear tearing a rotted log apart only a few feet away. We took photos and even with all the noise the bear was making, he heard the camera click and stopped what he was doing and looked us right in the eye. All of the authoritative books on bears seem to agree on one thing: if you're close enough to a bear to cause it to change its activity pattern, you're too close, and in possible danger. I signaled Pawn Power to get down and start up the trail as quickly as possible. He resisted a bit but conceded; this was no corn snake. I could tell by the look in the bear's eyes that it was very curious about what we were up to, and I couldn't get out of there quickly enough. Pawn Power did manage to get some great bear pictures. In the panic of the moment I had my camera settings all wrong and got blurry images of something big and dark in the woods; nothing *National Geographic Magazine* would have been impressed with. The photos looked more like those blurry images of Big Foot that crop up every now and then.

Figure 19: When a bear stares at you, that is a great time to change your plans. (Photo courtesy, Brendan Egan, A.K.A. Pawn Power)

Further up the trail were a series of sharp switchbacks, making it difficult to follow. At one point, I went left and even though Pawn Power was only a few feet behind me, he went right. Standing on the rocks twenty feet above him, I yelled that he was going the wrong way. He turned, answered me and started in my direction, so I turned and continued on. For some unknown reason, when he got to the point where we had just separated, instead of following me, he went back in the direction we had just hiked, not realizing it. When he didn't catch up, I doubled back to where I had last seen him and waited around for about a half-hour, but no Pawn Power.

Now I had to decide what to do. If he had somehow accidentally reversed direction (what I refer to as a "retro-blazing"), an easy thing to do on unfamiliar trail, he would be over a mile away by now, and I didn't want to retrace that much of the trail. Besides, our curious bear was back there. It is very easy to get turned around on the trail and retro-blaze. A trail can look very different going in the opposite direction and since the blazes are on both sides of the trees, they can create a false sense of confidence, especially on a cloudy day, or in deep, dark woods where there is little sunlight to judge direction.

The other possibility, one I didn't want to think about, was that he had lost his footing and fallen off one of the cliffs in the area. I scouted most of the ones near the trail in the area and concluded that he must have gone the wrong way. I continued north, stopping ever so often to carve my trail name "K1" and a directional arrow → into the dirt on the side of the trail with my hiking pole, hoping he would see it if he figured out his error. I continued on — there was nothing else to do.

I arrived in Daleville, Virginia late in the afternoon on our seventh day on the trail. Pawn Power and I had planned to take a zero day and stay at the Howard Johnson's but before going to the motel, I made a beeline for the Wendy's. Once my appetite was suppressed, I headed toward the motel and was pleased to meet up with Pawn Power. He told me he had in fact retro-blazed and when he realized the error, he found his way to a road crossing and hitched a ride to Daleville. I was relieved to see him.

The next morning Pawn Power called home and found out that a relative was seriously ill. He thought it would be best that he return home, but was devastated. He had been having a real adventure, and was really enjoying his trek, especially having a bear encounter and getting totally lost. He made arrangements to go home and we spent the rest of the day just resting and talking about the hike — I would miss him, as we hiked well together.

Ottie Cline Powell

On April 5, 1891 a schoolhouse had its youngsters go out to gather firewood. One of the children wandered off and became lost. Coming over the top of Punchbowl Mountain I found a bronze plaque dedicated to the child:

"This is the exact spot, little Ottie Cline Powell's body was found on April 5, 1891. After straying from the Tower Hill School House Nov. 9, a distance of 7 miles. Age 4 years, 11 months."

Figure 20: Ottie Cline's fate would haunt me for some time.

Even though the event occurred over one hundred years before, it still put a lump in my throat. It was sobering to think about what the poor child must have experienced. At that time of year in those mountains, the weather can be bitterly cold and with no food it had to be a tough way to die. He must have been a dedicated kid; the story goes that he still had the firewood he had collected when they discovered his body. His misadventure was a testament to how easily one can become disorientated in the woods, even the familiar woods that would have been around the schoolhouse. That simple memorial would haunt me for some time.

Coming down the mountain, I made camp at the Punchbowl Shelter. The shelter is situated right on the shoreline of Punchbowl Pond. Gradually other hikers showed up; "Yazzie," "Enoch," "Moccasin," "Liberty" and his sister, and "Sonny and Cher," were new faces. There was a familiar face as well: "New York Minute," who seemed to hiking at the same rate as I. I'd first met New York Minute back at the Catawba store.

After an early supper I put up my wire antenna into a tree and powered up my ham radio. My radio operation at the picnic table was a source of entertainment for my fellow hikers. Most of them had never seen a ham radio station, much less one as tiny as the one I was carrying. Using Morse code I chatted with a ham in Suffolk, Virginia and then another in Canada. It was a nice mental diversion and comforting to know that I could communicate should an actual emergency arise. Cell phone coverage in these remote areas remains rare and sporadic.

I retired around sunset, as did most of the hikers. Life on the trail is akin to life in the wilderness before electricity, i.e., getting up with the chickens and going to bed with the chickens. Hikers refer to sunset as "hiker midnight," and it might as well be midnight once darkness descends on the forest. I had just started to doze off when I heard a single frog "peep" near the pond, then a second later, another, then another and another and within five seconds thousands, perhaps millions of frogs were peeping. The uproar persisted for about twenty minutes and then, as if on cue, it ceased. Silence. I went right to sleep. About twenty minutes later the whole process repeated itself, starting with just one peep and then within seconds, a crescendo. Again, after about twenty minutes, total silence. This continued all night, making sleep very difficult.

Free Lunch

I was the lone camper at the Cow Camp Shelter on June 3rd. It was a nasty night, with lightning, rain and wind, so I slept in the shelter and planned on being up early so I could hike the thirteen miles to the Dutch Haus B&B in time for lunch. I'll do almost anything for a free lunch. The Dutch Haus B&B in Montebello, VA sponsors a free lunch for thru-hikers. Actually it's thirteen miles to the parking lot where the B&B sends a shuttle at 11 a.m. to pick up the hikers, and another three miles to the actual B&B. After being on the trail for two weeks, I was awakening around dawn in spite of my love of sleep. My plan was to be up at 4:30 and push hard so I could easily make the B&B in time for lunch, provided the terrain wasn't too challenging.

I set my watch for the allotted time and went to sleep. When the alarm sounded, I looked outside and decided to sleep another hour because I was in the midst of another summer thunderstorm. After another hour of dozing I got up and packed. It was still raining, but the lightning was subsiding and I went out to the tree where I had hung my bear bag. Returning to the shelter, I saw a bear up the trail in the direction I needed to travel. It seemed to be working on something in the nearby brook, so all I could do was sit and wait for it to finish.

Finally around 6 a.m. it wandered off and I was able to get up the blue trail back to the A.T. I was unquestionably behind schedule and the first two miles or so were considerably uphill; things weren't boding well for a record-setting time. However, once past the ascent, the trail was pleasant and reasonable and I started making good time. There were a number of slight downhill sections that I ran down, thinking that if I succeeded in shaving off time I might still make it. When I reached the Seeley Woodworth Shelter cutoff I knew I had about two more miles to the road. Unfortunately the guidebook isn't really accurate. The "road" is actually a dirt road, little more than a path and the parking lot is still a few miles down this "road." At the intersection of the road I met "Lemur" and "MacGyver," two thru-hikers that I had only briefly met previously. They told me they thought we had to go down the dirt road. Incorrectly, my instincts told me that this wasn't the road. It didn't look like a road, but they convinced me otherwise. Timing is everything on the trail and if they had not have been there, I would have gone the wrong way.

They too were trying to make it for the free lunch and had stopped to check their maps to make certain they were correct. The three of us now charged down the road to see if we could make the parking lot in time for the shuttle pickup. As we walked, MacGyver explained that earlier he had encountered three other young hikers who went down to the parking lot just ahead of us. He figured that they would be there on time and would certainly let the driver know we were coming. We really hustled, almost running. We finally reached the parking lot at 11:02 but there was *no* sign of the shuttle anywhere. How was this possible? The others had to have made it there before us, so where could they be?

Determined as we were, we decided to try and make the three miles to the B&B on foot. If we could get there before 12:30 there was a chance we could still get lunch.

Looking like marathoners with backpacks, we rushed down the road, now paved, with our tongues hanging out. Not only were we hungry, we were thirsty and hot.

We covered the two miles into Montebello center, which is actually just a camp store and Post Office. Once again, there was some confusion as to just where the B&B was located. While we were in the camp store parking lot a pickup truck pulled up and the driver asked us where we were headed. MacGyver explained our situation and the driver told us he was a former thru-hiker himself and invited us to hop in the back of the truck as it was yet another mile.

We flew down the road and made it to the B&B in time for lunch. We were graciously greeted by the proprietor, Lois, and welcomed in. There were a few hikers there that I knew and a few I did not. With a full stomach and tired legs, I decided to stay for the night. It was only then that I realized that I had covered the fifteen miles of walking in just over five hours — I was back!

Later, MacGyver and I tried to rationalize how we had miscalculated the shuttle timing so badly. I asked Earl, Lois' husband and driver of the shuttle, if he had made a pick-up that day. He confirmed picking up three younger hikers and he said that he customarily waits an extra fifteen minutes just in case there are stragglers, but these hikers convinced him that nobody else was coming, so he left at 11:00 sharp. MacGyver and I figured that these three wanted to get to the B&B before anyone else so there would be an abundance of food and it would be all theirs. This was very uncharacteristic of most of the hikers I had met, even very hungry hikers. Additionally, most thru-hikers showed respect for other hikers and often went out of their way to help each other.

At dinner that evening there was lots of lively discussion about the hike up to this point. Liberty, a hiker in my age bracket, and his sister, were there for the evening. His sister was lamenting the fact that she didn't have a decent trail name. Her brother, Liberty, was doing a thru-hike and she had joined him for a two-week stint. She was going home in the morning, so the evening meal was turning into a going-away party as well. She commented that her more athletic sister was always on her case about her not being athletic enough. She confided that hiking with her brother she felt like she was "a draggin' anchor." Simultaneously, several of us cried out, "That's it! Draggin' Anchor, that's your trail name!" She loved it. She couldn't wait to tell her sister.

Waynesboro

After reading the Bill Bryson's book, *A Walk in the Woods*, about his comical attempt at hiking the A.T., I anticipated Waynesboro, Virginia with a grin. It was in Waynesboro that his hiking partner "Katz" meets a married woman by the name of "Beulah" and Bryson and Katz were forced to leave town in a hurry, if you know what I mean. I wasn't in a hurry to leave town; in fact, New York Minute and I agreed to take a zero day there and ended up staying two nights.

The town is very welcoming to hikers and has an outfitter. Hikers who had not replaced worn and broken gear at Damascus certainly needed to do so by the time they arrived at Waynesboro. Many hikers stay at the Grace Evangelical Lutheran Church but New York Minute and I stayed at the Quality Inn. We had been hiking together for several weeks now and were getting along well. It was time to pamper ourselves and have a room with air conditioning, beds and a pool. We planned to refurbish our equipment, eat until we couldn't move, and rest.

We arrived on Friday night. On Saturday night the church was having a hiker get-together to celebrate the swarm of hikers that was descending on the town. Waynesboro realizes that these nomadic passers-through each spend far more than even the most spendthrift automobile driver. The hikers buy tents, hiking boots, sleeping bags, rain gear, clothes, food, meal after meal, and take advantage of everything the town has to offer, including purchasing a few beers.

The committee sponsoring the hikers' event arranged to have volunteers drive hikers to the nearby Staunton, Virginia shopping mall and movie theaters — nearby for an automobile, that is. For a hiker it may as well be the far side of the moon; 12 miles (19 km) away is at least a day's hike. About 80 hikers lined up for rides. We were each assigned to a vehicle for the ride over and were told that (in my carload's case anyway) a different driver would pick us up later.

We converged on the mall like a swarm of locusts. Unlike the usual shoppers dressed in slacks, clean shirts, nice shoes, dresses, etc., the hikers looked like stand-ins for an Indiana Jones movie that was playing that evening. Most, if not all of us, had come to catch a movie. It all seemed surreal being in a movie theater, sitting in a comfortable seat, loud audio, and a giant screen to stare at. To be honest, by the end of the movie most of us were ready for bed; it was only ten o'clock but way past hiker midnight. Our ride arrived late. We piled into the SUV and headed back to Waynesboro. New York Minute and I just looked at each other; the smell of alcohol was overpowering. At first I thought it was one of the hikers but then realized that our driver had been celebrating somewhere. This really became evident on the entrance ramp to the highway; it was a sharp curve and I was hanging on for dear life! A hush ensued, as we all realized this was no ordinary shuttle. I heard several seatbelts discretely snapping shut.

We swayed and lurched down the highway and were elated to have survived to make it back at the church parking lot. When the driver asked if everyone enjoyed the ride, New York Minute left his dinner on the lawn in reply. Gradually, he regained his sea legs and we walked back to the motel and retired for the evening.

Around 3 a.m. I had to get up to pee. On the trail I would often ignore nature's call at that hour because I would usually be up with the sun, but I planned on sleeping in, so figured it best that I get it out of the way so I could sleep. I very quietly got out of bed and walked through the darkness to the bathroom, not wanting to disturb New York Minute's sleep. I sat on the toilet to pee so as not to make any noise. Afterwards, I had to flush, but hoped it wouldn't be too noisy; I flushed. KA-WOOOSSSHHH! "WHAT THE F*CK WAS THAT?" New York minute sat straight up in bed and was in a state of shock. This was no wimpy trickling toilet; this was an industrial-strength behemoth. He had been out in the woods so long that the sound of a loud toilet had him in shock. Once he came to his senses, we both started laughing at his reaction. Other than that incident we slept well except for another time when New York Minute asked me if I heard a strange noise. There was a distinct rustling of paper and then we realized that there was a mouse in our trashcan. This was a nice hotel, and how it got into the room we couldn't fathom. Maybe it hitched a ride in via one of our packs. We decided to leave it alone; it could have the trash — at least it wasn't a snake.

Blackberry Milkshakes

When we had arrived in Waynesboro, a volunteer not only shuttled us but also took us on a guided tour of the town, pointing out landmarks and places we might find interesting. To me this volunteer represented the old America of my youth, someone who went out of her way to give far more than I ever could reciprocate. Now that we were leaving, another woman volunteer picked us up right on schedule and brought us back to the trailhead, asking nothing in return.

We were now starting to hit our stride on the trail. I say "we" because now I was regularly hiking with New York Minute. "New York" (as I called him) is an impressive 27-year-old software engineer that seems to have boundless energy. He was very determined and disciplined and unlike many of the guys I had met on the trail; I had a sense that he would finish regardless of the obstacles. He walked a bit faster than I, but tended to take more breaks so we ended up doing about the same number of miles each day.

Even though there was a huge difference in our ages, we shared many of the same interests: technology, web design, engineering and the outdoors. He is at that point in his life where he is ready for a steady female relationship and that topic came up often; once again my advice for him was about as useful as it was for George back at the NOC. Advice from a "celibate" married guy should always be suspect.

For some days we had been hiking through the Shenandoah National Park. The trail weaves in and out of the Skyline Drive and the Blue Ridge Mountains for hundreds of miles. Road crossings occur frequently and accesses to park restaurants become an almost daily occurrence. Aramark runs the restaurants and all seem to have pretty much the same fare: burgers, fries, sandwiches and so on, but their one distinguishing item is the Blackberry Milkshake. Hikers yearn for this treat long before ever having their first one. Rumors of the flavor and coolness probably blow the experience way out of proportion, but I can't say I was disappointed. I must have drunk ten of these elixirs and the last was as good as the first. I suspect the automobile customers just don't have the same experience as a calorie-starved hiker.

Figure 21: Blue Ridge Mountain bears are hungry, one tried to eat the A.T. blaze.

The Blue Ridge Mountains also mean bears. I was having frequent bear encounters, but they always took the same format: I spot the bear, usually before it spots me. I take out my camera to get "the picture." The bear spots me and runs off and I get a photo of the blurry butt-end of a bear. This performance repeated itself over and over. On the entire A.T. hike I had 38 bear encounters and did not get a single good photograph.

One of my most unforgettable bear encounters occurred just prior to the Gravel Springs Hut ("shelters" are described as "huts" as the trail gets more northerly; don't ask why). I was walking along alone, New York perhaps an hour behind, lost in thought going through thick growth that gave the trail the appearance of a tunnel. It was a very windy day and in thick brush in high winds there are often "cracks" and "snaps" as small twigs break under the pressure of the swaying trees. Off to my left I heard a significantly loud "crack," so much so that it startled me out of my daydream. I turned my head to the left and for a second I couldn't see anything, it was very dark— too dark? As my eyes focused I realized I was staring at the underbelly of a bear, a large bear. He was close enough that I could have reached over and tickled his navel. He had bent over a choke cherry tree and was using it as scaffolding to reach mulberries that were high above. Time froze; everything seemed to move in slow motion. I looked up and he looked down and then as much to say, "Hey, I'm busy, there are mulberries to pick." He went back to working on the berries, totally ignoring me. Stunned, I couldn't believe it! For a moment I considered taking a photograph but I would actually have had to back up because I was too close. Then I came to my senses and realized I was just given an opportunity to get the hell out of there. I walked away quickly, choosing not to disturb my busy friend. I skedaddled up the trail about seventy feet and stopped to reassess what had just happened. I could see the tree shimmering as the bear worked the limbs, gathering berries that must have been fifteen feet from the ground. I took out the camera, certain that this time I just might get a decent photo if the bear were to exit using the trail, since that was the most logical exit as opposed to the heavy underbrush.

I stood, camera at ready. The tree stopped its shimmer — this was it, the bear was leaving. I braced for the encounter, my heart pounding. Suddenly, there was movement on the trail, coming in my direction. As I readied to fire the shutter my eyes caught a glimpse of bright red color and then as they focused on the target, I recognized New York Minute. What? How could this be, just what the heck was going on here? New York shouted, "Hey, what's up K1, why the camera?" Flabbergasted, I silently signaled for him to come over where I was and then explained that he must have just passed a bear and as we talked the tree started its shimmer again. Apparently New York had just walked by the bear without seeing it. The bear must have sensed him coming and stood still as he passed, just as it had done for me. At first New York doubted me, but when the tree started shaking again as if Godzilla were doing acrobatics up there, he realized that he, too, had been fortunate. Shortly the bear hopped down out of the tree and went south, away from us, on the trail and disappeared — again no photos.

I had left camp early in the morning and I thought New York was still sleeping when I left, but it turned out he had left shortly after I had and was only about two minutes behind me when I had my encounter.

I was gaining a reputation among the hikers for my bear encounters. A few days later at the Rod Hollow Shelter we had another bear session. This time, it was early in the morning; New York had gone to fill his water bottles at the water source, which was perhaps fifty feet from where I was hammock-hanging. As I was packing I heard a very loud, nervous yell, "K1!!!" I grabbed my hiking pole and camera and ran in the direction of the yell, recognizing New York's voice. When I arrived there was a crash through the woods just ahead of New York, on the other side of the stream. New York came face-to-face with a bear on the trail and both were so startled that they both froze for a few moments until he yelled. Shaken, but unharmed, New York was regaining his composure just as I got there...Darn, no photo again, although I don't think that was a priority for New York. We both had to laugh at the thought of me running to defend New York, as if I could do anything against a 500-pound bear. I was starting to acquire a "Grizzly Adams" look about me: my hair was wild and unkempt, but then, so was the bear's.

Later that day I was hiking alone and came to a side trail that I took to make a cell phone call to Jane; it had been at least five days since we had talked. I went up a blue trail that led to a nice rock outcropping and had immediate service. After the call, I strolled further up the trail to see if there was a vista and I was gratified with a breathtaking look to the north. As I looked at the Skyline Drive far below I noticed a pickup truck in the parking lot that had at least seven sophisticated antennas in the bed. I immediately realized that this was a radio amateur mobile station. I carefully climbed down the cliff, walked over to the truck and seeing a man and woman inside, tapped on the passenger window. This was a very serious amateur radio station; it had more equipment in the front seat than a CIA monitoring station. I introduced myself to the occupants as K1YPP, and the man did likewise as Steve, K4GUN, and his girlfriend, Kristine, K4LIG. They were operating in a ham radio VHF contest. The high elevation parking lot was an absolutely perfect spot for such a competition.

As I climbed back up the cliff I heard them yell that they wanted a picture of me, so I turned and stood and they took a few photos. Upon returning home from the hike they sent me copies; I looked like something out of the Planet of the Apes; no wonder the bears didn't stick around. Additionally, back home I had a copy of an amateur radio magazine, QST, which had a full-feature article in it about the K4GUN truck that I had just seen in the lot — again, small world!

Doggone

Later that afternoon, at Snickers Gap, I strolled down the road to the Horseshoe Curve Restaurant. The hiker manual didn't say much about it. From the outside it wasn't terribly impressive, but hidden inside was one of the treasures of the Trail. The dining room has perhaps eight tables. The walls are completely filled with shelves of old, unopened beer bottles. There was every imaginable bottle possible, some ancient. I took a seat at an empty table (they were all empty at the time). The owner came over to take my order, a very pleasant and eye-catching woman. I ordered a beef plate and beer. As I waited, her two elderly dogs, sisters, came over to greet me. She asked if I minded and I replied, "of course not, this is so much like the English pubs I've experienced." As the dogs and I waited for the order, I looked closely at the beer cans next to me. One in particular caught my attention, it was a cream-colored can, very plain and just had the word "BEER" in capital letters imprinted on it and a one liner on the back that said, "Carling Brewing Co.," nothing else. I peered at it for some time and then realized that what I was holding in my hands was a G.I. issue, World War II can of beer. I was eating a late lunch in a beer sanctuary; it was an almost religious experience.

My order came and with military precision the two dog sisters went to work on me —long, solemn sighs, stares and moving from sitting to laying-down positions. It was obvious these two old pros had it down to a science; a dog lover such as I was no match for their technique. By the end of my meal, which was superb, one of the best I had on the trail, I realized that those two canines had duped me, a long distance hiker, out of a good portion of my meal, a sliver at a time.

The atmosphere in this place was overwhelming. I stayed way longer than planned and it was late in the day when I finally pulled myself from the seat and made my exit. I promised the dogs I would write, and not believing a word of it, they sighed, knowing they were losing a real sucker.

I hurried northbound on the trail; I was hoping to make it to the Blackburn Outdoor Center. I met up with New York Minute on the way to the Center and we crossed the West Virginia State line together, only to re-enter Virginia again. We did stop at the West Virginia sign for a photo op anyway; even though we wouldn't officially be in Harpers Ferry, West Virginia until the next day.

The Center has a large, modern building as well as a bunkhouse and a solar shower. There were many thru-hikers there that night and the majority of us slept on the screened-in porch. I treated myself to the solar shower; however, the water was frigid, since many had used it before me, what little warm water there may have been had long vanished. The solar shower has a tank on top of it that is dark in color and the theory is that the water will warm as the sun shines on the tank, but inexplicably every solar shower I saw on the trail had the tank located amongst tree limbs and leaves so there was no chance for any solar heating. What were they thinking? The good news was, I knew I was going to get a nice, hot shower at a hotel the next day in Harpers Ferry, West Virginia!

Figure 22: The author and New York Minute approaching Harpers Ferry, WV.

Chapter 8 - West Virginia

Harpers Ferry

Harpers Ferry, West Virginia is the psychological halfway point for thru-hikers. The actual halfway point is another hundred miles north of there, but Harpers Ferry is a favorite resting spot, historically significant, and the headquarters of the Appalachian Trail Conservancy. This makes it a much more interesting halfway point than some nondescript signpost in the woods. I was ready for Harpers Ferry. I hadn't endured all the hardships that the thru-hikers who started in Georgia had—the snow, the cold and the winter conditions. Nor had I gone as far in the same year. Regardless, I still felt the need for a few days downtime. I had now finished the 525 miles (845 km) of Virginia and my heart surgery seemed to be holding up just fine.

I noticed that on the long uphill climbs I just didn't have the "chutzpah" of the previous year. Although I was somewhat less aggressive in climbing, I was satisfied with my overall performance. On the level and downhill I could keep up with the best of them, particularly in my age bracket, so I was happy enough. I was starting to believe that I could actually finish this trek.

John Brown Lives

As I moseyed around town I noticed there were a number of photos of John Brown. You may recall that John Brown was going to lead a revolution/uprising of slaves and commandeered the Armory in Harpers Ferry. His short-lived revolt (a few hours) came to an abrupt end, as did he when they hanged him. During my time on the trail, my coif had grown long and my beard rivaled that of John Brown. Looking at pictures of this rebel and then at me, tourists declared that I was the reincarnation of John Brown. It was time for a haircut.

The barbershop was one of these boutique shops that do both men and women's hair. I thought my orders were simple: "make it slightly shorter and make me handsome." I guess the barber's vision of what would make me handsome was at odds with my vision of handsome. I started the previous year growing out a ponytail and was quite proud of it; I had never had one and liked how if felt and looked. I wanted to keep it long enough so that when I would let my hair loose it would fall down over my neck and ears and keep away mosquitoes. I came away from the salon looking like I had donated my hair to a good cause; there was very little left and it was cut at odd angles. There was nothing I could do about it. John Brown II was no more.

Shoes

My shoes were wearing out. The repairs I made in Waynesboro were no longer holding up and it was time for new ones. I have big feet, size 14 [US]. Upon entering a shoe store, or outfitter, my first question is not about style or model but "size." Rarely does a vendor have more than one or two in stock, if any. This was the case in Harpers Ferry; they had several choices but not in the style I really needed. I like a high-sided boot that gives good ankle support, stays dry unless the water is very deep and allows me to step from rock to rock without much give.

The current trend in hiking shoes is low-sided, expensive sneakers. As far as I'm concerned these expensive faux hiking shoes are inadequate for long distance hiking.

Since this was all that was available in my size, I purchased the shoes and wore them around town to break them in. Harpers Ferry is spread out and it seems that everything was over a steep hill. The old historic section was over one hill, the convenience store in another direction over another hill and the motel was in another direction over... you guessed it, another hill. It was supposed to be zero days, but with all the hill climbing I'm not certain I could make that claim; it was miles of walking each day. As comfortable as the new hiking shoes were, I was concerned about my ankles.

As is obligatory for any thru-hiker, I visited the Appalachian Trail Conservancy [A.T.C.] headquarters. The employees and volunteers of the A.T.C. coordinate all activities along the trail, both the areas under their jurisdiction and the areas controlled by other organizations. Personally, I think they do a marvelous job. They coordinate 2,176 miles (3502 km) of trail, about 250 shelters, 30 other member clubs, park organizations, private land owners, State Parks, National Parks, Federal Land authorities and so on. They publish numerous books and maps specifically for hiking the A.T. and overall, they get it right. There's plenty of criticism dolled out about their products, but considering all the challenges, and minimal funding, the end result is impressive.

At the headquarters I met John Fletcher, a very amiable and likeable gent who welcomed me to Harpers Ferry and took my picture for the record book. It was interesting to look back through the photos and see some of the hikers whom I had met along the trail, a few obviously way ahead of me. They have record books going back for years and it must be the most complete collection of hiker photos anywhere on the planet.

I mentioned to John that I was carrying a small amateur radio with me and his eyes lit up; coincidentally he is also an amateur, call letters N3NFO. He had me bring the radio to the A.T.C. and we went over it in great detail. He took a few photos and figured it might be useful for the A.T.C. magazine *The Appalachian Trail Journal*; they subsequently did a piece about it in the May 2009 issue.

He suggested I look up another amateur at the A.T.C. regional office in Boiling Springs, Pennsylvania when I got there. I promised I would.

On the second evening in town I set up the ham radio in a gazebo behind the motel. I made a few contacts but the signals were weak and there was lots of static. I was down in a "hole" near the river and the surrounding mountains were taking their toll on my peanut-whistle signal; but at least I made my contacts from West Virginia. The A.T. only has about six miles in the state, so there wouldn't be many other opportunities.

About halfway through my first contact I had to get up and chase away a few deer that were chewing on the antenna wire.

I'll Be Back

Two days in Harpers Ferry was just not enough. I'm a history buff and the town exudes history. There was just too much to see and not enough time to see it. The very fiber of the town feels like history. It changed hands during the Civil War as many as eight times. I can just see the families that lived there during that period: "Hey honey, look out the window and tell me if I should were blue or grey today?"

Figure 23: Harpers Ferry Spring House. According to local legend the North came here to get water during the day and the South at night.

Many of my hiking friends were on a journey to find a new area to call home; I found a place that I knew I would come back to — Harpers Ferry, West Virginia. Now it was time to cross the Potomac and get to Maryland.

Chapter 9 - Maryland

Talking Trash

It seemed that for every state on the A.T. I had some preconceived notion of what to expect: Georgia, the mountains; North Carolina, the trail wandering pointlessly; Tennessee, the Smokies; Virginia, supposedly flat (not!); and West Virginia, Harpers Ferry. Somehow in all this, Maryland was an unknown. It was impossible to know what to expect.

The only thing I had heard about the state was that a number of hikers take the "Maryland Challenge" and cross the state all in one day, about 35 miles (56 km). I wondered if this was because nobody wanted to stop there, or if it was just because of the distance and the possibility of making it across there in less than 24 hours. My personal forgone conclusions of Maryland had nothing to do with the trail. It seemed Maryland always had screwy, illogical laws that never made sense.

Leaving Harpers Ferry the A.T. follows the old C&O railroad bed for several miles and then turns up a steep grade and eventually levels off. The trail passes through Gathland State Park and right next to the trail are restrooms and soda vending machines. Not being one to pass a vending machine, I removed my pack and had two cans of pop in quick succession. I looked for somewhere to dispose of the cans and couldn't find any recycle bins or trashcans. I hunted to no avail. This seemed really weird. After a while a museum curator came out from a nearby building to invite several of us in. He briefly described the museum and it was tempting; he appeared knowledgeable and very enthusiastic. He had a nice way about him and I suspect the tour would have been time well spent. Normally I would jump at the opportunity to investigate historical matters, but it was late in the day, the heat had been oppressive and I just wanted to get on to the next shelter. I asked about trashcans and the curator explained, rather proudly, that Maryland has a carry-in/carry-out law; and to enforce it, they don't have any trashcans in the parks. My jaw dropped; how could this be? I asked, "Does this mean that a thru-hiker technically must carry their trash across the entire state? Better yet, if this were taken to the extreme, would we have to carry all our trash from Springer Mountain in Georgia to Mt. Katahdin in Maine?" He slid his glasses down his nose, and stared at me as if I had a screw loose. Fumbling for an answer he finally offered to take the cans and dispose of them, letting us know of course that he was doing us a favor and not to expect this as routine treatment. I appreciated his gesture, for otherwise we would have been forced to carry the cans with us; there would have been no other choice. It would seem to me if they want to enforce such foolishness that they could force the vendors to take away the empties, which would be the logical solution.

I'm certain the lawmakers were quite proud of themselves; they killed two birds with one stone by eliminating the trash removal jobs from the state budget and having the citizens bring home the trash in their automobiles to have it disposed of locally. The reality is, thru-hikers have nowhere to dispose of the trash. The less scrupulous park visitors, not finding a trashcan, just dump the trash in the woods where nobody sees them dumping it.

At another Maryland state park again there were no trashcans. Wanting to really get rid of the trash that was starting to stink in the summer heat and taking up room in the pack, I asked where I could "properly" get rid of the stuff. It was suggested that we "sneak" into the ladies room and get rid of it in the trashcan for the ladies sanitary disposables. This leads to an obvious conclusion, when hiking in Maryland be certain to hike with a woman. It appeared to me that the real "Maryland Challenge" is finding a trashcan!

Phallic Symbol

Maryland's Washington State Park has what is claimed to be the oldest Washington Monument. It is adjacent to the trail and the trail passes right through the park.

What is it about George Washington? There are several monuments to him along the trail and of course not far from the trail is the one in Washington, D.C. They're all tall and narrow. Then of course there is Mt. Washington in New Hampshire, the tallest peak in the northeast. Do these all have some phallic symbolism? He's referred to as the "Father of Our Country." I think I know why.

I was only in Maryland for one hot and steamy night. I was camped with a large collection of thru-hikers and most of us went to sleep without much regard for the weather, which had been hot and dry. At 3 a.m. a thunderstorm blew through and we all robotically got up to cover things, close up tents and keep things dry. It was amusing to see all the headlamps light up the forest. It reminded me of the eerie scene in the movie E.T., where the government agents were hunting for E.T. in the forest and the light beams frantically pierced the night fog.

Leaving Maryland one crosses another milestone — the Mason-Dixon Line, the famous but invisible demarcation separating the South from the North.

Chapter 10 - Pennsylvania

Potty Break

New York Minute and I were enjoying summer walks through boreal forests in Southern Pennsylvania. The weather was sublime, although very warm. The drought was worsening but tolerable. New York Minute had a drop box mailed to the South Mountain Post Office. The Trail crosses PA 233 several miles from the post office so we hitched a ride to town. "Town" consisted of several closed-down businesses, a shuttered convenience store, and a barely open tavern/hotel.

After New York crammed what he could carry in his backpack at the Post Office, we went to the tavern because the *Hiker's Companion* alleged it served food. The tavern was dark and dingy and the air reeked of cigarette smoke. Both of us have an aversion to the smoke, causing us headaches and occasionally nausea. The chemicals used in cigarettes today are much more powerful; these are not the smokes of my parents' generation. In spite of this, like dogs drawn to a dangerous prey, we sidled up to the bar, ordered burgers and fries and then waited in the shadows.

The order took forever. While waiting we were amused by the local regulars that were glued to the screens of the two TV's, engrossed in "Days of our Lives." Three old men were in a heated, beer-fueled debate about the soap opera and about a particular outfit one of the actresses was wearing. They were practically at blows arguing as to whether the actress had worn the same outfit in an episode a few days earlier. One argued she had worn a sleeveless gown, the other was certain it was pretty chiffon blouse and skirt. If I didn't know better it sounded like they were arguing over the outcome of a hockey game where the players were dressed in drag.

Having no gas masks, we grabbed our orders and ate outside to get away from the smoke. I thought the food was greasy, but nutrient-starved thru-hikers don't fret over such trivial matters. I've actually seen hikers drink olive oil with gusto, straight out of the bottle, to supplement their caloric intake. After downing our food we hitched back to the Trail. Since the convenience store was closed and I was low on provisions, we agreed to stop at the next road crossing about four miles north. I arrived at the road before New York and walked to the market; it was just far enough from the Trail that it didn't justify a hitch, but far enough to make me wish I *had* hitched.

After replenishing my supplies we decided to eat at the Italian Restaurant on the way back to the Trail. The establishment was bright and airy, contrasting with the earlier tavern. When my sub order arrived, I suddenly had the urge to get to the restroom. As I made my way to the room the urge became a five-alarm emergency. Fortunately, there was nobody in the bathroom; I blasted through the door in a full run, dropping my pants as I just made it to the seat. All hell broke loose with Montezuma's Revenge, taking my appetite with it. I returned to the table just as New York sat down with his order. In a repeat of my performance, he got up and started to walk, then run, like a man on a mission to the men's room. When he returned we realized that our earlier grease-fest had gotten the better of us. Whatever was in there was practically lethal; fortunately we had both jettisoned our loads and felt fine a short time later.

Figure 24: It may not appear so on the map, but Pennsylvania is only the halfway point of the trail.

Half-way

One of the first shelters in Pennsylvania is the Quarry Gap Shelter. It's very elaborate: two rooms, a covered area between them with a picnic table and a solid bear-proof locker for storing food. It even had hanging plants. If only more of the shelters were like this one; it was really homey and filled to capacity. There was a father and son team there from Israel, "Moses" and "Black Snake." Moses appeared to be about fifty while Black Snake is in his early twenties and looked very Middle Eastern, with wild, bushy hair and a dark beard. I had been leap-frogging them for weeks. I now had a chance to talk with them and they told me an amusing story about their first day on the Trail.

Arriving at the Atlanta airport, they found their way to the town of Dahlonega, near Springer Mountain without much difficulty. They were not having any luck hitching a ride from town to Springer Mountain. The locals would just slow down in their pickup trucks, gawk at them, and then speed off. Apparently, with all the paranoia of 9/11, someone called the police to report that a few terrorists were on their way to the mountains and there was no telling what damage they could do. They had backpacks, so quite naturally there was reason to believe they were going to blow up the mountain.

A police patrol arrived, took them into custody and hauled them to the station for questioning. They spent the better part of a day straightening things out. They even had to call the Israeli embassy! When it was clear their intentions were to merely get on the Trail and hike, an officer finally agreed to bring them back to the mountain. Fortunately the pair weren't too upset about the ordeal, but I had visions of them learning a new water interrogation sport. Eventually, this scenario repeated itself again in another town, but they were able to convince the officers to check with the Dahlonega office and they were cleared to continue.

The next day I reached the official half way point for the A.T. It was sobering to realize that I had been on the Trail for 36 days, plus 50 days from the previous year; a total of 86 days and was now only at the midpoint of the Trail. Looking at a map of the Trail can be deceiving. Pennsylvania appears to be way more than halfway up the Trail, but the Trail wanders so much in New England that the small geographical area of New England has many miles that are almost invisible on the map.

New York Minute and I parted ways shortly after the halfway point; he had a family function to attend and would be gone for several days, which meant I would pull ahead of him. I also planned some serious time off soon and he would then pass me. I was planning on spending the July Fourth weekend with Jane in Washington; she was flying up. I could tell New York was a bit emotional about our parting. We had hiked for about 5 weeks; he was losing his "Grandpa." We wished each other well and even though I felt we might see each other again, the chances were slim.

The next major town on the Trail was Boiling Springs, so named because it has an impressive fresh water spring that feeds a lake in town. The spring dumps 22 million gallons of water a day into the lake; hence the spring "boils." The water stays at a constant year-round temperature of 52°F; it doesn't freeze in the winter and is incredibly cool in the summer. The lake forms a picturesque setting right in the middle of the town. Many of the citizens can be found fishing there and they warmly greeted me as I passed. I really liked the town, people were very friendly and I was anxious to visit the A.T. Conservancy Regional office there.

As agreed to at the Harpers Ferry A.T.C., I looked up John at the regional A.T.C. office. He's a very active radio amateur and we hit it right off. I showed him the equipment I was carrying and we agreed to meet the next night on the air. He had work to do, so we parted and I went in search of food.

"Enoch" and "Moccasin," hikers I had previously met on the Trail at the Punchbowl Shelter, were in town with their friend "K-Bomb." We met at the Italian restaurant late in the day. It was warm and the air conditioning was out of commission so they had the doors opened. We were inundated with houseflies. In the woods we had become accustomed to their constant presence and hadn't really noticed them. The waitress came to take our order and apologized for the flies. For a moment we were all puzzled, with a "what flies?" look on our faces. New York Minute was almost never seen without wearing his mosquito net on his head, and I joked that if he had been there with us he would have had it on. We all had this vision him sitting there wearing his mosquito net eating pizza.

After eating I went back to the A.T.C., the favorite hangout for hikers passing through. There was a note on the bulletin board inviting hikers to stay in a local backyard on Race Street. The other choice was a campsite owned by the A.T.C. at the south end of town, right next to the railroad tracks. I checked out the backyard and it was very welcoming. The yard had numerous flowers and plants, lush green grass and plenty of shade. The family that lived there didn't even want us to knock, just set up camp as we wished. There was a backyard hammock next to a shed/playhouse so I put my hammock inside of the yard hammock so I could take advantage of my mosquito net. I settled in for the evening and went right to sleep. About 2 a.m. a big thunderstorm rolled through so I grabbed my gear and moved into the playhouse to ride out the storm, as did Moccasin. Once again generous trail angels provided for us, and to the best of my knowledge they were not hikers themselves.

The next morning I talked with some of the hikers that camped near the railroad tracks and with bleary eyes they described freight trains rolling through all night and blasting their powerful horns right next to the camp. They were certain the blasts were intentional, just to annoy them.

I left Boiling Springs and did the fifteen miles to the Darlington Shelter. Along the way I hooked up with a section hiker named Russ. We stopped for a break and he promised to pick me up in a few days at Duncannon and shuttle me to Baltimore where I could catch the train to Washington, D.C. to meet Jane for the long weekend. I left Russ at a road crossing and continued on ahead.

Just prior to my arrival at the shelter, I was caught in a heavy thunderstorm. The skies opened up and dumped on me; I was drenched when I got to the shelter. "Pony" and "Henry" were there. Henry is Pony's dog. They were from California and she and Henry were doing a long section hike up to the New York border. At a prior stop a few days before, New York Minute and Pony realized that they had attended the same high school in New Jersey; small world again.

I put up an antenna wire that night and put my station on the air. In no time at all I found John, WA3KCP on schedule on the forty-meter short-wave band. His signal was very strong since he was running a thousand Watts. I was running under two Watts. I made a few other contacts and retired for the evening; it was "hiker midnight."

The Doyle

In Maryland, without the support of the high-sided boots I prefer to wear, the rocks had caused me to twist my ankle badly and it hurt. I continued hiking through Pennsylvania but by the time I reached Duncannon, I had to take a few days to rest my ankle.

Duncannon is a sleepy town set into impressive hill country in central Pennsylvania. It's a favorite stop for many thru-hikers because it is a friendly place and there is the lure of the Doyle Hotel. "The Doyle," as it's referred to, is a trail icon. It was built by Anheuser-Busch in more halcyon days just over one hundred years ago and hasn't aged well. A succession of owners apparently milked it for what it was worth and overlooked maintenance in pursuit of profit.

The rooms are sparse, having just the bare essentials: a garage sale bed, chair and bureau and not much more. My windows were propped up with sticks. In spite of this, it is heaven for a thru-hiker. The showers are hot and the rooms are dry, except on the fourth floor where there are pails to catch rainwater from the leaky ceilings. The "maid" is an old guy with a unlit cigarette hanging out of his mouth, who also doubles as the maintenance crew. As a rule, most hikers are asleep early, so the place is quiet.

The Doyle's rustic tavern and dining room have an alluring appeal. If it were not for the cigarette and cigar smoke, they would be downright pleasant. I avoided the dining room during busy hours and would frequent it when there were not many customers. I have to admit they had some of the best meals in town.

I met a number of new thru-hikers while there and was especially amused by "Star Dust" who is from Brazil and a ball of fire. She is a bright middle-aged woman with a quick wit. I take pride in knowing a certain amount of history. One evening, after a few beers, I was on a diatribe about the Civil War. After putting my foot in my mouth several times, I came to realize that Star Dust knew far more about the Civil War than I did. On top of that, I made the mistake of claiming that Pulitzer was the inventor of dynamite, (it was Nobel); I didn't win any prizes that evening.

At one point I was telling her the story of my six-artery heart bypass surgery and Star Dust asked if she could see my incision; I said "sure," and lifted up my shirt to show her and the small crowd that had gathered. Satisfied, she thanked me (I suspect she doubted my story; most did. They simply couldn't imagine somebody hiking the Trail after that surgery.) I then explained to Star Dust that we have a tradition in the United States that if I showed her my chest, she would have to show me hers. Stunned for a moment, she quickly recovered and replied, "I don't have to; I'm not a citizen." You can't blame me for trying.

Duncannon is a nice place to walk around and just take in the sights. It is on the banks of the Susquehanna River and surrounded by picturesque mountains. It had the same feel as many other towns along Appalachia, the feel that it is just hanging on by a thread. The heartbeat is barely discernible and any shock at all could flat-line it. There are hints of former glory days, but they're long gone, along with the jobs, and it doesn't appear that will change any time soon.

During my zero days in Duncannon I managed to hike back south on the trail and spend several relaxing hours enjoying my ham radio contacts and meeting local hikers on the trail.

Washington D.C.

Jane's birthday is July 5th and we had agreed to meet in Washington, D.C. to celebrate. The timing was fortuitous; the ankle that I had hurt in Maryland needed Advil and time off to rest. As promised, Russ, the section hiker from Baltimore, showed up to drive me to Baltimore. After lunching at a Baltimore sidewalk café, he guided me to the train to Washington. He wouldn't take anything as payment for his generosity, so I promised to contribute in his honor to a good cause further up the Trail, sort of a pay-it-forward deal.

The train arrived in Washington in mid-afternoon and I found my way via the Washington Metro to Dupont Circle and then to the place where we were to stay. A friend of Jane's had graciously lent us the use of her Washington condo.

We had four blissful days — no phones, no meetings, and no interruptions, just the two of us! It was the July

4th weekend and the town was in a party mood. We were so happy to see each other that we hardly came up for air and mostly stayed at the apartment. Jane was shocked at how much weight I had lost, in spite of eating so much. I still had almost half the Trail to go. How much worse would it get? How much weight can a person lose before it becomes dangerous?

We strolled along the Washington Mall, enjoying the gorgeous temperatures, and abundant sunshine, hardly noticing the crowd or the festivities. We were getting reacquainted and in a honeymoon replay. It was such an emotional moment to be with my bride of thirty-four years again. For a few short days, the Trail seemed far away, a distant memory.

As is the case, whenever I go to Washington, I stop at the Vietnam Memorial. My brother's name is on the memorial at panel 49, line 23. Not many things make me emotional, but standing there staring at his name etched in that marble wall along with the names of 58,256 other brave Americans always chokes me up. I was carrying his Purple Heart Medal on this hike in his honor and it tore at my heart to realize just how much he meant to me. The forty years since he was killed in action seemed like the blink of an eye. In my mind's eye I could still see us wandering the trails of Connecticut, carefree and full of life. As Jane and I stood there, I couldn't help but think of those engaged in the endless war in Iraq; it brought me to tears thinking that our nation was allowing this to happen. "When will we ever learn? When will we ever learn?"

Figure 25: Honoring my brother, Thomas J. Blanchard, USMC, K Co, 3rd BN, 5th Marines, 1st MARDIV, III MAF. Killed in action, 7 August 1968. Panel 49, line 23.

Can't Get There From Here

With trail angel Russ's help, it took less than a few hours to get from Duncannon, PA to D.C. Returning to the Trail took more than fourteen hours. Sunday morning I escorted Jane to the airport via Washington's subway system, the Metro. It was tough to see her go knowing that it would be five weeks before we would reunite again, in Connecticut.

Since I was not leaving D.C. until that night, I returned to the condo. Even after hours of planning, the best connections I could find required my taking a 3 a.m. Monday morning Amtrak train to Philadelphia, PA, connecting to an Amtrak train to Harrisburg, PA, arriving there around 7 a.m. On Sundays the

Washington Metro stops running at midnight which meant that I had to get to Union Station before then and hang around there until the 3 a.m. train. On schedule, the train departed Washington and was full. The young man I was sitting next to had a bad case of sneezing and coughing; I kept thinking this was going to be trouble later, but I never did catch it.

In Harrisburg, I contacted someone listed in the *Hiker's Companion* for a shuttle to the Trail. He arrived at noon and I made it back to Duncannon by 2 p.m.. I immediately started hiking. The Trail crosses the Susquehanna River just north of town. The scenery is stunning and the Trail climbs quickly once across the river. I made the eleven miles to Peters Mountain Shelter well before sunset. It felt good to be back out in the woods and the injured ankle was feeling great.

Peter's Mountain Shelter had a tiny shelter nearby that was built by Earl Shaffer, the first person to ever do a thru-hike of the A.T. in 1948. Earl's shelter is very primitive and is a little taller than waist high. The original dirt floor had been replaced by plywood. A few weeks after I passed through, the shelter was deconstructed and moved to a history museum of the Trail.

To access water at Peter's Mountain, the Trail maintenance crews have placed over 300 stone steps down to the spring; I made certain to get plenty of water, as it was a very steep, long climb. At this shelter I met a new thru-hiker: "White Lightning" and a couple from earlier in Virginia, "Lemur" and "MacGyver." White Lightning had a similar injury to mine; he had pulled tendons in his leg and was having trouble walking. Fortunately, I had plenty of water and saved him the trip down all those steps.

Strike Two

The next day I was ambling toward Rausch Gap Shelter, lost in thought, when off to my immediate right I heard the alarming sound of a rattle! An angry four-foot long, black timber rattler was next to my right leg, maybe four feet away. I froze for a moment and then quickly jumped away; the rattler stayed calm and didn't strike. The snake was almost pitch-black. I later learned that in hot weather timber rattlers get darker in color. It was approaching nightfall and with the shadows I had not seen it. When my heart calmed down, I managed to take a few photos and then continued on, appreciating my good luck. Pennsylvania has a reputation for having the most rattlesnakes on the Trail and I hadn't given them much thought lately; I was brought back to reality quickly.

The Rausch Gap shelter has a plentiful spring right in front of it, but with the drought the spring was little more than a drip flowing into a stainless steel collection pan. The hikers patiently waited turns for water and, over the evening, everyone managed to gather sufficient water. By the next morning, even though it had not rained during the night, the basin was full and flowing steadily. I observed this phenomenon on more than one occasion but have not understood how or why they have more plentiful flows in the morning.

Helicopters

Lemur, MacGyver and I all camped at a tent site about 400 feet from the Rausch Gap Shelter. I slept very soundly in my hammock and didn't awaken during the night. The next morning Lemur asked me quite excitedly, "Did you hear the helicopter?" "What helicopter" I asked? "The one right over our heads about three o'clock this morning! It was right over your hammock." replied Lemur. Mysteriously, I hadn't heard a thing, which was so unlike me. I wished I had, for it would have been the fourth such occurrence since I started the Trail in Georgia. Lemur described the encounter: "The chopper came right down to the treetops; in fact its landing skids were right in the tree limbs. The noise was horrendous; I can't believe you didn't wake up. Everything was shaking! It hovered for maybe two minutes and then disappeared. It didn't have any lights on, either."

My three other encounters, starting in Georgia, were similar, each time they occurred late at night, chopper at treetop level, and then quickly vanishing. I have a theory that these are military or CIA choppers and they

- Are developing a personnel identification system that can pick out humans on the ground, identify them, and store the information for later retrieval. Identification was a major problem monitoring the Ho Chi Minh Trail during the Vietnam War. Hikers are the perfect test population; we're mobile, camp in different locations each night and are under a cover of forest. These are all the same properties one might expect of an insurgent, hostile guerrilla force.

Or

- Have perfected the system and are doing training exercises. They're using the hikers as targets to see if they can track them and re-identify them along the Trail. I wondered if they recognized me from the previous year: "Hey look, this guy is in our data base from last year. Hmm, looks like he's had heart surgery and see that grin, I'll bet he's not celibate any longer."

Well, maybe they're not that good yet....

Coincidentally, the first three encounters all had Boy Scouts at the campsites. An incident at the Wise Shelter in Virginia particularly stands out in my mind. I have mentioned this incident previously, but now, the rest of the story. A Vietnam era ex-Marine hiker, Kevin, arrived at the shelter and found that a band of Boy Scouts had taken it over. He ill-temperedly informed the troop leaders about the A.T.C. policy of not allowing groups to commandeer a shelter and chased them out. Later, a very strange thing occurred. Two adult scout leaders returned to the shelter to "apologize" and brought food as a "peace" offering. Then one of the leaders asked if he could take photos of the shelter; of course we had no problem with that; any normal hiker would not have even asked. Then, oddly, the two went off to the nondescript side of the shelter and took photos of the hikers, not the shelter. Later that night, around 2 a.m., we had the third very intrusive, noisy helicopter invasion. In fact, that chopper hovered directly over my hammock, off to one side of the shelter.

I can only speculate about these very odd goings-on. Was someone taking photos to match up the database to see how accurate the data collection is? Were the helicopters looking for Moses and Black Snake again? I can only guess. Subsequent conversations along the Trail revealed that *many* other hikers had experienced these same nocturnal visits.

501

The 501 Shelter is the last shelter before the severe Pennsylvania rocks begin. That night there was an eclectic bunch of thru-hikers staying at the shelter and, foregoing the comfort of my hammock, I decided to stay in the shelter, which is an actual building (as opposed to a hut), with a huge glass dome in the ceiling and bunks. There was a solar shower, but as usual, the water was like ice.

Some of the hikers I met there were "Bone Lady" (she's a taxidermist), "Slayer" (so named because she managed to fall on someone's tent one night and totally destroyed it, hence "tent Slayer"), "Uluru" (Australian aboriginal for "Ayer's Rock." He's a big guy!), "Thinker" and "Hell on Bad Wheels." This shelter is one of two on the Trail to offer pizza delivery and we each ordered a meal. Bone Lady mentioned that her younger sister, "Wild Oats," was also doing a thru-hike but was several days ahead and much faster.

As "hiker midnight" settled, everyone retired to bunks, like a bunch of kids after "lights out." The conversations went on for some time and as they progressed they became more and more humorous. Bone Lady in particular was quite funny. She described finding a "three-inch, blue rubber penis" on the Trail. Why three inches we pondered? We all started coming up with absurd theories as to how it came to be on the Trail: "Some hiker lost half his manhood," "A village somewhere is missing its blue penis," "a hiker was carrying it to use as a thimble in their sewing kit," "it was a spare tire in case a Viagra prescription ran out," and so on.

Port Clinton

Late the next afternoon, while hiking into Port Clinton, I stopped at a spring that was far down the side of a mountain, only to find it dry. Dried up water sources were becoming the norm. I worked my way back up the steep climb and met Slayer and Uluru, also looking for water. They were completely out and I only had a few tablespoons left so we continued on. A precipitous drop going down into Port Clinton accelerated our progress as we were trying to make it into town before the outfitter closed. As it turned out, there had been no need to hurry. Not only was the outfitter staying open late to accommodate the many thru-hikers, but they had also recently moved closer to the hiker's camp.

The town generously allows thru-hikers to camp at their town green/pavilion. It is a nice grassy spot at the end of town. A homeowner on the street to the campsite graciously sets up a hose next to his house so hikers can get fresh water. While getting water I stopped to talk with the older gentleman on his porch and found that he also had undergone heart artery bypass surgery. Because his surgery was more recent than mine, his progress was considerably behind mine and he found it difficult to believe that I could actually do this hike after surgery. I encouraged him to give it time and make certain to do the prescribed therapy. I wished him well and thanked him for the much-appreciated water.

This hike through Appalachia was giving me an entirely new view of America, a Norman Rockwell view that I thought had long ago died. I was meeting blue-collar, tough-but-generous people. They're not wealthy, but what little they did have they would openly share and often brought me into their homes and their hearts. Too often we roar down the highways and byways of this great country and see little more than billboards and fast-food establishments. The Norman Rockwell America is still there, but it needs to be observed on foot, or on a bicycle at a pace that allows us to actually meet the characters that Rockwell painted; they're real and every bit as interesting as we imagine them to be.

There were about forty people camped on the town green that night. I encountered a few new faces: "Cookie Monster," "Banjo," "Half-Elvis" and others whom I would continue to see on and off all the way to northern New Hampshire. It was July 10th and, according to one theory, a hiker should make Harpers Ferry, WV by July 4th to finish the Trail before winter in Maine, so with a week's margin I felt reasonably confident about my progress.

Physique

By this point, many hikers have dropped out for a variety of reasons: family problems, misjudged costs and subsequent running out of money, injuries, and predominantly: fatigue.   These nomads have been walking almost every day since winter and the physical demands start taking their toll. For others, boredom is the reason they drop off the Trail. It takes a unique mental attitude to keep at this everyday monotony: hot weather, cold weather, winds, rain, the same old food can all combine to be a self-imposed torture to many.

For most thru-hikers there are dramatic physical changes occurring. Males, in many cases, lose tremendous amounts of weight, particularly the faster ones. Their stomachs just cannot replenish the calories used day after day. They start looking emaciated, their faces drawn and the eyes sunken. Most of the men have forgone shaving, adding to their unkempt look. At this point I was starting to feel drained and at day's end I knew that I had to stop, eat and rest; I just couldn't push on. Then again, I was hiking further on average than at the beginning of my hike. Whereas in Georgia and Pearisburg, Virginia I was doing 7-10 mile (11-16 km) days, I was now averaging 17-mile (27 km) days.

Comparatively, the females have more stamina. Most also lose weight, but not as dramatically as the men. Many still have fat stores on their bodies and seem less distracted with getting enough to eat and more comfortable in their bodies. This is all the more amazing when considering that most women are carrying proportionally heavier packs than the men. For example, after receiving supplies from home, Bone Lady had at least thirty pounds of food in her pack, in addition to all of her other equipment. I, on the other hand, was complaining that my food supply was up to about twelve pounds. After lifting her food bag, I shut up.

Bone Lady and her sister Wild Oats were using equipment that looked like it came from a yard sale. Everything they had was outdated, like the very equipment I replaced before the hike. They were using what they could scrounge: older external frame packs, convenience store water bottles, heavy cookware and mostly regular street clothes not intended for hiking. In fact, one afternoon in New Hampshire I asked them where they found hiking dresses, since Slayer, Bone Lady and Wild Oats were all wearing similar dresses and not conventional hiking clothing. To my surprise, Slayer answered, "At Goodwill, where else?" She wasn't kidding. I was amazed that the dresses held up so well, right off the rack. I was quickly becoming convinced that I was hiking with some very tough women. By the time we got into New England a number of their male companions had left the hike, mostly due to injuries or they just couldn't take it any longer.

One afternoon a bunch of us were stopped at a shelter for a break. I knew there was a road crossing coming because there was trash lying around the shelter. Shelters that are near road crossings accumulate lots of trash from casual, local visitors and parties. Thru-hikers are meticulous about carrying out their trash. I was picking up trash and there was a piece of aluminum pole leaning against the picnic table and I complained audibly "I'm sick of jerks leaving their trash at the shelters. I'll haul this tubing out when I leave." There was a threatening explosion of expletives from inside the shelter, daring me not to; that bent and twisted piece of aluminum was Bone Lady's hiking pole. I didn't dare touch it!

Usually sleeping in shelters, these women had little to protect them from insects. At Lehigh Gap, Pennsylvania, Bone Lady and Wild Oats' Mom showed up to do a day of trail angel activity. Wild Oats took the day off from hiking to cook and take care of the passing hikers. Bone Lady, being a bit slower than her sister (everybody was "a bit" slower than Wild Oats) was hiking on but had stopped for lunch. I was looking at Bone Lady and realized that her skin was one continuous series of red bumps from constant mosquito attacks. If I hadn't known better, I would have sworn she had some exotic, rare disease! She swears like a drunken sailor about everything else but I never heard her complain about the bug bites.

Figure 26: Spectacular view looking back at Lehigh Gap, PA.

Moondog

At the Windsor Furnace Shelter, near a scenic vista known as the Pinnacle, I found messages that asked me to contact "Moondog." I had no idea who Moondog was. I suspected that it had to be a hiker ahead of me that had accidentally left something at one of the upcoming shelters and knew that I was following up behind. On several occasions previously that had been the case and I was able to retrieve items and bring them forward. I called Moondog's phone number and eventually we connected. Moondog was a member of our A.T.C. Florida club who has a place in Pennsylvania and whose trail name I hadn't recognized. He invited me to stay at his home and zero while passing through the area; now I had trail angels out looking for me!

Moondog had an interesting adventure on the day I arrived back on the Trail in Pearisburg. He had been out hiking the night before I arrived, in the area of the Wapiti Shelter. He found a campsite not far from a road crossing, and being tired, camped there. Most hikers avoid camping near roads since the town drunks tend to find their way there as well. The place was deserted so he pitched his tent behind some bushes and went to sleep. In the middle of the night a pickup truck pulled into the area and stopped. With the engine still running and the lights shining at the brush where Moondog had his tent, the driver started dumping stuff. The driver didn't see the tent; Moondog had intentionally placed it out of view.

Moondog figured this was somebody dumping his trash and yelled at the driver. A few obscenities passed between them, then the driver slammed the truck door and drove off in a rage. Moondog went back to sleep. The next morning he found his way home and noticed on the television that there was a story about someone shooting two fishermen, hijacking their pickup truck and subsequently getting into a high-speed chase with the police. The truck crashed and the driver was seriously injured and in the hospital. Moondog, certain the truck was the same one he had seen the night before, contacted the police. They had him show them the area where he camped and they found several black plastic trash bags with both men and women's bloody clothing inside. Oddly enough, the clothes did not belong to the two fishermen that had been shot.

The shooter eventually died of his injuries and the two fishermen survived their wounds. The investigation revealed that the shooter, Randall Lee Smith Jr., had killed two Maine thru-hikers back in 1981 at the Wapiti Shelter and had done 15 years in jail for that crime and then for some inexplicable reason was released from prison, only to attempt to do it again. Murder and crime in general is almost non-existent on the Trail, so this was big news in 2008. The section of the Trail where all of this occurred was closed off for several days, and hikers had to take alternative routes around the area. Moondog was one very fortunate individual!

Blueberries

The drought was affecting wild berry crops all along the Trail. I was finding wild blackberries, blueberries, mulberries, strawberries, black raspberries and red raspberries, but as a rule, with some exceptions, the crops were dismal and shriveled for lack of rain. There were a few isolated spots near rivers that had reasonable crops, but for the most part pickings were scant. I climbed Lehigh Gap, a formidable exposed precipice that rises about 1500 feet above a passing river. It was the most difficult hand-over-hand climb since Georgia. Once on top I was treated to a virtual blueberry festival.

The Trail for the next few miles was absolutely loaded with low-bush blueberries. The combination of the high peak and river at the bottom apparently creates its own weather and the wet clouds spill over the top of the peak and soak the plants. So, even though there isn't much rain, the plants get just the right amount of water from condensation and respond with the most prolific blueberry crop I have seen anywhere on earth. I removed my pack, sat down and ate blueberries for over an hour. This was serious blueberry eating, a handful at a time, there seemed no limit! I never strayed from the bush I sat in front of and ate non-stop. I finally couldn't eat another berry. I stood up, put on my pack and made a futile attempt to buckle it. My belly was so full I had to loosen the straps around my midsection so I could snap it. I later learned that these berries were growing right in the midst of mine tailings from a former nickel mining operation. The entire area is now part of a Superfund cleanup operation. I probably ate enough nickel to mint coins for the rest of my life.

Rocks

Pennsylvania is said to have the worst rocks on the Trail. Initially (in fact for almost half of the state) it lulls the hiker into a false sense of security with its really nice trails. Nevertheless, the second half of the state, starting near the 501 Shelter, does convince most that this is the nastiest section of the A.T. The rocks are not only everywhere; they are sharp and slippery when wet. Rumor has it that trail crews sneak out at night and sharpen the rocks; it was almost believable, as all the traffic hadn't dulled them in the least. In slightly more than one hundred miles the Trail totally destroyed my new low-sided hiking shoes that I bought at Harpers Ferry, WV. I was anxious to leave the rocks behind; New Jersey was rumored to be an improvement.

Chapter 11 - New Jersey

DWG

I was finally reaching another milestone: the Delaware Water Gap [DWG]. A subtler milestone was leaving the rocks of Pennsylvania and entering New Jersey. A 2,465-foot (751 m) bridge spans the expansive Delaware River and once across, I was in New Jersey. Prior to crossing I stopped at a pizza shop to order a large pizza. It was massive, so I shared a few slices of it with thru-hiking companions I encountered there. I kept two pieces for a snack later down the Trail; packing it in the very top of my backpack so it wouldn't get squashed. It was late in the afternoon, but I figured I could make that day's destination, the Mohican Outdoor Center by "night hiking." It isn't unusual for many hikers to night hike at this point in the trip. The terrain is finally improving; not long after leaving Pennsylvania the rocks get back to normal, and the Trail is reasonable walking.

I miscalculated the distance and ended up walking for about three hours in the dark. Normally this isn't significant, but there were warnings everywhere that this stretch of Trail has more black bears per square mile than anywhere else on earth. New Jersey doesn't have a bear-hunting season and bear sightings are almost guaranteed. I started thinking about the fact that I was carrying two fresh, aromatic slices of pepperoni pizza through the world's largest black bear population and it was disconcerting. To make matters worse, my batteries were getting weak in my headlamp and it was getting difficult to see the trail. The lamp was getting so dim I thought I would have to light a match to see if it was on! The trail was rocky and had precipitous drops and I was proceeding very cautiously. I breathed a big sigh of relief when I finally came to the road crossing that led up to the outdoor center.

The Mohican Outdoor Center is an expansive resort area offering an outdoor experience for weekenders and summer vacations. It offers boating, hiking and general outdoor activities to the regions nature-starved residents. It has bunk buildings, boathouses, community centers and campsites.

When I arrived it was too late to find any staff on duty at the office, but there was a sign that told me to make myself at home in the campground. There's no fee for thru-hikers, so I followed the trail out to the camping area. There was also a sign that warned of serious rattlesnake activity in the area and to stay alert. Black bears and rattlesnakes: this was a far cry from the stereotype of New Jersey that I had carried around in my head for years.

It was near midnight and as I stumbled around in the dark, one of the hikers was still awake and pointed me in the right direction to an empty site. I was wondering just how active the bears were around there when I looked down at the ground and my dim light showed the biggest pile of bear scat I had ever seen, right where I was hanging my hammock. I walked a few feet away to the bear-proof (if there is such a thing?) storage lockers and put my food bag inside and even with my poor lighting I could see bear claw marks all over the locker. I quickly went back down to the office building and ate my pizza there at a picnic table and got to bed as soon as I could. I did hear crashing and thrashing about all night around the area, but didn't actually see any bears. Surprisingly I had a splendid, if exhausted, sleep.

Old Crow

One of our Florida A.T.C. members, "Old Crow," advised me to call her when I arrived in New Jersey. Old Crow thru-hiked the A.T. in 1992 and offered to have me "zero" at her place. I contacted Old Crow by cell phone and we met at the appointed time in a roadside parking lot. To passers-by it must have seemed an illicit meeting: I came walking out of the woods resembling Harry Potter's "Hagrid", looked around to find the car with a good-looking woman in it, jumped in, and we sped off! Old Crow and her husband Bob treated me like a king. They have a wonderful spot in Pennsylvania, just over the New Jersey border. It is alive with wildlife: turkey, deer, black bears, and crows. Old Crow is a crow fan, hence the trail name. I stayed for a day and a half. On my second night there I had the pleasure of joining them for an outing at a local Italian restaurant with a bunch of her husband's high school friends who have stayed close for forty years. It was great to celebrate with old friends, and meet new friends, as well as get much-appreciated rest.

Old Crow dropped me back on the Trail in the morning and I managed to make it to the Rutherford Shelter near nightfall. The place wasn't very inviting but the mosquitoes were apparently thankful for companionship. Apprehensively I hung my hammock, not really certain that I wanted to stay there. It's funny how sometimes there is an intangible sense that something isn't right, but there is no certainty as to what it might be. Then I looked in the register and it appeared it had been several days since anyone had stayed there and the register had plenty of complaints about bear problems. Since there was nobody else around I repacked the hammock and decided to push on to the next shelter. Once again I found myself night hiking in serious bear country, but at least this time I had new batteries and no pizza.

At night most animal eyes reflect headlamp light brilliantly. My experience has been that shiny silver/blue colored eyes are deer, eerie golden yellow tend to be cats (large or small), occasionally insects show up as bright white or blue reflective spots (resembling ghostly eyes), and bears show up as green in bright lights and red in dim lights. This night had eyes staring at me almost constantly. It seemed everywhere I shined the light there were eyes. Some were odd colors that I hadn't seen before; is it possible New Jersey has werewolves? Fortunately none of the eyes were green or red.

I came upon the High Point Memorial Monument that night. It's situated at the highest point in New Jersey and resembles the Washington Monument at the Washington D.C. Mall, only shorter. It was erected in memory of the New Jersey veterans; I was surprised that it wasn't another phallic symbol to the Father of our country. The memorial is magnificently lit up at night; I wasn't expecting it and it had me awestruck to see something so dazzling in the darkness. A mile or so beyond the memorial I found the High Point Shelter. Bone Lady, Wild Oats and Slayer were already there and settled in for the night. I think they were a bit surprised to see me. They had been behind me, but must have passed me when I was at the Rutherford Shelter; they had missed the exit to it and continued on. So as not to disturb them, I set up my hammock away from the shelter and ate a late meal. It was a noodle dish and smelled really good and I was concerned it would smell really good to the local bear population as well, but none showed up. I was feeling smug; here I had been hiking through a huge bear population and other than some scat, hadn't seen a single one. I was beginning to think these New Jersey bear sightings were perhaps more myth than substance.

The next morning I was up at sunrise, ate breakfast, and I set up my ham radio. It was Saturday morning and I needed to make my contacts before moving on to New York State. I set up on the picnic table and made several enjoyable contacts. I kept an eye on the woods around the shelter; I kept hearing the distinctive crashing and crunching of a bear roaming in the area. I finally spotted a black bear spying on me, waiting for me to leave. As soon as I was a few hundred feet from the shelter, I could see it looking around the picnic table for food. New Jersey bears were no longer a myth.

The Outhouse

The A.T. often wanders across state borders; it's more influenced by geography than political will. In New Jersey the Trail comes within a quarter mile of Unionville, New York. I left the Trail and walked down into town and found the general store and ordered two large meat and cheese sandwiches. Just down the street there is a town pavilion with a gazebo. I sat and enjoyed my early evening meal. A stranger drove up, parked, and introduced himself as "Butch." He informed me the Mayor of Unionville would like me to join him at his home. Stunned at first, I was defensively cautious: was this possibly an ingenious scam? Warily I got into the car with him and as we drove to the mayor's home he filled me in on the ground rules: No swearing; ignore the dog as it is very shy and if ignored, is fine with people; soft drinks are free; there is one free beer per person; and any after that are twenty-five cents. Since my only requirement was to watch a fifteen-minute film and there was no mention of celibacy, it sounded do-able.

The mayor "Richard" was an amiable character and extremely generous. He took me on a tour of the residence and basically told me that his home was mine. It was wall-to-wall hikers, most of whom I knew, but a few I hadn't seen before. Recall that only a few minutes previously I had eaten a huge evening meal, now I was sitting down to a spaghetti dinner. I don't know where I put it, but I ate till I could hardly move. After eating, I showered and set my bunk up in the cellar. I had an upper bunk platform and it had a piece of thick carpet on it and was surprisingly comfortable.

Later we all assembled in the living room and watched a DVD of Paul Potts, the winner of a British show similar to American Idol: Britain's Got Talent. The mayor saw a connection between Potts, an opera singer, who against all odds, went on to win the talent show, and our challenge of hiking the length of the Trail. I felt that Potts had talent; I didn't see myself as having talent, but perhaps endurance? We hikers certainly faced challenges and at times the obstacles we faced seemed insurmountable, but regardless, many of us persevere and ultimately succeed. Our success depends on our own individual resources, resolve and strengths. Potts had to defeat his competition; our competition was the Trail itself and our inner selves.

In the morning, before leaving, I slipped the $20 I had promised trail angel Russ I would give to a good cause into the donation jar. Butch gave us a business card that showed the Mayor's place being referred to as the "Outhouse." I suspect it will continue to be referred to as the "Mayor's House."

Southbounders

I encountered my very first south-bounder [SOBO] at the New Jersey/New York border. "Rock Layer" started from Maine in early June and was hiking twenty and thirty mile days, every day! About six hours later I met my second SOBO, a friendly hiker from Tennessee and the next day I met my third SOBO and first SOBO woman, "Alpine Strider," a German hiker. She seemed very determined and was making serious time. These early SOBO's were in such a hurry there wasn't much information transfer, they were fleeting encounters and they were much more reclusive than their NOBO counterparts. Their reclusiveness is probably related to the nature of their hike. There are far fewer SOBO's than NOBO's, usually a few hundred a year at most. Spread them out over the month of June and early July, and that translates into at most a few a day starting. Theirs is a very lonely hike with little human contact unless they hike as a group and that's rare. Even though the NOBO hikers start in Georgia and face late winter conditions, they have a community ambiance or a sense of community to their hike and the weather does improve. The SOBO hikers start in the "mud and bug" season in Maine. In June, Maine's rivers and streams are still swollen from spring runoff and the water is frigid. Many of the river fords are deep with swift moving water. Contrastingly, there are few rivers to ford in the South. As the south-bounders arrive in the Middle Atlantic States, they encounter the hot summer drought conditions that are so prevalent at that time of year. Later, when they get into the Deep South they face the early winter conditions at the higher altitudes; essentially they never get a weather break.

A certain rivalry develops as the hiking season progresses. The northbound hikers start encountering the southbound hikers and they both have very different views of how the hiking world looks. A NOBO will ask a SOBO how trail conditions are up ahead, they may get a response such as: "Oh, it's not bad, pretty level and easy traveling." This same section of the Trail to the NOBO would be described as: "It's hell! Extremely steep climbs, boulders, bugs, river fords and freezing weather!" This disparity has more to do with their personal experience and their reference point; they have both had very different trail conditions up until this point. Gradually, in a joking manner, the NOBO's start claiming that the SOBO's lie about everything. I found as I progressed further north this would become a source of constant humor; "Those south-bounders, they all lie;" I'm certain they had similar thoughts of the NOBO's.

Lathered Up

I camped at the Wawayanda Shelter for my last night in New Jersey. The shelter is in the Wawayanda State Park. This state park is a very popular place for both New Jersey and New York residents to come and get away from it all. The park has a huge parking lot and is a very crowded place in the summer. The parking lot has a ranger station, numerous picnic tables and a tourist information building. The water source for the shelter is at a state park maintenance building at the parking lot.

I walked down to the maintenance building and filled my water bag and bottles. It was a very hot July afternoon and the water coming out of the tap on the side of the building was very warm. I decided this would be a great opportunity for a hot shower. My water bag holds about 5 liters of water and has a small spout that can be opened to use it as a field shower. I walked down off the parking lot into the woods and worked my way down into the forest so as not to be visible from the lot. I didn't get too far when I spied a female bear tearing a rotted log apart looking for grubs. She didn't appear to see me; I took her photograph, and then headed back up the hill toward the parking lot. The leaf cover was plentiful so even though I was fairly close to the lot I figured as long as I was quiet I wouldn't be spotted.

I stripped down and all I was wearing was my Crocs™ so I could keep my feet from having leaves stick to them. I stuck my hiking pole in the ground next to me, found a nice limb to hang my water bag on and started the shower. Since the bag is a limited water supply, I wet myself up, turned off the water, scrubbed with soap, working up a nice lather, and then turned on the spout again. At this point my body was covered in a good layer of soap bubbles and suds. My face was covered in suds so I rinsed my face and then turned to rinse my back. Stunned, I couldn't believe my eyes—there was the bear standing right in front of me, up on her hind legs! She was looking at me in complete fascination. She had the puzzled look of a child, looking at me as if to say, "What is he doing? What is that stuff on his body? Is it food? My, he's handsome!" (Well, maybe not *that* fascinated...).

For a moment I froze. Here I was, standing buck naked in front of a female bear just about as tall as I, maybe twelve feet away. Panicked, I decided that the best defense is a good offense; so I grabbed my hiking pole and charged at her, screaming at the top of my lungs; gambling she would turn and run. Notice a pattern here? Remember New Hampshire, hanging in my hammock screaming at a moose? At least there was no blinding light this time.

My gamble worked, she dropped down on all four and made for the hills with me in hot pursuit. She crashed through the underbrush, destroying everything in her path. Wanting to ensure that she kept going I made chase for a considerable distance; I wanted to make sure she didn't come back. In the ensuing chase the briars and thorns tore up my legs; adding to the intensity of my screams.

I stopped to catch my breath and regain my composure; my heart was pounding. It was then I looked up and realized I was standing next to the parking lot and a line of bug-eyed tourists were enjoying the show. All I could imagine were the conversations: "Hey Martha, check out the crazy thru-hiker. It must be mating season; did you see him chasing that bear? Poor thing, lucky he didn't catch her." Or "Henry, should we call the authorities; did you see all that foam? You don't suppose he has rabies, do you?" "I guess there's no telling what these thru-hikers will do in this heat."

I timidly retreated to my gear, dressed and as quietly as possible made my way back up the Trail to the shelter, avoiding the parking lot. The rest of my night was uneventful and I slept well; hopefully the traumatized bear did the same. New York State was next.

Chapter 12 - New York

Curmudgeon

Through northern New Jersey, the A.T. provides occasional glimpses of New York City. On the Trail in New York, as I walked through the sylvan landscape, it was hard to fathom that this section was so close to New York City. On the whole, the A.T. today is much more remote than it was at the time of its inception. Over its nearly eighty-year history, a good portion of the original A.T. has been relocated to be more in the backwoods. Paradoxically, in places it is a pseudo-wilderness, giving the illusion of being in the backwoods while, just through the nearby bushes, there is traffic rushing by.

In the densely populated areas, such as around New York City, the Trail is a masterful façade. Even though the hike goes through what appears to be thick forest it actually is only a narrow strip of forest, often only a few hundred feet wide. I kept wondering, "is it worth it?" Trail managers and maintainers go to great lengths to re-route the Trail to have the "appearance" of being in a remote wilderness; but urban creep is there, within earshot.

In the early days a good portion of the Trail was actually routed along country roads and back roads. Earl Schaffer and Grandma Gatewood spent a good part of their time meeting locals and staying with town residents they met along the way. These were chance encounters, not like my encounters where trail angels intentionally came to the rescue. One of my favorite moments on the Trail is my visit to the Horseshoe Curve Tavern in Virginia; I wouldn't have had that experience had the Trail not come down from the mountains at a road crossing.

Many other places in the world take a much different approach. In Europe, for example, many of the hikes intentionally find their way to an accommodating inn or hostel, conveniently located about a day's walk from the previous hostel. More often than not the hostel is located in a quiet village and combines the hiking experience with the cultural experience. Contrarily, the maintainers of the Appalachian Trail make a concerted effort to divorce the two and keep the hiking population as far away from town as possible. Why? I can't imagine that anyone's hike would be ruined with more opportunities to eat a decent meal, wash clothes and sleep in a comfortable bed. Besides, we are not always *really* out in the wilderness.

New York was just such a case. The Trail carefully weaves its way through the region avoiding small villages and towns as if hostile natives were waiting there to savage us. I recall one spot where I could clearly see that the forest had been clear-cut away, except where the Trail was. There was a narrow corridor of trees on either side of the Trail and nothing else on the hill up to the Trail and a dense village down below on both sides. It was really a green tunnel.

Another frustrating thing about the A.T. is that every year the trail maintainers add additional miles to its length. As the miles increase, it becomes more of a race to finish a thru-hike from Springer Mountain to Mt. Katahdin. Local contact and cultural experience decreases, while average daily distances increase and chance of injury also increases proportionally. I don't believe the A.T. was ever intended to be a race, but each year it seems to be more and more of a race against the clock.

On his third thru-hike of the A.T. at age 79, Earl Shaffer complained that, "relocations of it had made it pointlessly difficult." I couldn't agree more. I might also argue that for Earl, at 79, it just might be more difficult anyway.

At one point in Virginia, where the hiking was reasonably nice, I came to a huge rock outcropping. There was a blue trail that diverted off to the left, but the white A.T. blazes indicated an upward climb over this rock formation that was the size of a modern day millionaire's "McMansion." This route was a steep, hand-over-hand climb up the face of the rock and then an equally steep descent on the other side. When I got to the bottom I realized that the blue trail had merely gone around this impediment; there was no objective reason for climbing over it. The entire effort was pointless, and potentially dangerous. This sort of foolishness adds nothing to the A.T. experience and leaves one wondering about the sanity of those who route the Trail; is it someone's idea of a joke?

Virginia was replete with examples of this insanity. At another section in Virginia, the Trail climbs up onto a rocky ridge, meanders madly up and down and over huge boulders and then pops back down into the forest to continue as if nothing had happened. A few hikers joked that it appeared as if that the crew had brought in a bunch of five-year olds, given them a paintbrush, showed them how to paint a white A.T. blaze, put on some loud Disney music, and turned them loose. The Trail wondered about drunkenly and seemed to have no purpose.

It would have made more sense if the maintainers had followed the blue trails around these obstacles. Climbing over nuisance hurdles just for the sake of climbing over them detracts from the trail experience. These "bumps" may be fun for kids to climb during a Sunday outing, but add little to the hike.

In Harriman State Park in NY, I went through the "Lemon Squeezer," a split boulder that has a channel perhaps a bit over a foot wide. It is a well-known trail challenge and it is awkward to get through because the fifteen-degree lean weighs down the pack and makes footing a real issue. It was a fun, expected challenge but then leaving the Lemon Squeezer the A.T. climbs over a perpendicular twenty-foot wall that I called the "Lemon Drop." I had to remove my pack, tie a rope to it, climb the wall, and then pull my pack up after me. After all that effort, I found a sign indicating a shortcut around the wall, a blue trail. Had I seen the sign before climbing that wall, I may have taken the blue trail. One of the 2008 hikers, "Mr. Burns," broke a leg climbing this rock wall; it is that awkward. The climb for me, at least on that day, was just a nuisance, an impediment to getting to Maine. Perhaps it was the Trail just taking its toll on my mental state, or maybe I was becoming a curmudgeon.

Heating Up

By mid-July, the drought was getting serious. The Trail in New York west of the Hudson River follows high, long ridgelines of solid granite. Towns and villages are visible down in the valleys, but the Trail stays true to form and doesn't get near them. The high, rocky ground doesn't retain water so there was none to be found. I recall thinking that this was proving to be an unadvertised, challenging portion of the Trail. The difficult climbs, the lack of water, and the rocks weren't expected; the guidebooks failed to mention them.

Contrary to stereotype, I found New Yorkers to be friendly and warm. I appreciated their efforts to assist thru-hikers, especially in the midst of this drought. Often at road crossings I would find coolers with soft drinks and containers of water. Trail angels will often leave a notebook with these refreshments so hikers can leave notes. One such notebook said that the Tuxedo New York hikers had left the supplies. I had this vision of hikers all dressed in tuxedos hiking along; not even breaking a sweat, drinking champagne and having a merry time in the woods; perhaps the heat was getting to me.

At Greenwood Lake I followed the Blue Vista Trail down into town. It had been some time since I had found powdered Gatorade and it was an excuse to eat at a restaurant. The Trail did in fact have a wonderful vista and I took time on the way down to enjoy the awesome view. In town I immediately found my way to a café and had a late breakfast. I then went directly from there to a Chinese restaurant across the street and had lunch. After lunch, I hit a convenience store for supplies. Not finding powdered Gatorade, I drank three quarts of liquid Gatorade. My stomach was distended. Now I had to decide if I should hitch a ride up on NY 17A to the Trail or climb back up the steep Blue Vista Trail climb. The hitch would allow me to skip about three and a half miles of the Trail. This was the first time since I had started in Georgia that I considered such a thing. Hitching a ride and skipping a section is known as "Yellow Blazing:" following the yellow line "blaze" in the middle of the road as opposed to following the white blazes that mark the A.T.

It was tempting. After all, I rationalized, it was hot and the blue blaze to town was several miles and very steep; I could count the blue trail toward my total mileage. I started justifying reasons for hitching a ride and then the thought occurred to me that I'll probably only make this journey once and to skip even a mile of it would be cheating nobody but myself. I thought of my brother's Purple Heart Medal that I was carrying and the sacrifice that he made. How could I wimp-out because I was a little hot? His medal would miss some of the Trail. That settled it; I hiked back up the Blue Vista Trail and ending up enjoying it immensely.

When I arrived at the NY 17A road crossing, where earlier I had contemplated hitching a ride to, I rewarded myself with an ice cream sundae at the dairy creamery not far from the crossing.

Throughout New York I met large groups of hikers. This was vacation season and many school groups, church groups, and various clubs were enjoying the outdoors. It was also thunderstorm season and there were several occasions where groups of us would huddle together for a passing storm. At the Fingerhold Shelter a group arrived just as I did. I was avoiding a storm; they had planned on staying there for the night. As was my tradition, I handed out my hiker "business" card to a few of them. One young woman, a group leader, told me she was due to start a SOBO hike in Maine in a few days and she suggested we might actually see each other again. Sure enough, I believe it was in New Hampshire we did encounter each other again. Sadly, I forgot to make note of her name.

Bear Mountain

Strangely, considering its namesake, one of the few places I didn't encounter any bears was at Bear Mountain. The mountain itself, at 1,305 feet, isn't significant but affords nice views of the Hudson River Valley. There is a building at the top that in normal circumstances is open to the public with refreshments and tourist trophies, but they were in the middle of remodeling so nothing was open. Visions of a cheeseburger quickly faded and I headed down the mountain.

On the way down Motor Butt caught up with me. We'd been hiking together on-and-off since Pennsylvania. She was in a hurry to get to the post office in town and was cutting it close. I stayed with her and we flew down the mountain at a blinding pace. We made it to the park at the bottom of the mountain and had a difficult time finding the blazes for the Trail. It wasn't clearly marked and when we finally figured things out, we realized it was too late to make the post office.

We stopped at a refreshment bar in the park and had a burger and ice cream, then headed off to find the post office anyway. The Trail actually goes through the Bear Mountain Zoo. The animals are mostly rescued regional animals that have suffered injuries in the wild and are bought to heal and live out their lives in the protection of the zoo. Admission is free for thru-hikers so Motor Butt and I wandered through, taking little more than glances at animals that we had previously seen many times on the Trail. One animal that I did stop to view, however, was the bobcat. Since the big cats are reclusive, any I had seen on the Trail were merely ghostly wisps that vanished before I could distinguish much at all.

The exit to the zoo dumps hikers out to the entrance to the Bear Mountain Bridge that goes across the Hudson River. This is a large, mile-long suspension bridge and it was a thrill to be up so high with an unobstructed view. A few suicide-prevention phones on the bridge caught my eye. Are that many jumping from bridges? Do the potential suicides use the phone? It was food for thought....

About halfway across the bridge we realized that the village we were actually looking for was not across the river but on the same side as the zoo. We walked back to the beginning of the bridge and got our bearings and then walked back further to a traffic circle, which led to where the post office was. When we arrived at the post office there was a gentleman next to a pickup truck on a cell phone. He motioned to us to come over and then interrupted his call to ask if we were looking for a ride. We told him "no," and he explained that he was waiting for two thru-hikers and he was going to put them up for the night in his place. He thought perhaps we were they. He offered us the same accommodations and we agreed. As we stood there waiting for the other two hikers, "Banjo" and "Half Elvis" to show up, several others hikers happened into the parking lot and were extended the same offer. I was looking at the small Ford Ranger pickup truck that this man had and was getting just a bit skeptical about how many of us could fit in it.

This was beginning to look more like a Shriners clown act. The truck had one of those small rear-seat cab sections, but even with that it was getting crowded. We also had the packs to consider, and they're not insignificant. Additionally, a few of these hikers were carrying packages from the post office. Banjo and Half Elvis arrived with more hikers, making us nine hikers and the driver, plus packs. Additionally, it is illegal to ride in the bed of the pickup truck in New York and we were going fifteen miles away to Tuxedo. Undaunted, the driver, John, got us all into the vehicle, hid a bunch of us under the packs in the bed and off we went. I ended up in the bed laying in a rather convoluted fashion and couldn't get my head down out of sight. Miraculously, we made it without getting stopped.

As we arrived at John's home the skies opened up and drenched us before we could get everything into his garage. We stripped down and gave him our wet and dirty clothes, which he took to wash. After explaining a few ground rules about keeping the house clean, he turned us loose to relax and freshen up. He must have a humongous hot-water tank; we all took showers and never ran out of hot water. He had a computer there for us to catch up on email, big screen television and soft drinks and beer. His dogs were just elated to have all this company. Later, his wife Sue came home from her veterinary business and treated us all to Chinese food and wouldn't take anything in return. There had to be at least $40 worth of food, if not more. Between the food, hot water, gas, breakfast the next morning and drinks we had to be costing these people a fortune. Not only that, they were doing this almost every night as the thru-hikers passed through town!

Unbeknownst to John and Sue, we took up a collection and made a card to leave for them to find, hoping it covered expenses. The next morning John drove us back to the trailhead in three runs since we had different destinations. I was on the first run. Unfortunately, John forgot to bring his wallet and, being almost out of gas, asked if he could borrow enough to get home. I willingly pumped twenty dollars of gas figuring it was payment for the help I received from my Baltimore trail angel, Russ. Of course this twenty was on top of the twenty I had deposited at the Mayor's house in Unionville, NY; Russ was making me pay dearly without even knowing it.

After crossing the Bear Mountain Bridge, the Trail climbs steeply out of the Hudson Valley and the terrain changed dramatically from what we had experienced in western New York. The Trail became much less rocky and far more pleasant to walk on. Where it had been endless miles of substantial granite ridges, it was now more paths through boreal forests; this was more like the trails I grew up with in Connecticut.

That evening at the Dennytown Road campsite I managed to lose my bear-bag-hanging rope. The rope was a forty-foot length of tough nylon that usually slipped through the limbs of trees with ease. On this evening, as usual, I tied a small rock to one end and tossed it aloft but as it looped over the chosen limb it swung around a second smaller limb and instead of going earthward it wrapped around the smaller limb several times; it was there to stay! I tugged and pulled and unsuccessfully tried every trick in the book. I felt like Charlie Brown and his encounters with the kite-eating tree. To my dismay, I did this in front of a full audience of other hikers, not on some night when I was alone at a shelter somewhere. After many years of practice at throwing ropes and strings into trees, I could usually place the rock right where I wanted it within one or two tries. Of course, I was usually alone when I did this. Murphy's Law is nothing if not consistent.

The next day I came to another landmark, the Appalachian Trail Metro North Railroad stop near NY RT 22. Earlier that day I had met thru-hiker "Longwe Tru" and I waited at the rail stop to see if she was interested in hitching a ride to a deli that was about a mile south on RT 22. The approach to the rail crossing comes across a vast swamp. Puncheons (heavy cut timbers) were laid strategically to allow nimble hikers a route through the swamp but every step has to be measured; missing a step was immediately rewarded with a waist-deep plunge into the swamp muck. While I was there a man with receding hair, a short, trim beard and a wrestler's build came to update the stop's bulletin board. He explained that he worked at the nearby A.T.C. Regional Headquarters and he was updating the hiker information. His trail name was "Sasquatch" and he offered to give me a ride to the deli since he was heading that way after finishing the board. I asked if we could wait for Longwe Tru and he agreed. He had an activity that night so wouldn't be able to hang around to give us a ride back to the Trail, but one-way was better than no way. I figured it might take Longwe Tru some time to work across the puncheon network, but ultimately she made good time and arrived shortly.

Longwe Tru and I piled into Sasquatch's car and were ferried to the deli. The deli was actually more of a country store and had a few young employees working the deli side of things. Longwe Tru and I placed our orders and somehow the staff got things mixed up; I had the correct sandwich, but on the wrong bread and the same for Longwe Tru. We told them it was no big deal, we would take them anyway and they graciously did not charge us for the subs. We bought a few other things and went out to the picnic tables to devour our purchases.

Longwe Tru had started from Springer Mountain on my birthday, March 17th. She was the quintessential thru-hiker, always smiling and upbeat. She was also well-prepared, confident and seemed very at home on the Trail. Her background included working in Borneo as a teacher (her trail name derives from Melanesian Pidgin describing a "very far distance") and time at a Mt. Everest base camp; she was no stranger to out-of-the-ordinary environments.

After eating, Longwe Tru noticed that a van had come down the road from the trail direction and the driver ran into the store. Figuring he would return back to from whence he came, she brazenly approached him and begged for a ride back to the Trail. Strangely, this man had never heard about the A.T., but willingly offered a ride back to the Trail. We scrambled to gather up our stuff and hopped into the van and off we went. We gave the driver a quick summary of the Trail and its history before he dropped us off. In all, we made the round trip quicker than if we had our own vehicle, since we would have had to park and lock it. I commended Longwe Tru on her skill at finding a ride. Since my hiking rate was quicker than Longwe Tru, I went on ahead.

For my last night in New York I stayed at the Wiley Shelter where there was a good-sized crowd of thru-hikers. Earlier that day most of us had hiked past

Nuclear Lake. At one time this lake was used as a cooling source for a nuclear power plant; hence the name. The lake is in a beautiful setting, remote, pristine and tempting for a swim. With the current drought and water being at a premium I was tempted to get some water there, but had enough and didn't. I don't like using lake and pond water; it is usually not very pure and can have considerable contaminants. The authorities claim that Nuclear Lake had been given a clean bill of health but somehow that played a part in my decision. Then, near the north end of the lake, just before the Trail turns back into the woods and leaves the lake, I noticed there was a large, bloated, dead deer lying in the lake, perhaps seventy-five feet off shore. It most likely had caught a hoof in some rocks and drowned struggling to free itself. That night, at the shelter, I asked if anyone there had gotten his or her water from Nuclear Lake and Cookie Monster replied, "Yeah, I did." I then asked, "Hey Cookie, did you notice if it had a slight venison flavor?" He just grimaced at me.

Two of us hung hammocks that night and then about 4:30 a.m. a fierce thunderstorm blasted through. "Bilge Rat," the other hammock-hanger, and I high-tailed it for the shelter to sit out the storm, figuring it would be a safer place to be should a tree get knocked down or struck by lightning. As I sat there I kept wondering how Longwe Tru was doing. It had to be pretty exciting out there alone in the forest with this fierce storm. I would learn later that she often camped alone along the Trail and seemed to prefer it. I recalled my five-day hike in New Hampshire and the charging moose and found that I really did enjoy the company of others at night, to each his or her own.

The next morning I would make it into Connecticut, the 9th state and New England at last!

Chapter 13 - Connecticut

Kent

I was born and raised in Connecticut, so it really felt like I was coming home. The border crossing had a nice sign greeting hikers and a box containing pamphlets with information about the region and the Trail; I was impressed. The downside of being in Connecticut was that the State is paranoid about open campfires. Understandably, during drought conditions there is reason to be fearful, but Connecticut was extreme.

Connecticut has a policy that allows no open fires along the Trail. I personally did not have fires that often, having started only five campfires on the entire hike, but every now and then I appreciated a fire, particularly for drying wet clothes. Conversely, if clothes are wet and everything else is wet there is probably not much fire danger. Every campsite and shelter in Connecticut had signs plastered everywhere prohibiting fires. This prohibition made no sense to me. I really thought this ban was excessive; it smacked of Maryland and all its screwy laws. Through all of the other states there were no problems with hikers having fires but in Connecticut we were apparently incompetent. It just seemed a case of overkill. Maybe I *was* becoming a curmudgeon, but I couldn't help thinking that all those signs would make a really great fire.

Like near many other borders, the Trail meandered back and forth between Connecticut and New York before settling for good into Connecticut. I was back in New York for the moment, when I encountered Bilge Rat and Cookie Monster talking with a hiker known as "Tank." They were drinking beer and Tank cordially offered me one as well. He was doing a short section and figured he would "trail angel" and do his version of Johnny Appleseed. This was no supermarket run-of-the-mill beer; this was local microbrewery stock, really good, and I really appreciated it on such a hot day. After consuming the beer I put the bottle in my pack and hiked on. It never occurred to me to give the bottle back to Tank so he could collect a refund on it, I just figured that he wouldn't want to carry out the extra weight. Thinking about it, I realized he might have just thought me a cheapskate!

The seasonal weather patterns were absolutely changing. Afternoon thunderstorms were becoming the norm and the rivers and streams were extremely swollen. This all happened over a period of just a few days. The shelter registers from just the week before had notes about going for nice swims and enjoying afternoon frolics in the river. The Housatonic River was now a mud-tinted, raging series of rapids and angry falls, nothing I wanted to venture into.

At The Mt. Algo Lean-to (for some reason, in the north, shelters are referred to as lean-to's) I met four SOBO's. They told of countless miles of mud and water going north. I in turn related stories of drought and parched earth going south. It was almost as if we had all been hiking on different planets. We had been in our particular environments so long it was difficult to envision anything different; how bad could it be?

I went into Kent that evening; a town about a mile's walk from the lean-to. The four SOBO's had all bought hot meals at the deli in town and I offered to take their trash back to town for them since going south they would have to carry it about eleven miles to the next trash drop. I don't know why, but I had this sinking feeling that if I hadn't taken the trash they would have left it there — I just hope I was wrong.

Kent is a quaint, picturesque little village in western Connecticut. I liked it, but I had the nagging feeling that it suffered the same lack-of-middle-class malady, as did Sarasota, Florida. Everything in Kent glittered: the jewelry on the walkers, the shiny new cars and homes right out of Better Homes and Gardens. As I walked around Kent I observed a number of very well-dressed locals walking their "designer" dogs: mixes of Poodles, Shitzu, and Pomeranians. Others were driving gleaming BMWs, Mercedes, Lexuses, Porsches, and Hummers. I had the feeling I would have to be careful to not be mistaken as a homeless person and swept up by a patrol.

In recent years my adopted hometown, Sarasota, was nominated the "Meanest City in America" by the National Homeless Coalition because of its attitude toward homeless people. In Sarasota, at one point, falling asleep at the beach was cause for arrest. There was such uproar from the citizens that the city backed off, but it left a stain on the city's reputation. I can't say that Kent had such a reputation. The people were very nice; I just felt very out of place.

The walk from Algo Lean-to to my next camping site, Silver Hill, was exceptionally enjoyable. It was one of those rare places along the Trail where the guidebook said it is "flat" and "easy," and it actually was! The Trail follows the Housatonic River for a few miles and it was a joy to actually walk casually upright, *Homo sapiens*-like. Near the end of the day, the Trail climbs up a long hill and it was here that I passed two hikers utterly struggling. As I approached them from behind, I gasped at the size of the pack one guy was carrying. It was huge, at least twice the size of mine, if not bigger. Sherpas would refuse to carry it! He labored under it like some cartoon character carrying an automobile or refrigerator on his back. I asked where they were headed and they said they were going to the same camp I was headed for.

At that point they had maybe two more miles to go; they never arrived. I guessed they turned back, sank into the ground, or stopped on the Trail to camp. They were just out for the weekend. I can't imagine what they were carrying: a full-sized gas grill perhaps? I considered that would be a way around the campfire laws.

The Silver Hill campsite is convivially pleasant. After I arrived, a number of others showed up: Longwe Tru, Bilge Rat, and White Lightning, as well as a few section hikers. The campsite comprised a large, open, grassy area, a nice covered pavilion with picnic tables, a hand water pump and a great view of Western Connecticut. It would have been a perfect place for all of us to sit around the campfire, but then I've already bemoaned that situation. I wondered if they have Campfire USA (formerly known as Campfire Girls) in Connecticut. Instead, we sat around wearing our headlamps and had a deep philosophical discussion about water bottles and filters. This led to a confession circle resembling an Alcohol Anonymous meeting. Everyone was jokingly describing bad habits that they exhibit in public. When it came Bilge Rat's turn he solemnly looked us in the eye and declared, "Well, you see I'm an alcoholic... with a hiking problem." That cracked everyone up and it was off to bed; nobody could top that.

I climbed into my hammock and attempted to make my Connecticut ham radio contacts. The location was perfect, the antenna was up nice and high and yet mysteriously I was unable to raise anyone on the radio. It was a Monday night and all I could imagine was that something very interesting was on the television and nobody was around. Even though Connecticut only has about 52 miles (84 km) of Trail I knew there would be more opportunity to make radio contacts. Before I could do that, however, I was planning to get off the Trail in Connecticut for a few days and visit my younger brother

Ernie in Thomaston, and then meet Jane for a few zero days.

Strike Three

The A.T. runs up along a high ridge near Lime Rock Park, a motor sports racetrack. I didn't expect it to be terribly active on a Tuesday, but I could hear the track for many miles before it came into view. The throaty roar of big American V8's, the whine of high-revving Japanese engines, and the distinguished song of the European engines made for a strange serenade in the middle of the forest.

Mindlessly I was stepping over a log about the size of my thigh when there was a moment that seemed to happen in slow motion. As I lifted my foot to step over the log, my neurons signaled my slow brain that this was no ordinary log and that perhaps I should cease forward motion and rethink the procedure. This log had a strange pattern on it. Gradually — it seemed like eons — my mind registered that I was attempting to step over a snake, a very large, make that an *enormously* large rattlesnake! I numbly eased my foot back and then stepped back a few steps—the snake didn't move. Was it dead? It was lying directly across the Trail and looked every bit like a log. After a few moments the creature noticed me and then slowly wriggled slightly off of the trail, unenthusiastically rattling at me a few times and then, as if deciding that it wasn't doing a very good job as a rattlesnake, it went into a full-blown tizzy! I was stunned by the size of this creature. It was a Timber Rattler and contrary to what many think, Connecticut has more than its share of them. These snakes usually don't get very long, four or five feet tops. This one was nearer seven feet or more! With Pennsylvania rattlesnake country well behind me I had been just drifting along on the Trail without being on guard for the slithery creatures. After this incident I was back on red alert.

Figure 27: Large rattlesnake in northwestern Connecticut.

In 1963 my mother, an immigrant from Ireland who had never seen a snake in the wild, went out in front of our house to work in her small garden and was bitten on the arm by a rattler. She got to the hospital and the first question they had for her was, "Mrs. Blanchard, did you bring the snake?" (They like to have the snake to identify which anti-venom to use). She let loose with her Irish temper: "What do you bloody well mean, 'Did I bring the snake?' *I* was the one bitten, not the friggin' snake, you fool! Besides, it made a funny rattlin' sound, does that tell you anything?" Diplomacy was not one of my mother's strengths. Fortunately, she did get assistance quickly and, other than a bad headache for a day or so, recovered well. If you knew my mother you might wonder if the snake didn't get a headache.

The next day I was in an old chicken coop that my brother Tom and I had converted into a clubhouse, reading the *Guadalcanal Diary* by Richard Tregaskis. I was lying on an old couch when I heard a "swishing" sound on the concrete behind me. I figured it was my brother Tom and told him to "cut it out." He didn't, so I turned to look and there on the floor was a rattlesnake, maybe four feet long. Panicked, I threw the book at it and it slithered out the door and I never saw it again. I'm certain it was the same one that got my mother.

My current rattlesnake was an imposing creature. I took a few photos of it and then made my way down the Trail hoping nobody else happened upon the reptile. This was once again a reinforcement of that adage about hiking: "long periods of boredom, interrupted by moments of sheer terror."

Coming into East Falls Center I encountered Longwe Tru and her long-time hiking partner, "Willow." They had not been together for a few weeks. Willow had lost too much weight and had gotten off the trail to build back her strength and was now ready to return to hiking. Looking at her I was concerned that maybe she should have taken more time; she was a wisp of a woman and looked almost frail. But she had high spirits and seemed determined to get to Katahdin; who was I to rain on her parade? The two had met at Trail Days in Damascus, Virginia in May and had been hiking together since. The three of us hiked on for about another mile and found a nice spot next to the waterfalls. The falls were roaring; they were almost at flood level and the water was spectacular. We "stealth" camped next to the Trail. Stealth camping is a term for camping just about anywhere that isn't a designated camping site. The falls are situated near a residential area and, though it was secluded, we were close enough to homes to see their lights through the leaves. My biggest concern was, with all the noise from the falls, that I might not hear a bear, or helicopter for that matter, during the night. I consoled myself figuring that neither would be a concern since we were actually surrounded by homes.

After we set up camp, I moseyed down to town to see if I could find pizza and soft drinks. The *Hiker's Companion* indicated these were available in town, but when I got down there, I found the pizza shop had gone out of business and it looked like the rest of town wasn't too far behind. It was such a contrast to Kent: the buildings were run-down and in need of TLC, but I don't think that is going to happen anytime soon. The streets were empty and looked lonely. I managed to get to the local liquor store a few minutes before it shut for the day and picked up a few soft drinks and hauled them back to camp. We cooked up our trail food and had effervescent drinks to accompany dinner. It wasn't pizza, but satisfied, I climbed into my hammock and slept well and the night was uneventful.

In the morning I packed up, took a few photos of the falls and headed north. Early risers Longwe Tru and Willow were already gone. I caught up to them on a long downhill coming into Salisbury. I offered my good-byes since I was getting off the Trail for a few days. I wasn't certain I would see them again since I was going to be spending as much as a week off the Trail.

Can't Get There From Here

My brother, Ernie, seven years my younger, lives in Thomaston. My plan was to visit him for an evening then get to Bradley International Airport near Hartford to spend a few days with Jane. I now had a logistics problem to solve: getting from Salisbury to Torrington to pick up a rental car.

Travel in the United States without an automobile can be torturous. Salisbury is not terribly far from Torrington, maybe thirty miles, but it may as well be on the moon. I walked to the post office in Salisbury to ask about possible transportation. I inquired of three elderly women who were in a conversation in front of the post office about rental cars. One woman, Deanna, suggested that the garage in town might have a rental and offered to drive me there. I accepted and warned her that I was a thru-hiker and that with the warm weather I was getting "ripe;" I really needed a shower and clean clothes. She assured me that wouldn't be a problem.

The garage didn't have anything but suggested I try Lakeville, the next town, "only" about four miles away; they had a rental office. This wonderful woman offered to take me there, totally out of her way. I humbly accepted; I hated to see her ruin her day running me around. As we drove along I noticed that gradually she put on the air conditioning and gradually increased the fan and then started opening the windows a smidgen at a time...I did warn her, didn't I?

Lakeville *did* have a local rental office, but they didn't have any cars in stock. I had asked Deanna to leave me there; not knowing if they had cars or not, I didn't want to burden her with my troubles any longer, and by that point her air conditioner was on full blast. I walked over the local IGA market and bought a snack to munch on and while in the checkout line I was chatting with the young lady at the cash register. I asked her if she knew of a way to get to Torrington without a car. A fellow in line behind me, Mick, piped up with his English accent and offered to take me to the next town, West Cornwall, as he was going that way. I was inching my way to my destination. He had a carpentry business and a van, so I threw my pack in and enjoyed a nice ride to West Cornwall. I had just been there the day before, as the Trail passes near the general store and I had gone to town for breakfast; now I was going back.

At the general store I found a piece of cardboard and, using a black marker that I carried, I fashioned a crude sign that said, "TORR" indicating I was trying to get to Torrington. As I was making the sign two young guys at the picnic table asked what I was doing. I explained and they offered to take me to an intersection on Route 4, which goes directly to Torrington. They were mountain biker enthusiasts, my other favorite sport, so Mike, the driver and his friend Chris discussed local riding conditions until they dropped me at the intersection. I tried hitching for about twenty minutes at the intersection until a young lady in a Jeep, Keelie, stopped and offered to take me to Torrington. It seemed I never had any of my young male hiking friends with me when these young ladies would come along to help. She had one stop to make along the way and then, even though she wasn't going there, took me to the other side of Torrington to the car rental company.

In all, it took about two and a half hours to get to Torrington, just about as long as it would have taken me to do it on a bicycle, the standard that I measure transportation by. When I went into the car rental office I found out that they would have come out and gotten me in Salisbury. I made plans with them to return me there when I returned the car.

The next week off the Trail was bliss. Jane arrived at Bradley Airport. We then proceeded to visit with my daughter in Massachusetts, my brother in Connecticut, and to eat heavily for a week. I re-supplied and bought new hiking boots that I thought would take me to Katahdin; after all it was only another 689 miles (1110 km). One mistake that I made during this week of zero days: I didn't rest much. I was so busy running around seeing family and friends that I was exhausted when I returned to the Trail.

Hey Dennis

When I returned to the Trail at Salisbury it was late in the day. As promised, I did get a ride back with another wonderful young lady from the rental car company; maybe I'm just a Babe Magnet? She dropped me off in town and I picked up an ice cream cone and headed for the Trail. The next lean-to was only four miles away so I just strolled along and enjoyed the sunny, warm afternoon. About half-way to the lean-to, climbing up some steep rocky sections I heard someone behind me yell, "Hey Dennis...Dennis." Even having grown up in Connecticut the odds of anyone recognizing me after thirty-five years were slim. Certainly none of the other hikers knew me by my real name. I waited for the caller and when he and his friend caught up, I realized it was a young member of our Florida A.T.C. He didn't know my trail name, nor did I know his. His moniker was "Borders" and his sidekick's was "Worm." Borders was so-named because he would celebrate every border crossing on the A.T. with a party, usually a party involving substantial quantities of beer, and sometimes they would go on for days. He had a reputation for serious trail parties.

We camped at the Riga Lean-to that night and caught up on old times. Borders looked emaciated! The majority of males, by the time they get to New England, have given up shaving and just let their beards grow. I suspect that Borders would have looked even worse without the beard; it camouflaged his gaunt face and made it appear fuller. As thin as he was, he is one of those rare male hikers that hardly lose weight on a long hike. He was so thin when he started that I couldn't see how he had any to lose; overall he lost perhaps five pounds. Maybe it's possible that fueling your hike with beer has some advantages that modern science hasn't stumbled upon yet.

Later that evening I managed to put up an antenna and made one feeble ham radio contact, but at least I met my self-imposed requirement of one contact from each state. I went to sleep, exhausted from a week of zero days, and slept twelve hours!

I was on my way to the Massachusetts border when I happened upon a tent tarp hanging from a branch adjacent to the trail. At first I didn't see anyone around and stood staring at it, puzzled how it got there. Then I heard a distant nervous voice claiming ownership of the tarp. Looking down toward the stream there was a camper next to his tent; then it made sense, he was drying the tarp after the previous night's rain. I suspect he thought I was going to take the tarp, little did he know I had absolutely no place to carry it. Later I met this same chap, his trail name is "Walky Talky." Walky is close to my age and we have much in common: he is a serious bicyclist, loves hiking, and enjoys talking. His wife, Nancy, gave him his trail name because she says he likes to "walk and talk." Walky has a nice pleasant Georgia voice and I never tired of hearing him talk; he always had something interesting to say. The next night we would camp together in Massachusetts at the Hemlocks Lean-to.

Chapter 14 - Massachusetts

Talk

The week off the Trail put me in with a new batch of thru-hikers. It was also the peak of the hiking season in the Northeast and there were section hikers everywhere. The Hemlocks Lean-to is inviting, up on a hill surrounded by pine forest. The building is new and spacious. Strangely, it's only a tenth of a mile from the Glen Brook Lean-to. I never checked out the Glen Brook, as I was happy where I was, but some of the other thru-hikers went over to check on the residents there. Borders and Worm went off for while and I was alone until a group leader and troop of young hikers showed up.

I found the leader intriguing. He was a Welsh soldier, bound for Afghanistan. To help get in shape for duty he was carrying an immensely heavy pack, mostly used military gear that had to weigh at least eighty pounds. In spite of this, he was cheery and absolutely the most talkative human being I have ever encountered. He talked continuously from the time he arrived until long after I had gone off to my hammock and drifted off listening to his drone. The next morning several of the others were all bleary-eyed and exhausted looking; he had talked relentlessly into the wee hours of the morning! I hope he never gets captured; the enemy won't have to pump him for information, they will be asking him to please shut up.

Leaving the Hemlocks, on the way to the Mt. Wilcox Lean-to, I met a young, dark-haired woman named "Bar Fight." I wasn't certain how she ended up with that name; I can only imagine that perhaps she inspired a few events of the same name. The Mt. Wilcox site has two lean-to's about a hundred feet apart, one older than the other. Most of the hikers went past the old one to stay at the new one. Walky Talky and I stayed at the old one and as a huge thunderstorm rolled in we both put our hammock and tent in the shelter. It was a fierce storm; lots of cracking lightning and torrential downpour. After my experience the previous year at Cherry Gap, I was observably nervous and I think Walky sensed it.

Unlike down South, we were getting heavy rains every day. The rivers and streams were filled to capacity, with minor flooding here and there. The Trail was getting spongy and in places mucky. We were hearing stories from SOBO's about extreme mud and appalling hiking conditions. We would brush it off with a joke about "southbounders are always lying anyway," but confidentially we suspected that wasn't the case.

Upper Goose Pond

The Lean-to's in the Northeast were proving very different from those to the south. Many were newer and grandiose. Upper Goose Pond was just such a case. The lean-to, more like a hiker hotel, was a two-story building with doors and windows, complete with kitchen, gas stove, fireplace, tables, and bunks. There were even two privies. It was the hiker "Ritz."

The caretaker, Peggy, was gracious and made everyone at home. She briefed each hiker on the ground rules of the place, such as keeping things clean, helping out with chores, etc., and then invited them in to stay. A large group of Israelis had just left and I was hovering between shifts. The Israelis were all young women and most of them were knockdown gorgeous and amiable. New York Minute was nowhere to be seen; his timing was impeccable.

Since the water source for the lean-to is across the pond, it is retrieved once a day by hikers who volunteer to canoe to the spring and back. The caretakers volunteer to stay at the lean-to for two-week stints. They choose to make either a breakfast or an evening meal for the hikers; Peggy opted to make pancakes for breakfast. I was regretting that I hadn't picked some blueberries along the way; they would have been a splendid addition. There were perhaps twenty hikers hungrily attacking the pancakes in the morning and I can't recall ever eating that many pancakes in my life. Walking out of there I felt like a burdened pack animal, even before I put the pack on.

Dalton

I was really enjoying Massachusetts. The forests are alluring, with plenty of places to stop for food and a lean-to system that was well above-average. The locals were pleasant and I felt welcomed everywhere. I had a 21-mile (34 km) day coming into Dalton, Massachusetts and averaged well over three miles per hour for the last nine miles – I was really starting to hit my stride.

There are two hiker hostels in Dalton, one's published in the *Hiker's Companion*; I stayed at the unpublished one. On the way into town I encountered Cookie Monster and he described the unpublished one as "funky;" that suited me. The place was mobbed with hikers. I ended up sleeping in the rafters of the garage; there was no room in the house. The owner was very generous and didn't turn anyone away.

Late in the day someone set up a Slip-'N'-Slide in the backyard on a nice downhill grade and it was amusing to watch a bunch of twenty-something hikers having a ball drinking beer, and sliding down the hill. The males were looking extremely lean, almost like refugees, while most of the females were in great shape. I'm sure most of these women would kill to keep those figures once off the Trail; it must have been liberating for many to eat copiously without gaining weight. Our sedentary lives are cruel to the human body. Typical American diets are capable of keeping a lumberjack in good form, but office work and light labor just doesn't burn off those calories.

Later that evening the hostel owner drove us to Lenox, Massachusetts to an AYCE (pronounced "A-cee," hiker lingo for an All You Can Eat buffet). We spent two hours eating and were still stuffing our faces when they closed the place and we had to leave. In addition to our group, there was another group from the other hostel; I wondered if the AYCE made any money that night. It was just unfathomable that such lean bodies could pack away so many calories!

The Party's Over

As I hiked to the next town, Cheshire, the beautiful weather progressively turned nasty; violent thunderstorms drenched the afternoon. I stopped at Diane's Twist, an ice cream and sandwich shop on the outskirts of town, as much for food as to get out of the storm. As I sat there eating an Italian sandwich, Walky Talky showed up and so did "Party Animal." I had heard Party Animal's name from time to time, but we had never met. The name intrigued me — was he the male counterpart to Bar Fight, a twenty-something good-looking woman? Party Animal turned out to be another old codger like myself. What's in a name? This was his second or third thru-hike and he looked tired and dragged down by the weather.

The local Catholic Church offered thru-hikers lodging at its gymnasium. With the current weather, we were ready to be indoors. We made ourselves comfortable at the gym and discovered they had a well-stocked hiker box. There were shelves of goodies and useful provisions: soups, crackers, nuts, cookies, couscous and so on. I was surprised to see this much stuff so far north; most of the hikers that make it this far north know how to provision, so hiker boxes are usually sparse.

Party Animal left to call his significant other and was gone for a very long time. When he returned he quietly announced he was getting off the Trail, just like that! Walky Talky and I were stunned. Party Animal had come all the way from Georgia and we thought he was making good time, but the mud and weather was just proving too much; it wasn't fun any longer.

When the hike is no longer fun, it's time to quit. Fun is a subjective quality. The weather can be killing you, freezing or hot, high winds, or ice. The Trail can seem unending, but as long as you're mentally challenged and enjoying it, you're having "fun." When it becomes a job with too many overtime hours, it's time to quit and Party Animal was smart enough to know that. I wondered if I would be smart enough. I almost wasn't, with the angina, and it could have killed me. I admired Party Animal and when I later saw how tough things were getting, I realized he made a good judgment call. There's a saying, "Hike your own hike," and he did.

The Trail was certainly getting tougher and tougher. In New England I noticed a new trend taking place among many of the younger hikers: shortcuts. There are many places one can skip lengths of the Trail if desired. Blue trails that circumvent obstacles and big climbs, roads that shortcut the Trail, power lines and even hitching rides can shave precious miles and ease the pain. I was starting to observe more and more of this. The desire to "get it over with" was overpowering the desire to "hike it all."

Another technique that some employ, that doesn't skip any of the Trail but can certainly make the hike more agreeable, is "slack packing." There is some of this available for the entire A.T., but much more in New England, particularly the northern end. Slack packing is quite simple: get a ride out from a hotel or hostel in the morning to a point on the Trail and then hike back to the origin, or vice versa, start out hiking in the morning and then get picked up in the evening and hauled back to a hostel or hotel. Slack packing allows a hiker to just carry the day's needs: some food, snacks, water, and rain gear. Often a hiker can borrow a small daypack and end up carrying very little weight. Since the pack is so light, the distances covered per day can increase dramatically and shave days from the entire hike. The downside of slack packing is cost; the ride and staying indoors can be expensive. Those who can afford it and are not purists frequently start slack packing in New England.

Thus far I hadn't opted for slack packing, but it was starting to look inviting. By this point most hikers had done some slack packing; would I? To be honest, I was still having too much fun just hiking along each day, the complexity of making connections and being somewhere on time for a pickup just didn't appeal to me. Other than that, I had no problem with it.

Shelter Blaster

I was approaching Mount Greylock. At 3,491 feet, Greylock is the highest peak in Massachusetts. Previously I had ridden my motorcycle up there, but had never walked it. The approach has several short steep climbs before climbing in earnest. It was around lunchtime and the skies were threatening again when I stopped at the Mark Noepel Lean-to about three miles before the summit. I hadn't yet made my ham radio contacts for Massachusetts. The altitude was good for reception so I decide to give it a try.

I strung up a wire into a nearby tree and set the radio equipment on the picnic table in front of the lean-to. The lean-to roof covered the near side of the table. As soon I had things set up, it started to pour. At that same moment a bunch of young thru-hikers showed up to get out of the weather and have lunch. Someone in the bunch had a loud CD player and fired it up during lunch. They were having a great time talking loudly and joking. One of them had a case of noisy farts, causing some serious laughter, and in combination with their music and rain beating on the metal roof, I couldn't hear anything in my headphones. I decided to cook up lunch and wait them out; after all, they were in the majority. I didn't want to offend them when they were having such a good time. The storm let up in about an hour and the party continued for another hour. I was beginning to think I should just put the radio away and try somewhere else when they decided to go. I enjoyed their company and they were pumped with energy but it did squeeze my time to get on the air, make at least one contact, and then get over Greylock and to the shelter on the other side before it got too late in the day.

Finally I managed to get on the air and talked to Lou, WB3AAI, in Sandy Ridge, Pennsylvania. We had a nice contact and his signal was strong and made for easy listening; of course that's only if you think Morse code is "easy listening." I packed things up and headed back up the Trail. The Trail was becoming quite muddy now. All this rain was really soaking in and with all the hiker traffic, it was starting to have the consistency of bread dough.

About a half-mile from the Mount Greylock summit all hell broke loose! Heavy rains whipped by blustery cold winds bit at my body like thousands of tiny knives. I wear glasses and finally succumbed to removing them, as I just couldn't see with them on. Lightning was flashing all around me like some July Fourth celebration gone terribly awry. Trembling, I reached the top, or at least I was fairly certain it was the top; I couldn't see my hand in front of my face for rain and the clouds I was now actually walking in. There is a tall granite war memorial at the summit, but I could only see a few feet of it at the base; the rest disappeared a foot from my head. The visitor room inside the memorial was closed. I was starting to shiver, so I decided it would be best to get down off the mountain.

Under these conditions it was difficult to follow the trail blazes. Visibility was zero, and the rain and wind were physically pushing me around. A short distance from the summit memorial, I found a shelter called the Thunderbolt Shelter. A sign indicated that it is for emergencies only and I didn't consider this an emergency, but perhaps I should have. I was shivering and soaked. The shelter was gorgeous, with multiple woodstoves and benches, but it was off limits for use? I went back out into the raging storm. It seemed even more furious! Water was flowing down the trail in a steady torrent, at least a foot deep. The flow follows the trail since the entire mountain is a solid piece of granite and it doesn't seep in; the excess water eventually finds somewhere to flow off the mountain, but most of the time it followed the trail, like a raging brook.

I had never actually been hiking in such fury. In the storm at Cherry Gap the previous year I was shielded somewhat by the shelter. Here I was exposed to all that nature could throw at me, and it was pitching everything it had! My normal rapid walking pace had slowed to a crawl; the water was so deep and rapid that I couldn't see where I was stepping. Each step was carefully placed and calculated; there was no room for error. I didn't want to end up under water. A thunderstorm draws up huge volumes of water, accelerates it upward to the top of the "thunderhead" and then the frozen water starts the return trip to earth. Sometimes the trip is so rapid and the volume is so heavy that the water collides with the earth as hailstones; I wasn't in hail, but this water wasn't far from having just melted and it was frigid; my legs were going totally numb. My walk was like that of Frankenstein, stiff-legged and animated.

After about a mile I could see something moving up ahead, also walking like a zombie. It was a SOBO. He was going up the mountain. He was obviously in a bad state; I'm not certain he even saw me. I gave him a grunt of a greeting and he said nothing, just moved on past with a distant, painful look in his eyes. I hoped I didn't look that bad, but figured that I might.

Whenever I came upon terrain that was level it would be filled with water, forming a temporary pond on the trail. At times the water was up to my crotch and most of the time over my knees. I had lost all feeling in my legs and feet, and was getting very concerned. I knew I was in the early stages of hypothermia and was worried that I wouldn't know if I was in the more advanced stages. Most deaths due to hypothermia don't occur in vast arctic regions or on the world's highest peaks, but in conditions such as I was now stumbling through.

It took me close to two hours to do the three miles down from the summit. I was exhausted and shivering. I found the sign to the Wilbur Clearing Lean-to and made for it. I overshot the turn for the lean-to and ended walking about another half-mile before I realized the error of my ways and turned back. Was I really that gone already?

I staggered around the corner of the lean-to and I was startled to find it full of people. As my eyes focused I realized it was mostly youngsters, early teens, and a few adults. It was one of these camp groups that hit the Trail during the summer. Puzzled, I couldn't figure out why they didn't even acknowledge my presence. Then it dawned on me, the place was already full and there was fear that perhaps I might try to find space with them; I was a wet dog!

The picnic table was completely covered in gear: packs, shoes, raincoats, and cooking equipment. The ground around it was also littered with gear, much of it sitting in puddles and mud. I *had* to sit, and being ignored wasn't helping my mood, so I just pushed a bunch of stuff aside and sat at the picnic table, with still no reaction from anyone.

I figured the first thing I had to do was get something warm in me. I fired up my stove and boiled water and drank down two helpings of hot chocolate and then made couscous and downed it hot enough to scald, but I didn't care, I needed heat. Gradually, as I warmed, I started absorbing the discussion going on behind me. They were sitting in a large circle and the leaders were having each kid recite something about how they would change the world for the better. The first kid I tuned into was saying, "I'd make the world a better place by reaching out to the elderly and homeless. I'd help feed them and keep them warm and sheltered." I was awestruck; here they had an opportunity to do just that (if I'm "elderly" at 61) with someone not more than six feet away. My body was trembling so badly when I arrived that they had to see it. The next youngster proclaimed she would, "seek out those that need help in this world and offer them assistance in any way I could."

As the water dripped off of me and my body temperature rose from "ice" to "slush," I grabbed my pack and set off to hang my hammock. I got it set up and then unpacked my nice warm, dry sleeping bag and climbed in and spent the next hour warming up. After that I went back to the lean-to; they were still saving the world in there. I was too frozen earlier to grab my stove and dirty cookware; I cleaned things up and went back to nirvana in my hammock, happy that I had saved myself. It rained monsoon-like all night long.

Eat Fest

The next morning I hiked down to North Adams with "Kirk," another young man I met along the way. We had a nice walk into town and parted ways once there. I walked up the road to the Friendly's restaurant and went in for a late breakfast. I just couldn't control the eating. I didn't have a scale, so couldn't weigh myself but I strongly suspect that I had shivered off many pounds the previous day and I felt emaciated. I spent two hours in the Friendly's eating *continuously* and spent $30; that's a lot of breakfast! The restaurant workers were obviously accustomed to serving hikers; they marched me to a table in the back as far away from the rest of the customers as possible. I can only imagine that with all the water, sweat, and dirt I was an olfactory experience that had no rival. I didn't find this form of segregation offensive; I can only imagine how repulsive I must have seemed.

While in the Friendly's I overheard a conversation that the storm the night before had dropped a record-setting 11" of rain! These storms we were hiking through were extraordinary; their power and water content were beyond description.

I left the restaurant and walked over to the nearby supermarket to re-supply. Following that I drifted into the Chinese restaurant next door and ate for another two-hour session. The staff kept watching me go back to the buffet counter and refill over and over. I felt badly for them; business looked slow and I was eating the profits, but I was starving. It was a matter of survival.

Strangely, I seemed to be eating more than most of my peers. I couldn't rationalize it. Some seem to get along on a much lower calorie intake but there were a few of us that were the proverbial "bottomless pits." Eating wasn't a luxury; the scale was proof of that. Opportunities to weigh oneself are not frequent on the Trail, but the belt is a good indicator. I started out the hike in Georgia wearing a belly bag that I purchased from the Florida A.T.C. It has a cute backpacking alligator logo and was perfect for carrying my camera, hiker business cards, change, and my brother's Purple Heart. As the hike progressed I kept adjusting the belly bag tighter and tighter. By North Adams, MA I had run the adjuster to the end. Now, it was so loose that one afternoon it worked its way down around my knees and nearly tripped me. I took it off, tied a knot in the strap and put it back on; it fit nicely. In Maine I had to tie *another* knot, my waist being down to a Barbie-like 25 inches.

While in North Adams the sun finally came out. I walked over to a Little League ball field, hung all my wet clothes and gear on the fence around the field and lay in a dugout facing the sun. I dozed off for about an hour and when I awakened everything was nice and dry for the first time in at least a week. Feeling "tanned, rested and ready," I left North Adams and another state; I was in Vermont later that day.

Chapter 15 - Vermont

Dog Days

The Trail was rapidly tuning into a mud bowl. The constant rains of the last few weeks were taking their toll on the Trail. The rain, combined with the peak of the hiking season was the "perfect storm" for trail damage. Anything that wasn't granite was mush, and with the traffic the mush was getting deeper and deeper. To add to the misery, the mush would often be hidden just below a skim of dark water, making navigation nearly impossible. In the beginning I attempted to sidestep the worst of it where I could, but eventually accepted the fact that there was no avoiding the mud.

Vermont is renowned for its 272 mile (436 km) Long Trail; a predecessor to the A.T. and, some argue, the inspiration for it. Under normal circumstances, it is a fabulous hike and I may someday return to hike its entirety, but in the late summer of 2008, it was a disaster! It reminded me of the photos of WW I where cannons and mules are mired up to their axles and bellies in syrupy mud and the troops gazed out of the photo with that look of total loss, knowing there was nowhere else to turn. On a number of occasions I lost my footing, what little there was, and ended up knee-deep in slime; there just was no avoiding it. Nothing in my lifetime of hiking and mountain biking compared to it. Maybe Party Animal had called it correctly after all.

I arrived at the Story Spring Shelter (yep, we were back to "shelters" again!) to find a huge number of campers. Since there's a road about a mile or two away and it was a weekend, the weekend crowd was out. It was already dark and there were a few folks hanging around a campfire. I struck up a conversation with them. One heavyset man confessed it had taken them five hours to get the fire going because the wood was so wet. Generously, another weekender, "Dan," offered me a hamburger. I declined, figuring I was taking food out of the mouth of a hiker. When I later learned how much gear he was carrying, I would have eaten a half dozen to lighten his load. As friendly as Dan was, he had a dog that wasn't terribly friendly and growled and barked at every passer-by. He was constantly yelling commands at the dog to behave; the dog would respond by barking louder.

I went off and set up my hammock in the woods. The woods were thick and dark and my headlamp batteries were in need of replacing. Fortunately Jane had suggested that I wrap highly reflective tape around my hiking pole and each night I would put the pole next to the hammock so I could find it in the dark. On this night I had trouble finding my way back to the hammock and the tape saved me.

I went back to the shelter and just sat and watched the activities for a while. This shelter was a virtual village: there were people from all walks of life, ages, and ethnic backgrounds. It was an interesting cross-section of America. I enjoyed just sitting and watching everyone go about their business.

Dan was very entertaining. All of his equipment was military surplus, *everything*. Camouflage uniform, combat boots, cooking gear, tent, etc. He even had a WW I bayonet. I couldn't imagine how he packed all the stuff that he had into the site. He kept the dog on a short leash so he had some control. The dog, perhaps a German Shepard mix, was very nervous. For some reason I can't explain, Dan set up his tent right next to the path to the privy, so close in fact that he had to reel the dog in every time someone wanted to use the privy. It developed into a routine: hiker approaches to use privy, dog barks, dog is reeled in, hiker passes, dog relaxes. Hiker returns, dog barks, dog is reeled in, hiker passes, dog relaxes and the whole process repeats itself each time. Dan didn't get much sleep that night; after all, people use the privy all night long.

The next morning I was one of the last to leave the site. I sat with two others and had breakfast when Dan was finally packed up and leaving. He was a memorable sight: he had the dog on a short leash, two hiking poles, the most massive backpack I have ever seen, even larger than the fellow in Connecticut (I didn't think that possible), and two large military chests. I would have trouble lifting one chest and he had *two*! He apparently had his car parked a few miles away and he had evolved a technique for getting to it through all the mud. He would step on the stepping-stones that were scattered throughout the mud. He would grab one chest and drag it to the next stone; the dog barking the whole time. Then he would double back and grab the next chest and haul it to the first one, then repeat the process, yelling at the dog the whole time for barking. It was an extraordinary comic and absurd scene, indeed.

As he disappeared ever so gradually from our sight, we broke into a spontaneous laugh, as it was a sight like none of us had ever seen. It was particularly notable since, from what we could tell, he was only there for an overnight camp. If he did a thru-hike he would have needed at least 30 Sherpas to handle the load. Thinking back, I'm certain one of those fellows in the WWI photos of the mud had to be one of Dan's forefathers; that would explain the bayonet. Maybe instead of a dog, he might try a mule.

Piss On It

The William O. Douglas Shelter is named for the nation's longest-serving Supreme Court judge. He hiked the entire A.T. during his lifetime. I left my hiker business card on the sign for the blue trail to the shelter in case Walky Talky happened along. I knew he was behind me somewhere and I wanted to meet up with him again. I made my way to the shelter to find it was empty. I set up my hammock and later two weekend hikers arrived and set up off to the other side. Later Yazzie showed up. I had been seeing more and more of him lately.

Yazzie hung his hammock in the shelter hoping nobody else would show; he didn't relish having to take it down and hang it elsewhere if things got crowded. It was a good call; nobody showed. With his twisted sense of humor and easy-to-be-with nature, Yazzie makes a great hiking partner. He is one of the nicest people I've ever met. He has a big heart and was always offering to help out with any difficulty. In our conversations over the last 1000 miles (1610 km), he divulged that most of his career as a doctor was on Indian reservation and that, after his hike, he was going to Iraq as an Army doctor. Needless to say, because of my heart condition, it was comforting to have him around.

As I looked at his hammock hanging in the shelter, I wondered why there was a hole in the side of it. The hole looked intentional, carefully sewn, not something an errant bear would have produced. When I asked him about the hole, Yazzie replied, "I hate getting up in the middle of the night to take a piss." I laughed so hard I thought I was going to pee! Then he added, "Yeah, it's practical, but it's hell when you leave your backpack under the hammock."

The next night I stealth-camped and put my antenna wire up for my Vermont radio activity. I had one very weak contact with a station in Virginia and he could barely hear me, so we didn't persist. I tuned around for a few minutes and then hooked up with Bob, K2OGT in New York state and we had a nice conversation for about a half-hour. He was thrilled to be working me under such primitive conditions. It was comforting to me to know I could find somebody, if needed, regardless of where I was. I had no cell phone service here at all.

Green Mountain House

The next morning I found my way into Manchester Center. To a hiker's sore eyes, this was a wonderland! There are two outfitters, restaurants in practically every other building, and the Green Mountain House, a seasonal hiker hostel. I walked into town and stopped at the first café I spotted, The Green Mountain Café, and ordered their largest breakfast. I walked out of there and ran into Walky Talky. He had to get to the post office, so we agreed to meet at the Breakfast Is Up Café. I had already visited the outfitter and picked up what I needed, so I hiked over to the café and sat on a bench at the bottom of the stairs. The café is on the second floor of the building. It was a wonderfully sunny Sunday morning and I just sat and enjoyed the ambiance of the village.

Manchester Center is one of those "yuppie" towns that are sprinkled around New England, like Freeport, Maine and North Conway, New Hampshire. It has all the outlet stores and is a real draw for the New Yorkers just beyond its borders. Nonetheless, it was genial and welcoming. There were a number of stunningly beautiful young women and at the same time the hordes of overweight Americans; how can they possibly co-exist? Sitting there, I enjoyed listening to the tourists. The fairly steep stair climb to the restaurant was proving a challenge to average American tourists that were already carrying substantial weight without a backpack. Time and again they would approach the climb, look up the stairs and then decide that maybe they didn't need breakfast that badly, or they would wander off somewhere else where the food trough wasn't so difficult to reach. It then dawned on me that perhaps we could get the country into shape by putting all eating establishments on the second or third floor, with stair access only. Fortunately for the restaurant, there were still a number of patrons that could make the climb. When Walky Talky arrived, we hustled up the stairs with our packs and enjoyed an outstanding breakfast, my second that morning.

Following breakfast, Jeff from the Green Mountain House drove us to the hiker hostel. One of the Florida A.T.C. members, "SkyWalker" (a 6' 11" man whose last name is Walker) had recommended this gem of a hostel.

The hostel is actually Jeff's home, which he turns into a hostel for hikers in the summer months while he lives in the smaller building on the property. In the winter, the hostel becomes a place for his family to visit and enjoy the ski country surrounding West Manchester. This upscale hostel was new and clean. To keep it smelling sweet, Jeff requested that the hikers place their smelly hiking shoes in large plastic tubs with covers, and keep them there until they left. This made me recall the time I roomed with New York Minute in Waynesboro, Virginia and had to keep my boots outside because they stunk so much!

Walky Talky and I did a Near-O in West Manchester. We managed to wash clothes, dry things out, and spend some time in town just roaming around and eating. In the evening we dined at the Sirloin House and had a sweet, attractive young lady wait on us. I was still in awe of how many gorgeous women there were in the town. Was it the water or maybe the air? Whatever it is, they should bottle and export it.

The next day my pack was heavier than usual. I was getting paranoid about not having enough food. Since I was eating so much more, it was difficult to judge how much food to pack. Even with the challenging terrain and the ever-present mud conditions I was going farther and faster each day. I'd estimate the mud was reducing the daily mileage potential by about a third. We were all starting to walk with a gait like that of a zombie, trying to land on rocks and logs that would offer at least some support. Walking was more of a dance, one where each step was a balancing act and failure meant a foot stuck in the mud and occasionally falling and getting soaked in the slime that the Trail had become.

This was an unfortunate situation, because Vermont under normal conditions has spectacular views and terrain. Rather than taking in the sights, we were concentrating on not losing a boot in the sucking mud. More than once my leg sunk into the mire up to my knee and I had to use great care to pull my leg out and not lose my hiking boot. The black goop would hold on like some gigantic leech, sapping both strength and willpower.

The topography was also changing dramatically. The climbs were getting steeper and longer and the rocks larger, but we were still in mud. Walky Talky and I crossed the pedestrian bridge over the Clarendon Gorge, a spectacular raging flow of water. The manual indicated that the Clarendon Shelter was not too much further, exactly a mile. We figured we'd be there in fifteen minutes, twenty tops. It took us over an hour! After crossing VT 103, the Trail climbed an unbelievably sharp climb up what appeared to be a former avalanche. Huge boulders as large as houses were strewn about, and the

Trail meandered upward through them. The climb was taxing and, in the heat of the day, tiring. We were relieved to reach the shelter just before a nasty thunderstorm blew in. This thunderstorm was massive, not the normal run-of-the-mill thunderstorm. Lately, none of the storms were run-of-the-mill.

The shelter was packed with thru-hikers. We were discussing lighting when suddenly there was a huge "CCRRRRAAACCCCCKKK!!!" The strike had to be directly behind the shelter. It was loud enough that most of us ducked or cowered down. The odd thing is, there was NO flash of lighting—none. We were all puzzled. Sound travels at about 1,080 feet per second, so you can judge how far away a bolt of lightning is by counting approximately a second per 1000 feet, or five seconds a mile. This bolt was obviously very near; it had to be within at least 50 feet but there was no flash at all; there was nothing to count.

Storms blew through all night. In spite of the lightning I stayed in my hammock. We were now living in a world of wet, night and day. Even with all the rain I had managed to avoid actually hiking in it but I still had to walk in the results of the rain. Everything was waterlogged and damp. Stepping on dead wood resulted in a muffled "sqwook" instead of a crack; starting campfires was difficult and clothes and equipment were damp and sticky; even the mildew was growing mildew. It was difficult to wipe my glasses clean; the cloth was damp and would just streak the glasses, smearing everything around. The Trail was becoming a very different environment from the drought in the South. Since this rain was not normal for the North, we were experiencing a new world. The hikers in 2005 had similar experiences further south, now it was taking place in Vermont. Was this the result of climate change? Only time will tell.

Even though I was far north and it was late in the season for SOBO's, I was still meeting a few. I suspect the muddy conditions had them way behind schedule. I thought it would be a terrible plight to be that far north and have to worry about making it to Springer Mountain so many miles to the south.

In spite of the fact that no official trail organization sanctions records on the Trail, every now and then someone attempts to set a new record traversing it. In Southern Vermont I encountered just such an attempt. I had heard rumors that somebody had started out at Mount Katahdin and was attempting to *run* to Springer Mountain in record time. The runner and his "lead runner" passed me on their way south and I have to admit it seemed a credible attempt. The runner was going so quickly that he had passed his lead runner; the lead runner was too slow for him. A series of lead runners had volunteered to help with the effort so the record runner doesn't have to figure out where the Trail goes and lose valuable time with a wrong turn. These guys were flying, but I heard that a few days later the runner gave up. With all the mud he was already eight days behind schedule and knew that it was futile, that he couldn't make up that kind of time. If conditions didn't change I was getting concerned about making Katahdin before winter myself.

Somewhere after Mt. Greylock in Massachusetts I had encountered "Zero-Zero." Zero is legally blind and doing a thru-hike of the A.T. To tell where the Trail was, he contrasted dark vs. light and used his hiking poles as feelers. Whenever he came to an intersection he would either try to feel the print on the signs (the task was eased if it was engraved) and, if he couldn't figure it out, he would just sit and wait until someone showed up to read it for him. In spite of his visual limitation he was a very fast hiker, which made up for the time lost because of his handicap.

Another hiker, "No Amp," had me puzzled by her trail name. I had seen her entries in the registers for a month and gradually caught up to her. She told me she came up with that name when she had to get off the Trail for an infected, injured toe. The toe was so bad her surgeon recommended amputation. She decided to be good to it and take a break and see if it could heal on its own; fortunately for her, that was the case; hence "No Amp." All the time I thought maybe she was referring to not using an amplifier to sing or something of that nature.

Figure 28: Spidey in Vermont. Black and White just doesn't do it justice. Imagine wild flowers everywhere.

At one point in Vermont I was resting on a hot, flat granite area with a spectacular view. "Spidey," a petite young lady thru-hiker, was coming up the Trail and I took her photo. It ended up being one of the nicest photos of the entire hike; I caught her with a big smile, surrounded in wild flowers and green and greenery with a backdrop of a Vermont valley far below. It was just one of those wonderful spontaneous moments that couldn't be planned.

At the Churchill Scott Shelter, near Rutland, we had a surreal experience. Walky and I arrived there in late afternoon. A couple that had at least a half-dozen kids, several still in diapers, and the rest not much older occupied the shelter. They looked like a throwback to the Woodstock era or even the Great Depression. I had the distinct feeling they had lost their home and had nowhere else to live; so there they were, perpetually on the Trail.

They had commandeered the shelter. After a while, Zero-Zero showed up as well, and we all camped up the hill from the shelter. There was a tent platform there and Walky and Zero put their tents on the platform and I hung my hammock in the nearby woods. This platform was an island surrounded by mud, but then everything was surrounded by mud. None of us dared to be in the shelter, it would have been terribly uncomfortable and crowded with all the baby equipment; it looked like a nursery. During the night there were screams unparalleled by Fay Ray in King Kong coming from the shelter; we figured at least one of the kids suffered from "night terrors," a malady that some kids suffer. There didn't appear to be any other reason for the screaming. The kids made noise all night long and, even at the distance we were from the shelter, it meant for a restless night. One certainly does see and hear some weird things along the Trail.

The next morning Walky and I parted ways once again. He was meeting family from Rutland and would be off the Trail for the day. I figured if I didn't hurry too much he would eventually catch up.

Pink Blazing

I was huffing my way up a steep trail one morning when I met a large pack of SOBO's. I moved over to let them pass. Protocol says that the climbing hiker has the right of way and the descending hikers should make way for the climber. That never made sense to me; the climber should pull over to rest and catch his breath. Anyway, I pulled over and as they passed and we said our quick "hello's." I heard a voice that proclaimed, "Hey, I know you, you're...you're..." and I filled in, "K1." He said, "Yeah, K1; we met last year, down South." I recognized him more by his voice than physical being – he was a changed man!

As you may recall, I hiked with "First Timer." in North Carolina, in my first year of the hike. He was the one carrying a seventy-pound pack that was lightened at Neel's Gap; he had the fifty pens and five stove canisters. I had last seen him with friends and a bottle of wine at the NOC and it turns out he didn't get much further. First Timer also had the propensity for getting dirty by just sitting still.

His new trail name was "Honey." He was tidy, beard trimmed nicely, looking quite the distinguished hiker. I couldn't believe the transformation; what could cause such a thing? Then he introduced me to "Dusty," as cute a hiking partner as I have ever seen. It was then I realized Honey was "Pink Blazing." Honey had found the love of his life and was doing a SOBO hike with her. Pink Blazing is the term used for men that fall for a woman on the Trail and their world changes. Honey looked great and after a few minutes of bringing each other up to date, we were on our way. I walked away in amazement; now that was some real trail magic.

1927

The Trail pops down into West Hartford, Vermont and goes right through this village consisting of just a few buildings. As I passed the town library, I noticed the sign out front that proclaimed, "Building was donated by Hartford, Connecticut after the 1927 flood." The library was not far from the river and I was wondering if the current conditions would once again lead to destruction. I also marveled at the fact that Hartford, CT had shown such generosity. We don't see much of that any longer. I wondered if this library were to wash away today if anyone would offer an outstretched hand to help. After hurricane Katrina, New Orleans did not receive much help beyond the meager and late Federal assistance; there wasn't a nationwide swelling of sentiment to jump in and help. I'm afraid this sentiment of large-scale compassion as demonstrated in 1927 is forever gone.

I stopped at the deli in town and had several wonderful subs, drinks and deserts. Yazzie happened along and we chatted for some time. For the last few hundred miles he had taken to filming things along the Trail and interviewing hikers. He even modified his straps on his backpack so that he could carry the camera where it was readily accessible. He asked me a few questions and I wasted more of his tape. We had an interesting interview at the Green Mountain House a few days before. He filmed me doing my spiel about the things that one finds in a hiker box, especially the white powder. We had a good laugh about that and I hope to one day see that footage.

Figure 29: A Vermont barn pops the question. I wonder if Leslie said, "Yes!"

I hiked on to the Happy Hill Shelter. I spent so much time at the deli that I ended up night hiking for over an hour. It was the 22nd of August and the days were already getting noticeably shorter. I arrived at the shelter where there was a bunch of thru-hikers enjoying several bottles of wine. They were having a nice time and invited me to join them, but I was tired and full, and just wanted to sleep. It was my last night in Vermont and even though the mud was a killer, I had enjoyed the state and hoped to maybe one day hike the Long Trail.

Chapter 16 - New Hampshire

College Bound

I was anxious to get to New Hampshire. I was born and raised in Connecticut, but spent most of my adult life in the Granite State. My kids were born and raised there and I have a real affinity for the state, nutty politics and all. Having lived in Florida for a few years, I summarized that New Hampshire had prepared me well for the politics and elections there. I have often joked that New Hampshire is the only Southern state north of the Mason-Dixon line.

New Hampshire has the largest State House of Representatives of any in the Union. According to the state website, the N. H. House of Representatives is the third-largest parliamentary body in the English-speaking world. Only the U.S. Congress and Britain's Parliament are larger. As of this writing they have 392 legislators, representing about 3,000 state citizens each. If the U. S. House had this amount of representation with its current population, there would be about 115,000 representatives.

Dominated by picturesque Dartmouth College, Hanover is the first town one encounters entering New Hampshire on the A.T. The college quad is on one corner of the main intersection in town. I had made no plans about where to stay, so naturally I went off to eat first. Afterwards, I walked around town and met up with Walky Talky and Zero-Zero. Walky called a motel south of town and arranged for a pick-up. We all agreed to take a zero day the next day. I never needed to be convinced to zero; I loved eating too much.

We settled into the hotel and hitched a ride back to town. Of course, after re-supplying we went to eat. The town was literally crawling with hikers. I can't imagine the financial impact the hikers have on communities along the Trail, but it has to be substantial, at least for a few months each year. Restaurants notwithstanding, there is the motel business, re-supply, equipment replacement, and transportation. The interesting thing is: other than the outfitters, I didn't see much support of Trail hikers by merchants. I know there is some, but in proportion to the business coming into these towns, I don't believe it comes even close. Some towns go all-out: Damascus and Waynesboro, VA certainly come to mind, but many of the others seem to simply *tolerate* the transient population passing through for a few months each year. There's a healthy population of trail angels everywhere, but with some effort, businesses along the Trail could profit by paying more attention to hikers. The Trail organizations constantly struggle to find funding for maintenance and new projects; it'd be brilliant if some in business would take note of where a good portion of their summer traffic comes from.

The Quad

I decided to get my radio contact done on my zero day. I walked down to the Dartmouth College Quad. It was a Saturday and the weather was picture-perfect. There was a tinge of autumn coolness in the air even though it was only late August, and the sunshine was intense. There were college students everywhere, lounging around on blankets, playing Frisbee, reading, or sitting in small groups just absorbing the day.

It was too crowded and busy to use a weight to throw wires into a tree; I was afraid I might conk someone on the head. I just strung the wire in a few tree limbs above a park bench and figured I would give it a try. It had to be the absolute worst antenna configuration and location of the entire hike. The wire was about seven feet above the ground and I was at a low altitude in town, not far from the river, surrounded by mountains. I had my doubts.

Surprisingly, within a few minutes I was engaged in a conversation with station KE3V, Kevin, down in Pennsylvania. He was running low power too, about 5 Watts, but we had reliable communications; I couldn't believe my ears. This technology was really impressive. Surely the college students that afternoon took me to be either a very eccentric professor, or a government agent spying on them. They warily watched me with sideways glances as I sent Morse code with my right hand and strained to hear the signals with my small earphones. Since I now had my self-imposed New Hampshire obligation out of the way, I decided that I didn't need to carry the radio through the White Mountains, so I shipped it ahead to Maine.

Hanover is where many of the late season thru-hikers pick up cold weather gear. Even in the summer months, the White Mountains in New Hampshire can have snow and deadly cold winds. Jane had shipped my cold weather gear to the post office in Hanover. Additionally, since some of my clothing was absolutely wearing out, I stopped at both L. L. Bean and EMS in Hanover and picked up a few new things. I couldn't believe it; I met a floor manager at EMS, "Venture," and he had already finished his thru-hike, *that year*! It was the 24th of August and he was already back at work, while I was still moping along at the beginning of New Hampshire.

One of the new pieces of gear I purchased was a sleeping bag liner. This amazing device is extremely light. The material looks like black sheer mosquito netting. That evening, I showed it to a bunch of the thru-hikers and made the mistake of commenting, "Hey, you know, my wife would really look good in this, it's see-through."

Simultaneously, several responded, "K1, you've been out in the woods too long!"... Maybe I had.

I had not yet been cold in the hammock, but I didn't want to wait and find out that I didn't have sufficient insulation. The liner was a good decision; it *did* warm up the sleeping bag dramatically and there were several nights in freezing temperatures where I really appreciated it. The weather was still warm so I didn't use it every night, just occasionally. I also purchased new long underwear, and with the fleece that Jane sent me, I felt ready.

Hexacube

Heading north from Hanover, I camped at the Hexacube Shelter. Engineering students from Dartmouth College had built this shelter. As engineering types are wont to do, they couldn't just build a shelter; it had to be different. They built it as a hexagon and it had four enclosing walls and two open ones. The center of the building has a large support pole going from the floor to the roof. When I arrived, there was a quandary: the hikers who were there couldn't resolve how to best use the floor space so they could all fit. They had tried several hodge-podge layouts and nothing was satisfactory. They hoped that with my engineering background I could come up with the best configuration to lay out the sleeping bags. I studied it for a moment and then just told them to all sleep with their heads at the center-pole, with their feet radiating out like the spokes of a wheel. It was as if I had invented sliced bread. They all had that "Why didn't I think of that?" look on their pusses. I walked away chuckling to myself.

Walky showed up and we camped on a hillside some distance from the shelter. The slope was extremely steep and we had to use caution when doing our evening ritual. Walky almost lost a pot at one point and we both had this vision of it rolling all the way back to Hanover.

Next morning, I sat on a log to have my breakfast of several mini-bagels with cream cheese. Further south it was too difficult to keep cream cheese. It would go bad in the summer heat, but now that the nights were frigid and the days cool, it kept well.

As I sat on the log eating, a chipmunk hopped over to greet me. This little critter had obviously worked the crowd before and knew the routine. I called to Walkie Talky and told him I was going to do a little experiment. I figured it was familiar with human food and, even though it's illegal, I held out a piece of my bagel to test the theory and the critter came right over and grabbed it out of my hand. It ran off with the prize and I continued eating.

I had my plastic bag of bagels by my foot. Shortly the chipmunk came back and with no hesitation ran right up to the bag and immediately attacked it like a little buzz saw! Experience had taught it exactly where the goodies come from and it wasn't wasting any time. I jumped up, yelled and ran after it to scare it away. It ran just far enough to stay out of reach and then sat and chattered at me, cursing me up and down. All the while, Walky was cracking up at our antics and admiring the little rascal's impertinence. The lesson I took away from this was simple: don't feed the animals. Transpose this incident to an animal the size of a bear; instead of sitting and chattering at me, it would be tearing my head off for a bag of bagels.

Whites Only

The approach to the White Mountains involves climbing over the "foothills" of Mt. Cube and Smarts Mountain. They're not especially big mountains, but were a precursor of things to come. New England had been relatively easy to the south, but was now changing dramatically. Long climbs were becoming the norm and one starts sensing that this is just a warm-up exercise; the real thing still awaits.

At NH Rt. 25 I decided to go to the Welcome Hiker Hostel in Glencliff. The hostel is an old farmhouse that has been converted to host hikers. There is also a Quonset hut garage that has some beds in it for sleeping. Everything in the hostel is Spartan. Like many of the hostels, it runs on the honor system. There are cooking grills, a fridge, outdoor shower and a community room to gather in. There is a shuttle to the nearest town (Warren, NH) for basic re-supply.

Warren exemplifies the nutty NH politics I mentioned earlier. Going through town, the driver pointed out a Redstone Missile prominently displayed in the center of town. It is an actual, deactivated ballistic missile. The Redstone was all shiny, nicely painted, well maintained and incongruously glistened in the sun. It was in stark contrast to the surrounding village, where most of the buildings looked like so many others throughout Appalachia: run-down, paint peeling, and in need of repair. Why is it that towns such as Warren can find funds for such massive follies as a missile, but characteristically can't find sufficient funds for their school systems?

Henry T. Asselin donated the missile and brought it to Warren from the Redstone Arsenal near Huntsville, Alabama in 1971. He supposedly did this to honor long-time New Hampshire U. S. Senator Norris Cotton, a Warren native. Cotton was renowned for having voted against the Civil Rights Act of 1964. One can still detect the subtle racism in the region. For example, next to the post office there is a door that has painted on it, in large letters, "Whites Only." I suspect there's an excuse, such as a laundry or storage area that has "white only" goods stored there, but the message seemed pretty clear to me.

Moosilauke

The "roller coaster" terrain since the A.T. left the Long Trail in Vermont was training for what was to come. Mt. Moosilauke looms large from Warren, almost ominously. There's tangible electricity in the hiker atmosphere that nobody talks about. There was a sense that we were about to embark on a hike different from anything we had yet experienced. The White Mountains, or "The Whites," as they are dubbed, are not as dramatic as the mountains of the Western United States, and the Whites are certainly nowhere near as tall. (Mt. Washington, at 6,288 feet, is puny compared to its western cousins.) However, what they lack in size, they make up for in stature. Their proximity to large population centers, i.e., New York, Boston, Ontario, and Southern New England provide more access to hikers than the western mountains can. This access allows visitors to roam these auspicious peaks in unrivaled numbers. An outgrowth of this popularity is numerous trails and roads into the area. Virtually all of the White Mountains can be accessed during a one- or two-day hike.

The entire region is "eye candy," with spectacular views from almost any peak. Even though the southern Appalachians in Georgia, North Carolina, and Tennessee boast numerous peaks, many higher than the Whites, they are tree-covered and offer no perspective as to the surroundings; the hiker sees nothing but a wall of trees. The Whites offer magnificent panoramas at practically every turn, unless obscured by weather conditions.

The weather in The Whites is not to be trivialized. The mountain range is situated between the cold arctic blasts that pour down from Canada, and the warmer air over the Atlantic Coast. The collision of the two produces spectacular weather patterns indeed. The higher peaks in the range can experience snow any day of the year. Once I rode my motorcycle up the access road to the top of Mount Washington. The temperature at the base of the mountain was 95° F while at the top it was a balmy 28° F, certainly cold enough to snow. It was also so windy that I had to be careful not to blow right off of my motorcycle.

White Mountain winds are legendary. For years Mount Washington had the highest wind speed ever recorded on earth; a blustery 231 miles per hour (372 km/h) was recorded on the 12th of April, 1934. What never occurs to many is that there are scores of peaks in that surrounding area that are also subject to similar gusts. The Appalachian Trail goes over dozens of peaks with nearly identical conditions. Foolish is the hiker that enters this region, even in the heat of summer, without being prepared.

Mt. Moosilauke is the first taste of The Whites for the NOBO's. Its 4,802 feet (1464 m) are deceiving. There are no gradual switchbacks traversing the face of the mountain; the straight-up rocky ascent makes for slow progress. Often the hiker reaches an area that appears to be the top, only to discover that it is a ridgeline and the peak is still a mile off. This deceptive pattern repeats over and over again all the way to Mt. Katahdin in Maine.

On top of Mt. Moosilauke I met up with Walky Talky, Zero-Zero and, even in September, a host of SOBO's. The weather was picture-perfect: total sunshine, mild breezes, and clear air. We took a bunch of photos and enjoyed a snack and break. Since I had lived in the region for years, I had previously climbed Moosilauke several times but had never seen such a view. It seemed every time I had been there in the past, the weather had been atrocious and visibility had been about an arm's length so that day was a real treat. It was also a real eye-opener, for we could see where we were headed and it was all non-stop mountains to the northeast.

While up there, I used my cell phone to call Kathy, KD2VX, a ham radio friend that I had never met. The year before, when I had set out to do the thru-hike she had sent me an email on my trailjourals.com account suggesting that I should contact her when I got into the White Mountains and that she could "trail angel" for me, if needed. Fortunately she answered the phone. I told her that I would be crossing NH RT. 112 that evening and asked if we could meet up. She was thrilled and said she'd be there. I asked if Walky and Zero could tag along and she graciously agreed.

Kathy is a hiker as well as a ham and lives in Waterville Valley, NH. She has completely hiked the Maine section of the A.T., all 282 miles (454 km). I warned her we wouldn't smell too good, but she knew what to expect and that didn't deter her in the least.

The climb down the east side of Moosilauke is very different from the west side; in fact it is different from most mountains as it is loaded with steps. The Dartmouth College Outing Club maintains the region's trails and as part of their work they've installed hundreds of wooden "steps" on Moosilauke. The steps are sections of large railroad ties split diagonally and bolted to the angular granite surface that is Moosilauke. Picture a large parking lot, sloped at a 45-degree angle with step sections bolted to the surface at reasonable stepping distance, such is the Moosilauke descent. The Trail runs next to a raging river with waterfalls for most of the descent and the watery mist makes the wood wet and slippery. It was challenging for Zero-Zero, but trooper that he is, he did it. Walky Talky worked with him and talked him through the more difficult sections.

We arrived at the NH 112 road crossing where there was a trailhead parking lot and Kathy promptly arrived. Even though we had never met, we immediately felt like old friends. We loaded everything into her vehicle and drove down to Lincoln. Kathy (trail name "Kit Kat") and I were engrossed in a conversation steeped in amateur radio lingo and jargon and after while I realized that the two guys in the back were really quiet. Then it occurred to me they didn't have a clue as to what we were talking about; it may as well have been Chinese. We all broke into a laugh over that. It was a side of me my fellow hikers hadn't seen. Technological discussions are foreign to most hikers; our lives are much more primitive and filled with more fundamental considerations such as how clean a privy is, cooking methods, and where to find re-supply. I was a bit amazed that I could drop back into a normal engineering discussion so readily.

In town, we quickly raided the local market for re-supply and then Kit Kat took us to dinner at an upscale Chinese restaurant. Dressed as we were, I was concerned they wouldn't let us in, but business was slow. I think they might have let us in naked. It was a feast to behold and we stuffed ourselves. Kit Kat refused to let us pay for our meal and grabbed the bill. In return she allowed us to take her down the street and at least buy dessert at an ice cream shop. At the ice cream shop we did a photo session and enjoyed our treats and then had to head back to the trailhead; Kit Kat only had a limited amount of time to spend with us and had to get back to Waterville Valley, and it was getting late.

Figure 30: Trail Angel "Kit Kat" in Woodstock, NH.

She dropped us at the trailhead and we said our good-byes. It was only a short visit but we all felt as though we were losing an old friend; she was so good to us and we did so little to reciprocate. After she drove off, we hiked back up the Trail a ways and found a nice spot to stealth-camp. During the night I recalled hearing muffled noises but didn't awake enough to pay much attention. The next morning Walky Talky told me that Zero-Zero had been up most of the night vomiting. He must have unknowingly had seafood in his meal and, being allergic to shellfish, had a bad reaction. I waited around a while and finally headed out. Walky Talky agreed to keep an eye on Zero-Zero to see if he'd be okay.

Directly across the street from the trailhead the Trail climbs sharply for a few thousand feet. The two of them only got a few hundred feet and Zero had to turn back, he was just too ill. He went back to the road and hitched to town to take a few days to recover.

In New Hampshire, I started seeing lots of hikers slack packing. The terrain is tough and I think many of the males in particular were weighing the amount of effort needed to finish versus the miles left. There was also an anxious feel to things—the feel that we're *almost* there, only another four hundred miles or so. Playing against this sentiment was the extremely rugged country we were hiking through; the mountains, hills and swamps seemed to be endless. Autumn is earnestly in the air. At this point, we all had the Katahdin Park closing date in mind; to hike all this way and not summit was becoming a real fear. Personally, I wasn't too worried. It looked like I would make it by around the end of September or early October, unless something went wrong—and what could go wrong?

Franconia Ridge

Walky and I figured we would get a head start on Franconia Ridge by climbing up to Liberty Springs Tent Site and walking the ridge first thing in the morning. The ridge covers a series of significant peaks all in one day: Little Haystack, Lincoln, Lafayette, and then over to Mt. Garfield. The ridge stays at a considerable altitude with many of the peaks near 5,000 feet. Weather can be a determining factor on successfully making it across all in one day. We hoped we could start early and avoid any serious afternoon thunderstorms.

A few years previously, I had been caught on Mt. Lafayette with Jane, my two young teenage kids, and one of our daughter's friends, Katrina. It was a beautiful day for a climb and then right near the summit a thunderstorm blew in out of nowhere and we became separated, me with Katrina and the rest of the family at the summit. Dangerous lightning played all around us and the winds climbed to near 100 mph! I hunkered down with Katrina and tried to shield her from the flying stones and rocks that were pelting us, and the family did likewise at the summit. We were literally inside the storm and I was concerned for the family but couldn't do anything to help. Fortunately, they weathered the storm well and nobody was injured, but it was once again a sharp lesson about conditions in those mountains at any time.

We enjoyed the stay at the camp. The site manager, "Claire Bear," was extremely amiable and loquacious. She told us her term at the station was almost finished and that she was setting sail for an Antarctic science station for a year to manage their waste disposal and environmental concerns. I feel she'll be good at it; she seemed very dedicated.

Early the next morning, Walky finished his hot morning coffee, which he traditionally cannot start the day without, and we were on our way. The climb wasn't bad and the day started out sunny, but quickly became socked in with cloud cover. We would later learn the clouds were just in the mountains; the valleys were sunny. With the clouds came serious wind gusts that I estimated to be a sustained 50 mph, with serious peaks of 70 mph or more. Walky, who was ahead of me, was struggling with the wind, leaning sideways such that he reminded me of a drunk leaning against a lamppost. I kept wondering if the wind were to suddenly stop, would we just fall over? We couldn't even carry on a conversation; the roar of the wind was deafening. If Walky was more than a few feet ahead of me, I would lose sight of him. Thank goodness there were lots of well-placed blazes, otherwise it would have been impossible to pick the best route. I'd crossed this ridge a number of times over the years and knew that you didn't want to wander too far off in a few places; there are dramatic cliffs and drop-offs to contend with and the wind could easily force one over the edge.

Work-for-Stay

Walky and I were tired, it was getting late in the day, and we were not looking forward to setting up camp. Luckily, we were not far from Gale Head Hut, one of the huts operated by the Appalachian Mountain Club [A.M.C.] in the White Mountains. The A.M.C. offers a bunk, evening meal, and breakfast at the huts and they are usually booked well in advance. However, for a thru-hiker on a budget, the huts are an expensive luxury. Keep in mind that these are very primitive locations, located far from roads, electrical service, or everyday conveniences. Most of the food and supplies are ported to the huts by the staff and trash is carried back down off the mountains in special backpacks.

Since staffing at the huts is usually minimal, the A.M.C. offers "work-for-stay" to thru-hikers. Thru-hikers that arrive early have the opportunity to work at the hut in exchange for meals and a place to sleep. Walky and I hoped that perhaps we could do so at the Gale Head Hut. When we arrived, there were a number of younger thru-hikers already there, but as luck would have it, they took us on.

The staffs at the huts are referred to as the "Croo." Walky Talky was quickly enlisted with the cleaning Croo. It was readily evident that they were running out of tasks for all the thru-hikers present and I was concerned they would have a change of heart and send me out into the woods again. The Croo manager, an amiable fellow, interviewed me to see where he might employ me. He was visibly flummoxed with what to do with me. He asked me if I had any particular skills. Figuring I had nothing to lose, I offered to "manage the parking lot, or maybe the casino, or to be a life guard at the hot tub." He looked at me a bit cockeyed, certain he ended up with the class clown. "Hmmm," he offered thoughtfully, "hey, you can be our speaker this evening, we don't have one." Often the huts have a scheduled speaker, but fortunately for me, they didn't have one this evening.

Most hikers would rather freeze to death at night outdoors than do public speaking. As a longtime member of Toastmaster International, I was excited about the opportunity until the Croo manager added, "Oh, by the way, almost all of the guests tonight are from Quebec, Canada, and I'm not certain if they all speak English." "Great" I thought, "maybe freezing wasn't such a bad option after all!"

With only an hour to prepare, I was able to structure the presentation to my satisfaction. My goal was to be as humorous as possible and to keep the audience's attention, as I knew they'd be tired from hiking. I sat down and roughly outlined the bullet points I was going to address. While I was preparing, the hiking guests started arriving. It became evident immediately that these folks were in a partying mood and that they apparently knew each other well. Some were speaking English, some French. I went over to one couple that seemed fluent in both and told them about my dilemma. I was told not to worry, that everyone was comfortable with English and that if there were a problem they would do an on-the-spot translation for me. They also told me that the guests were all related; it was a yearly gathering of an extended family, thus explaining the party atmosphere. I was also warned that the group tends to have a short attention span. I interpreted this to mean that they would be easily bored.

A small group of hikers from Maine arrived as well, increasing the audience to around fifty people. It was evident that this was a "high-energy" audience, laughing and joking. I needed to be in sync with them or I would lose them, and I didn't want to disappoint these folks. My Toastmasters experience taught a basic premise: know your audience. They were tired from the day's hike; a lecture on various types of tent seams would have them asleep in minutes. I needed to entertain and yet give them useful information.

After I finished my notes, I cleaned up as best I could. Thru-hikers rarely have spare clothing, so I had to wear my hiking clothes, which was not so bad; it had me in character.

I was scheduled to speak after the evening meal. The room was quite noisy until the Croo manager started the evening's program and introduced me. As they quieted, I hoped I could keep it that way. In proper Toastmaster fashion, I greeted my audience. Next, I knew I had to connect with them, create some common bond. We were all hikers, that was too obvious, but since my lovely wife, Jane, is of French Canadian extraction (her native tongue is French) I proudly announced that I was married to a French Canadian. There was applause, hooting and hollering — we now had something in common, and I had succeeded in connecting.

I explained to them how Jane is a prankster and worked hard to prepare me for the hike. In the evening, as I was working on my computer, she would sneak up behind me and growl like a bear or bellow like moose or wiggle a rope on the floor behind me like a snake. One evening I felt ice pellets and water hitting me; she was putting it into a floor fan directed at me. I asked, "Just what are you doing?" she replied: "Getting you ready for Mount Washington."

I recounted how every Sunday we wash our bed sheets and make the beds. One Sunday evening, when Jane had already gone to bed, I went into the darkened bedroom. I pulled back the sheets, put my hand on the bed and realized that there was something on the sheets. I couldn't imagine what, and then I heard "tee-hee" on the other side of the bed. I turned on the lights and found a bunch of rice in the bed. I looked at her and asked, "What's this?" "It's mouse droppings, of course, just like those in the shelters on the Trail." My audience loved it, and I could see they were taking her side in the conspiracy against me. They were engaged!

I continued with descriptions of animal encounters on the Trail, weather difficulties and the beauty of the Trail, trying to paint a picture with words. The Croo had hoped I could speak for at least half an hour; at one hour I went to questions and answers and finally we had to stop for lights out. They were a wonderful audience; engaged, funny, and a joy to be with. I went to sleep satisfied that it was "mission accomplished."

Figure 31: The AMC builds some serious "huts" in the White Mountains. This is the Gale Head Hut.

Crawford Notch

The next day we hiked through spectacular country; every turn of the Trail was a new panorama of mountains and valleys, streams, waterfalls, and pristine country. I'd been given a second chance at life with my heart surgery and it was here, more than anywhere else, that I was overwhelmed with the knowledge that I was truly living the gift. It was so exhilarating to breathe the cool fresh air, feel the warmth of the sunbeams and take in all that was around me. It was as close to a religious experience as I have ever had. All of the magnificence that this planet has to offer was right there before me and I was living a dream, absorbing it and appreciating it. For all the suffering, body pains, cold, heat, thirst, and weariness it was worth every step, every penny, and every breath.

At day's end Walky and I ended up at the trailhead parking area at US HW 302. The A.M.C.'s Highland Center was about three or four miles to the north. The lure of a room and hot shower was enticing, so we tried to hitch a ride there. We had no luck getting a ride. After a while a car pulled in, and the driver was a previous thru-hiker, "Rock Dancer." He opened his trunk and had all sorts of goodies for making sandwiches, and fruit and drinks to share with us. We feasted. As we were enjoying all this, two other women hikers, "Sprite" and "Freckles," showed up and told us they had another hiker, "Papa Sarge," coming to pick them up. They were going south and offered to take us to the Crawford Notch Campground. We agreed.

The campground was perfect. They have a hiker cabin, hot showers, hot food, and hiker re-supply. It was a notch above most of the campgrounds I had experienced along the Trail, as they really understood hiker needs and catered to them. It cost far less than the Highland Center would have, and we had all the creature comforts we could wish for. Once again, going with the flow on the Trail proved most prudent.

Mt. Washington

The owners of the Crawford Notch Campground graciously gave us a ride back to the trailhead in the morning. Our goal for the day was Lake of the Clouds Hut. The hut is over a mile before the summit of Mt. Washington, but we didn't want to get to the summit because there is nowhere to stay once there and it would have been late in the day. Once again we had a spectacular day for hiking: not too hot, plenty of sunshine, and great vistas. New Hampshire truly is a jewel for hiking and even though I had lived there most of my life, I was still in awe of the breathtaking beauty.

Much of the day's hiking was above the tree line. The Trail is replete with rocks of every shape and size but in spite of that, it is reasonably navigated. My Florida lungs were feeling the altitude and I couldn't push too hard without heavy breathing. I'd noticed that since the heart surgery my uphill climbing ability had changed; I could climb at a fairly steady pace, but couldn't climb as quickly as I once did. One hiker, a nurse, at the Mayor's Place in Unionville, NY commented that it might be caused by the beta-blocker medication that I now had to take. Maybe she was onto something. At sixty, I had previously been able to keep up with the twenty-something's on the hill climbs. Now I had to settle for climbing with my age peers. It was a consolation I was willing to accept in light of the situation. Regretfully, I concluded that this also meant an end to my serious mountain bike racing.

We arrived at the Lake of the Clouds late in the day. The Croo there was generous and was taking in all the hikers and giving them work-for-stay. We were all thankful for that; if we couldn't stay, we would have had to hike down several thousand feet to below the tree line to camp, and then come back up again in the morning, an undesirable task after hiking all day. I once again got to entertain their guests with my NOBO hiking presentation that I did at Gale Head Hut.

Snow Plow, an amusing hiker I've mentioned earlier, was at the hut. In conversations we had along the way, we found we had much in common. She is a young feminist; no, we didn't have "young" in common, but we did have similar political leanings and she had a very subtle sense of humor. On the surface she appeared gruff and put-offish, but she was actually extremely likeable. She looked really tired and depleted at Lake of the Clouds. Around mealtime she was shuffling across the floor from the kitchen carrying a coffee and soup and managed to spill a good portion of it on the way to the table. As she sat, she muttered to no one in particular, "I do work-for-stay just so I can clean up after myself."

Snow Plow always seemed petulant and when I asked her about it she told me, "I like to stay at a certain low level of pissed-off at all times, that way I never lose it and blow my top!" Maybe she's onto something. During all the years we had the Cold War, neither side went over the edge; maybe the State Department could learn from Snow Plow.

After eating, I went outside to take in the spectacular sunset and sky. I just stood there in awe of it, along with a dozen others. We just stared and were humbled by the whole thing. The air was cold, near freezing, but there was no wind, just absolute silence. The sky was ablaze with color and we were only a few feet below a blanket of clouds that extended just beyond the mountain, like the brim of a hat over your forehead. After the sun disappeared I hung around for a while just to take in the evening. Soon the stars were out and there is nothing that describes the night sky in high mountains. The stars seem almost within reach. They were painted so thickly on the dome above that they actually seem smeared together, there are so many. The Milky Way is aptly named from such a vantage point.

Objects that cannot be observed from most of our terrestrial planet because of ambient light literally decorate the sky like some misplaced Christmas ornaments; nebulae, clusters, and galaxies, such as the M31 Galaxy, are visible with the naked eye. When I lived in Southern New Hampshire, I needed powerful binoculars to just make out M31. In Florida I can't even find it. Here, on the slope of Mount Washington, it leapt out at me! How many young people today grow up never realizing that there is such a spectacle above their heads? With so many lights creating an atmospheric camouflage, the beauty of the night sky goes mostly un-noticed by most of the residents of the industrialized nations. Instead, many have a star-field screen saver and no inkling that it relates to something far more spectacular. Nor do they realize that the power used to run their computer contributes to the light pollution that erases the night sky.

As awesome as things were outside, it was also cold and getting colder. I went inside the hut and readied to bed down. The guests had gone off to the bunkrooms and so the thru-hikers make do with whatever is available in the main room; sleeping on the floor or on the tables. I grabbed a table near a window so I could stare at the sky until I fell asleep. Things quieted down quickly (normal for tired hikers) and I was soon in that twilight zone between being asleep and being aware. Movement caught my eye and nudged me back awake. To my left a ghostly form seemed to be hovering over me. As my eyes adjusted, it appeared to be a human form but in a very peculiar position. There was a leg skyward and another off at a bizarre angle that made no sense. The body had the appearance of a crashed aircraft where the parts were identifiable enough, but in disarray. Finally, I could make out a head in the heap: it was Wild Oats. I asked just what on earth she was doing. She explained she was doing her nightly yoga before going to sleep. This is the young lady that was typically doing half again as many miles as most of us every day and she still had the energy to work out before going to sleep.

Wild Oats was going through the New Hampshire section for the second time. She had already done it a few days previously, but got so far ahead of her sister, Bone Lady, that she figured it would be fun to come back and do it again and catch some of the peaks that the A.T.

didn't cover on the first pass. Unbelievable. Wild Oats is a professional dancer and she gave me a whole new respect for that profession! Once I realized that it wasn't an angel, or worse, hovering over me and that I wasn't on my way to my creator, I peacefully dozed off.

The next morning dawned clear, cold, and windless — a perfect day for hiking to the summit of Mt. Washington. Excitedly, we all took care of any chores and were on the Trail at first opportunity. Since I had given a lecture the previous night, I had completed my obligation toward my work-for-stay, but I helped the others so we could all leave together.

The stretch from the Lake of the Clouds hut to the Mt. Washington summit is exceedingly deceptive. It is slightly less than two miles and is only about 1,200 feet of climbing, but many have died out there from exposure. There are plentiful signs warning the unwary to turn back if not prepared. Thru-hikers are usually prepared, but many week-enders and section hikers have been known to get into serious trouble in this stretch. The weather on Mt. Washington is highly unpredictable. On several weekend hikes with my family, we had made it to the Lake of the Clouds Hut, only to be turned back by the Croo because the weather was prohibitive. We didn't want to become another statistic. On other hikes, the weather was superb and the walk up was a treat.

Figure 32: Mt. Washington from the Lake of the Clouds Hut.

I was excited; this time I was hiking the Appalachian Trail as a thru–hiker — there was a special significance to this day. I had a bounce in my step and could hardly contain myself. The walk up never seemed so easy. I would get ahead of the others and stop and wait and just absorb the experience; it was exhilarating. Arriving at the summit was absolutely glorious! The view was unimpeded, the wind was still at bay and the air had warmed up to a balmy 50 degrees. As remote as the summit is for hikers, it is a virtual tourist haven. The world's oldest cog railroad services the summit, as well as a van shuttle service, a National Weather Station, and a New Hampshire-operated automobile road. The operation is a money maker for the state: railway tickets cost near sixty dollars round trip, shuttles are about forty one-way, and about thirty for an automobile. In spite of the costs, the place was mobbed. I had hopes for a nice meal at the cafeteria but those hopes were dashed when I found that all they had was hot dogs and frozen pizzas cooked in a toaster oven. Years ago I seemed to recall a much larger menu. I had a few hot dogs and then went up to the viewing platform at the weather station. I knew there was an Internet web cam up there and had checked it often from down on earth. I knew that it took a photo of the platform area about every fifteen minutes, so I hung around up there and when I thought that a photo had been recorded, I called my wife, Jane, and told her to check out the Mt. Washington website. Sure enough, there I was waving at her. Her first comment was, "You're so skinny — what happened to you?" How could I explain that I was eating all that was humanly possible and still not keeping my weight up? If she was certain I was *that* bad seeing me on a web cam, I began to wonder just how thin I was. Was I going to make it? For a moment I had doubts, but then I put them aside and relished the moment — I was on Mount Washington and could see Maine!

Returning inside the building, which is a rather formidable bunker to protect it from some of the harshest weather on the planet, I found a poster on a wall that listed the names of over 170 people that have perished on Mt. Washington and the surrounding area. The causes of death were breathtaking: fell 4,000 feet, fell 2,000 feet, fell 1,000 feet, crushed in landslide, froze to death, and one that I could really identify with: heart attack; there were lots of those. My heart was still pumping along nicely, so I figured if I didn't join one of the thousand-foot clubs, I might just make it.

There is also a museum, post office and tourist shop. I had been to the museum many times and, as a thru-hiker, I was not going to load up on Chinese-made trophies to haul down the mountain on my back. I checked the weather log. It was 50°F (10°C) with 10 mph winds. On that same day, a year previous the temperature was 10°F (-12.2°C) with 80 mph winds. I considered myself one lucky individual. Hopefully, I would get out of the Whites before my luck ran out.

It was time to go. The Trail descends next to the cog railway for about a mile. Even though it is illegal and the penalties are rather stiff, several of the young lady thru-hikers "mooned" the cog rail train; those passengers got more than they bargained for. There's been a history of these occurrences and I suspect they'd have to build a tunnel to prevent it. I can just imagine the tourists going home and showing off their photos of the "wildlife" in New Hampshire.

Figure 33: The A.T. near Mt. Madison. The region is sparse and desolate but spectacularly beautiful.

Pinkham Notch

The region going north from Mt. Washington is mostly above the tree line. It is barren and rocky, but spectacular. The weather that day was perfect and everything was eye candy. I hiked with the others for some time, but was so into moving right along that eventually I left them behind. I stopped for a while at the Madison Hut and enjoyed the best lemonade on the Trail. The caretaker took great pride in her lemonade and the effort was greatly appreciated.

Snow Plow, Bone Lady, Wild Oats, Slayer and others arrived in late afternoon and the place was filling up. I think some of the thru-hikers stayed on to do work-for-stay, but I was anxious to get moving, enjoying the hiking too much to stay. The climb out from Madison Hut is a near-vertical wall and most of the female hikers flew by me on the way up. I hiked with Walky Talky for some distance but eventually we parted on the downhill side of the peak. On the way down I passed "Bigglesworth." I had been reading her entries in registers for weeks; we finally met. She's a soccer coach and soccer talent scout and filled me in on all the latest in college soccer and the Olympic Team. This was the year of the Olympics in China and I had not really followed any of it, being too busy with my own events.

As the day wore on, I found myself hiking alone again. Around nightfall I came up to the Osgood Campground. The young women that had passed me earlier were setting up camp. I was still feeling full of energy and thought I might continue on, even if it involved some night hiking. I asked Wild Oats what she thought of the upcoming Trail section to Pinkham Notch; I should have considered whom I was asking. "Oh sure, K1, it's not bad at all, mostly downhill, an easy trail." Recall that Wild Oats was doing her second pass at New Hampshire because she wanted to kill some time while she waited for her sister to cross the state. Reassured that it was an easy walk, I struck out for the Pinkham Notch Visitor center with visions of hot showers, a sit-down evening meal and a warm bed.

I immediately ran into trouble. The Trail was poorly marked and with the twilight I missed a turn and started down a blue trail that wasn't marked for about a mile. The trail was rough, muddy and overgrown. The going got tougher and tougher until I finally spotted a blue blaze on a tree. Now I had to turn back and traverse the same rough trail I had just covered, losing about an hour in the process. When I finally found the proper turn, night had fallen.

The Trail meandered like grazing mountain goats had blazed it! It was a maze of intersections; none indicating which way the A.T. went and the only way to tell was pick a trail and go until finding a blaze: white, for the A.T.; blue, the wrong trail. It crossed a number of raging mountain streams and climbed over vertical rock walls. At one point I came to a simple stream crossing. The stream was perhaps ten feet across and not very deep, but one wrong step could prove disastrous. There was a waterfall to the left that had a vertical drop of maybe twenty feet and the crossing was slippery. Additionally, the A.M.C. (the A.T.C. is just as guilty here) had trimmed a fallen fir tree that was across the stream. Trimming it was not the problem; the problem was the *way* they trimmed it. This sapling was perhaps four inches in diameter and was originally covered with limbs. Instead of trimming the dead limbs off flush with the surface of the trunk, they left about four to six inches of the limbs sticking out. This practice had been a pet peeve of mine since starting the Trail. The theory as I understand it is that it looks more "natural." Whenever there was a low-hanging tree trunk or limb that was close to the Trail, the maintainers would slice off the limb at an angle, leaving a punji stake sticking out to impale skin, knock out an eye or at least hook a passing garment or backpack; I had the scars on my head to prove it.

As I crossed the stream in the dark, the loop on my shoelace caught around one of the protruding, sharpened limbs. Before I could gain any control I hurtled through the air, my foot firmly affixed to the tree, and landed backwards onto the tree itself! Several of the sharpened stakes pierced my leg and one into my arm. Thankfully, my backpack protected my backside. At least I didn't go over the waterfall. I was beginning to understand what the clerk at L. L. Bean was talking about when he suggested my backpack might not last the whole trip.

I got up, released my shoelace from the limb and limped to the shore. I cleaned up my wounds and started shivering from the cold bath. I didn't want to linger and get much colder, so I continued on. Eventually the Trail did improve as I neared the notch and the highway. As I neared the Pinkham Notch Visitor Center I could see its lights and knew my day's hike was coming to an end. Suddenly, out of nowhere a cow moose bolted across the trail in front of me. When I walked into the lights I could understand why the moose was spooked; I was a frightful sight, all covered in mud and bloodied. I wondered if the staff would think me some tramp and send me on my way.

I went into the reception area and an attractive college coed greeted me and acted as though I was a crown prince arriving for a room. She set me up with a room and offered that I should call if I needed anything. I dragged myself to the room on the second floor and concluded that if Wild Oats ever suggested that something was easy, I would really, really question it. I know she meant no harm, but she hikes at a level beyond mere mortals.

The next morning I was up early and had breakfast at the café with some hikers that I hadn't seen in a while. It was great to see Longwe Tru and Willow there; I hadn't seen them since Connecticut. They looked well and were as jovial as ever. They'd gotten ahead of me when I took a week off the Trail and I didn't expect to see them again. I hung around, hoping to meet up with Walky Talky and the female hikers from the previous night. Just before I was leaving, the ladies did show up and confirmed that they had not seen Walky or Bigglesworth. This surprised me; I didn't think they were that far behind. I decided to head out anyway, assuming Walky would catch up somewhere.

Leaving Pinkham Notch, the Trail follows the shoreline of a pond. One thing I was learning in New England, that I hadn't really noticed in all the years I had lived there, was that when a trail follows a shoreline, it means walking on boulders, big and small. Every time the trail would come to a pond or lake in New Hampshire or Maine it would mean lost time due to walking on rocks, roots, or both. Of course, there was always a quantity of mud in the mix just to make things slippery and challenging.

Just as it did in the Southern states, the Trail would inevitably head *south* for miles; keep in mind I was supposed to be heading north. There is a mathematical postulation that goes, "The shortest distance between two points is a straight line." Zero-Zero once stated he had a variation on that; "The A.T. is the longest distance between two points!" Eventually the Trail turned up into Wildcat Mountain and left the mud.

There is one short section on Wildcat Mountain that is narrow, steep (hand-over-hand) and tough. If you lose your grip and fall to the left, you could easily join the 2000' Club on the list at Mt. Washington. I was ever-so-carefully working my way up this rock face; sweat pouring from my brow, blurring my vision and taking slow, controlled breaths to make certain I didn't do anything foolish. I was about halfway up this challenge when I heard a cheery voice behind me, "Oh, Hi K1." I looked down and could make out Wild Oats coming up behind me. I froze in position because it was obvious that she had no fear and was casually walking up the face of the mountain. I clung there and watched as she hopped by, not using any hands and continued on up out of sight in moments. As I hung there, I started doubting my sanity: "Did I just see that?" For all my brawn, strength and testosterone, there is no way I could compete with that performance. I was really starting to admire these young ladies and their strength, stamina, and skill.

Pushing on, I finally arrived in Gorham, New Hampshire, the last opportunity to take a zero day before heading into the remote Maine wilderness, not that New Hampshire was exactly a metropolis. I enjoyed a zero day in Gorham, repaired gear, ate, and replaced my hiking shoes.

Kit-Kat came up to help with my zero day and ferried Longwe Tru, Willow and me around town. She drove me to the two outfitters to find shoes. The only shoe the outfitters had was a low-sided sneaker style-walking shoe. Since I wear such large shoes, I had to take what they offered. Kit-Kat had gotten my ham radio walkie-talkie from my cousin and now I felt ready for the last state.

While in Gorham, I learned that Walky Talky was leaving the Trail. His wife had a medical emergency and he had to return to Atlanta, Georgia immediately. I heard the news through the Trail "grapevine" and didn't get to see him before he left, but I was really disappointed for him. To be this close to Katahdin and have victory snatched from his grasp must have been frustrating, but I was also proud of him. To be there with a loved one in their time of need is *far* more important than any trail.

I wondered how many more of us would have something beyond our control change our lives and our goals? We were all now going into Maine, the toughest and last state on the Trail.

Chapter 17 - Maine

Fourteenth State

The next day was more of the same, PUD's (Pointless Ups and Downs) through spectacular country. Late in the day I came over a rise and there it was, the last state border crossing: Maine!

I made it to the Carlo Col Shelter and met another hiker there by the name of "Chipmunk." We were the only two there and the weather looked like it might get nasty during the night, so I hung my hammock in the shelter, and he did the same with his tent. Longwe and Willow came down to the shelter and decided to continue up the Trail further. As a rule they preferred stealth camping and didn't seem to enjoy the atmosphere around shelters even though they are both very friendly.

It was a cold night, during which the wind picked up, and by morning there was a light rain in the air. Chipmunk was considering taking a zero day at the shelter; the forecast was for far worse to come.

We parted ways and I worked my way up the trail. Almost by the minute the weather was deteriorating. The winds were starting to really howl and the rain was coming down in buckets. The storm was a remnant of one of the hurricanes that had worked its way up the coast and the climb over Goose Eye Mountain was really tough. I didn't have adequate rain gear for this weather. I *did* have a rain poncho that went over my pack and me simultaneously. Unfortunately, I couldn't wear the lower leg sections of my hiking pants because they would just get soaked with the runoff from the poncho and then fill my hiking shoes. Normally I was contented to walk barelegged and tolerate the cold, damp conditions, but these were unusual circumstances. The wind was biting and it actually stung my skin. The weather stations were reporting 80 mph gusts at the higher elevations and I was at the higher elevations, and not well-prepared for them.

Goose Eye Mountain was also a battle. The wind tore at me like a rabid dog, yanking my poncho in several directions at once. There were a few moments where it felt as if the poncho would come apart at the seams, but it held. I removed my glasses, fearing they might blow off my head. The roar of the wind was deafening as it pushed me around like a rag doll. In some of the wide open rock escarpments, I got down on all fours, and crept along, my pack feeling like a great sail on my back catching each gust. I feared being tossed and going over the edge and tumbling down a vast slanted slope of granite, my body never to be found.

After inching my way over Goose Eye Mountain, I decided to stay at the next shelter even though it was still mid-morning; it was fruitless to try to continue. I arrived at the Full Goose Shelter and there were already a few others there. One was "Wild Flowers," whom I had met back at Spy Rock, just outside of Montebello, Virginia and hadn't seen for months. I settled in and didn't even bother with the hammock; I just wanted to be out of the wind and rain. I crawled into my sleeping bag and finally warmed up.

Eventually another group showed up, "Papa Bear" and his three sons, the "Preacher Boys." They were Mennonites and had some very interesting homemade equipment. Their portable wood stove made from a gallon can immediately caught my eye. It had an inner can lining it and there was a small door at the bottom. When needed, they would attach a battery-operated fan to pump air in through the door and even with wet wood they would have a nice hot fire going in no time. They too, were chilled to the bone. Even though they did have rain gear, they didn't yet have their cold weather gear. It was waiting for them at the Caratunk, Maine Post Office one hundred and twenty miles north, so they also decided to stay at the shelter. It was then I realized that I had only covered 4.7 miles (7.6 km) that day; it felt like five times that!

Later in the morning, Longwe Tru and Willow showed up and decided to call it quits too; it was proving to be a fierce day. The shelter was crowded but we managed well. New York Minute was prophetic when, in an earlier telephone conversation, he emphatically told us to expect "some *shit* in Maine!"

We spent the rest of the day socializing, eating, napping and scaring each other with tales of Mahoosuc Notch, which was not far ahead. I had been reading about it since before the hike. It was always depicted as a formidable and terrifying section of rockslides and boulders. Mahoosuc Notch is only 1.1 miles (1.8 km) long, but for the uninitiated it can take several hours to traverse. I wasn't certain of what to expect, but I figured by this point in our hike we could deal with it. I was appreciative of the fact that I delayed getting into the Notch until the next day; the weather was atrocious and undoubtedly would have made the Notch even more taxing.

Mahoosuc Notch

There is a sign at the entrance to Mahoosuc Notch. I don't recall what it said exactly, but I don't think it indicated much about what was to come. New York Minute confessed to me that somehow he had never heard of Mahoosuc Notch and when he started going through it, he couldn't believe his eyes. I found it comical that he had never heard of the most famous mile on the Trail; somehow he didn't get the memo.

In reality, Mahoosuc Notch is an interesting anomaly but nothing to get emotionally worked up about. The Notch is just that, a deep notch between two very high ridges. The rocks and boulders are a collection of things that have tumbled down from the cliffs above over the millennia. As I was pawing my way through, I was anxiously anticipating the next delivery, envisioning myself as the coyote in a Road Runner cartoon smashed by the fallen boulder. There is no "ground" in the Notch, just boulders varying in size from Volkswagen Bugs to apartment buildings. It is without a doubt a jumbled rock scramble. Overall the Notch was enjoyable; this was simply a change of pace from "trail" hiking, a "time out" to go play in the rocks and caves.

Figure 34: Mahoosuc Notch. Yes, there is a trail through there. Note the white blaze.

Since Longwe Tru and Willow entered the Notch just behind me, I left for them arrows built from scraps of broken sticks to show the route I had taken. In many places there is more than one way to go and some approaches are better than others. Occasionally, I chose the more difficult route only to discover that there was an easier way further on. Even with taking my time and putting down arrows, it only took about two hours to do the 1.1 miles (1.8 km), not too bad I thought. Next came the "Arm."

A SOBO had warned me that the Mahoosuc Arm was more dreadful than the Notch. I later read in Mary Julyan's 1993 book *Place Names of the White Mountains* that the "Arm" in "Mahoosuc Arm" simply means "a subsidiary summit of the mountain."

The Mahoosuc Arm is a vertical climb of about 1,500 ft. up mostly smooth granite. Auspiciously, shrubs and trees have grown on the surface of the granite, allowing footholds and handholds. It is incredibly steep, and I was very cautious climbing. Any mishap could result in a long freefall before coming to a brutal stop against a tree or rock outcropping.

Upon reaching the top, not clear about the definition of an "arm," I asked a local southbound section hiker how far it was to the "Mahoosuc Arm." With a look of wonder, as if I had just gotten off of an alien spaceship, he told me that I had just come up Mahoosuc Arm.

I ended the day doing a few hours of night hiking. It was getting very cold and I was seeing frost on leaves as I approached Bald Pâté Lean-to (yep, we're back to lean-to's). Papa Bear and The Preacher Boys were there. Papa Bear, being the great dad that he is, had given most of his gear to the boys to keep warm and he basically stayed up most of the night keeping the fire going. He was really anxious to get to Caratunk to get their cold weather gear. I was still warm enough in my hammock. When I arrived in Maine, Yazzie had given me a small piece of foam sleeping pad that I would place where my butt would rest in the hammock and that was sufficient to keep me comfortable, even with below-freezing temperatures. The pad was only about a foot and half wide by a foot long, but it worked great.

The next morning was very cold. I dressed quickly and got on the trail as soon as possible so I could warm up. There was frost everywhere; it was apparent we were getting very late in the hiking season. It was a nice hiking day, but windy. At Bald Pâté Mountain I encountered the remnants of another hurricane passing through. There were not many clouds but a tremendous change in atmospheric pressure and the winds were fantastic! Bald Pâté is one huge domed slab of granite and the winds made progress a perilous dance requiring hugging the bare rock surface and leaning into the wind while looking for footing. Ex-Marine "Bull Dog" passed me going up and seemed much more sure of himself. His stocky, muscular build seemed much better suited to the terrain than my tall wind-sail build, and he quickly disappeared over the top.

Pine Ellis Hostel

At a road crossing, East B Hill, a few others convinced me I should go into Andover with them and stay at the Pine Ellis Hostel. The driver, David, showed up with some excellent lemonade and that clinched it; I'm a sucker for good lemonade, and I gladly piled into the shuttle. It was a long drive to Andover, but worth it. The hostel is an old home and there were hikers stuffed everywhere.

When I arrived somebody told me that a fellow by the name of "Slo-go'en" was there and I should look him up because he was a ham radio operator. When I heard the name, I knew that he was more than that; he was the designer of the very Morse code radio that I was carrying. His call letters are KD1JV and he is something of a celebrity in the world of low-power ham radios. I was thrilled he was there; we had met briefly a few times over the years and had emailed on occasion. Slo-go'en lives in Berlin, NH and was out doing a long section in Maine. Earlier in the season he had done a long section down South and I suspect he must be near completing the whole Trail by now. I ran upstairs and the door was open to the room so I popped my head in and greeted him. It was a thrill to see someone from my 'other' world. He was holding up well and enjoying Maine. In some ways, section hikers have a tougher time than thru-hikers. Section hikers never go long enough distances to have their bodies really adapt to the trail, so they essentially hike the whole thing in some degree of beginners' pain.

I felt a tad embarrassed explaining that I didn't actually have my radio with me right at that moment, that it was somewhere in the mail system and would eventually meet me up near Katahdin. Slo-go'en didn't seem phased by that; he's done enough long distance hiking to appreciate what I had done. In fact, he wasn't carrying a radio at all, so I didn't feel too guilty.

The next day I left early with a full van of hikers. I did 13 miles and it all seemed rather easy. Along the way I hiked with Bigglesworth, my soccer coach friend. She talked me into slack-packing the next day, which would mean another night at the Glen Ellis. I'm easy, what can I say? At day's end David was there again with the lemonade and the van and we went back to Andover.

That night a bunch of us chipped in to get a shuttle to Mexico, Maine. Andover has very little for re-supply and shopping. Even though Mexico is another of those

Appalachian towns that is hanging on by a thread, it does have a Wal-Mart and an assortment of eateries. The thread in this case is the mill in town. I didn't ask, but assumed it is a pulp/paper mill. I usually avoid Wal-Marts but it was the only store in town. I had some time to kill in the shopping mall parking lot and I watched the shoppers coming and going. It occurred to me that if the mill were to cease operation, the Wal-Mart would soon follow. This town no doubt once had a Main Street dotted with small businesses and merchants, but was now vulnerable, dependent on the one big-box store in town for all its goods, and much of its employment. The old business model had been destroyed in a single generation! I was seeing this all up and down the Trail; it's a worrisome situation. What happens if the economy tanks? (But wait, that could *never* happen!) I talked to a few locals and the ones that didn't work in the mill worked in larger towns to the south, Portland, Lewiston, and Augusta to name a few, which are hours away. I kept getting this disconcerting feeling that the entire system is being held together by some very thin threads and it wouldn't take much for the whole thing to unravel. I hope our leadership knows what it is doing. Little did I know what the coming years were to hold.

David drove us to the Chinese restaurant, which was mobbed. In addition to our crew, the other hostel in Andover had a bunch of hikers there as well. "Leaping Turtle" was extremely generous; he bought three Pu-Pu platters to share with everyone. As busy as the place was, the staff was very efficient and we were all taken care of without much wait. As usual in such places, I stuffed myself until I couldn't walk.

Slack Pack

I had promised Bigglesworth I would slack pack to help her with the cost of the shuttle. The more that ride in the van, the less it costs per individual. My pack wasn't actually that "slack." I took out the hammock, most of the food, stove and a few other items and ended up with a total pack weight of maybe twenty pounds. Of course I still carried warm clothing, as well as rain gear; this was Maine after all. It was a nice autumn day and the day passed quickly. The last few miles down to ME 4 were very steep and with just enough water on them to make them very slippery. While we thought we would be an hour or two early for the scheduled shuttle pick-up, we now were worried we'd be late! Each step had to be measured carefully as one misstep could end in a painful injury and a trip home. We were too close to the finish line for that. We did arrive on time, but just barely.

Zero-Zero was amazing; even with being legally blind he was able to keep up with us with assistance. We took turns talking him through the really difficult sections. The master at giving directions, though, was Bigglesworth; she was a natural. She had a sense for guiding and describing that none of us achieved. All the while she was issuing directions to Zero-Zero she would also manage to carry on a conversation with the rest of us; it was masterful. The *Hiker's Companion* indicated that at the end of the day we would have to ford the river, but when we got there we found stepping stones adequate to make it across with care and nobody got wet feet.

Gone to Heaven

Enough goofing off with hostels and slack packing; it was time to get serious. The weather prediction showed the remnants of hurricane Ike were to arrive during the day, and the morning was already foreboding. The winds were whipping and the rain was building. Zero-Zero was in a terrible mood; he realized he had lost his ATM card and a sock. He was really upset because he is meticulous about where he puts things since he can't see. We couldn't find either item and had to move out. A number of us were shuttled out to the Trail crossing at Maine 17. The driver, David, attempted to do a group photo of us getting back on the Trail but it proved nearly impossible. The winds were whipping, we were in the clouds, and it was difficult to even *stand* in one position. I think he finally captured something in the camera and we scurried for the cover of the forest. Once on the trail, the vegetation did cut the wind and we could at least walk upright. Zero had his own personal hurricane brewing and most of us were too cowardly to face it, myself included. We walked quickly to put space between us, hoping he would calm down later. Yazzie stayed with Zero and the rest of us bailed.

As I walked into the maelstrom, I saw some movement on the trail ahead. An elderly woman appeared, adorned in full rain gear and pack. It was difficult to get a good look under the conditions, but I'm certain she had to be near eighty! She gave me a bubbly, "*Good* morning!" as if she normally went for a walk in a hurricane. I asked if all was well and she indicated that she was going to the road crossing we had just left. Her husband was meeting her there. She was out doing a section and obviously thoroughly enjoying herself. I had glimpsed a vehicle at the road fading in and out of the clouds and asked if he was driving a pickup truck. She said, "Yes." I told her he was already there and we parted ways. I couldn't fathom her cheery attitude in the middle of this hurricane.

The rest of the day was atrocious. The wind and rain turned the Trail into a mini version of what we had slogged through in Vermont. There were huge ponds of water on the trail and the wind forced me to pay constant attention to staying upright. By day's end I was ready to get back into another town. This was a change in plans. I just wanted to get to somewhere where I could dry things out and start over. I made it to a trailhead parking area at Maine 4 and stopped to cook a meal. I figured my pace that day had been quick, in spite of the weather. If I cooked something to warm me up and kill some time, then Zero-Zero, Yazzie and Bigglesworth would catch up and we could all try hitching a ride into Rangeley. I waited close to two hours and there was no sign of them and daylight was fading.

I got down onto the road and attempted a hitch a ride to town. Traffic was light and in perhaps forty-five minutes only fifteen vehicles had passed, and none showed any interest in picking me up. As I was standing there, a vehicle came from the opposite direction, from Rangeley, and stopped across the road. A hiker, White Lightning, hopped out and the driver rolled her window down and asked if I wanted a ride to town. Wasting no time, I climbed aboard and she did a U-turn and we were heading for Rangeley.

Lori is a woman somewhat older than I, spunky and full of life. She explained she had picked up White Lightning in town and brought him out to the trailhead even though she had not planned on driving that far. She actually lived on the other side of Rangeley at Mooselookmeguntic Lake. Her mission wasn't complete yet; she was driving back into town to pick up some SOBO's at the Laundromat and was taking them to where they wanted to stay, a free hostel that basically offers a place to throw a bedroll. Lori offered that she had a spare cabin that I was welcome to if I wished.

I was in Maine, home of Stephen King, and I had previously read his novel, *Misery*, where a woman picks up a man in distress and tortures him and keeps him hidden away in her home on the prairie. It was later made into a movie starring Kathy Bates and was convincingly real. I sized Lori up and figured I was bigger but I'd just keep my eyes open.

In town we picked up the two SOBO's and she made them the same offer of her cabin, but they declined. I decided to live on the wild side and take her up on the offer; why not, the trail hadn't failed me yet. How bad could it be?

We drove out of Rangeley, turned down some smaller back roads, which turned into smaller dirt roads that turned into little more than double-track paths, to arrive at a cluster of rustic lakeside cabins that epitomized the ideal L. L. Bean concept of the cabin by the lake. Lori started explaining to me when she was having dinner and where I could find sheets but I was so lost in the beauty of the place that I didn't hear a thing she said.

The cabin cluster comprises twin cabins that share a wall and plumbing. I had one whole cabin to myself. It had five beds, a loft, a full bathroom, kitchen, a wondrous living room with a woodstove, and even a library. I kept pinching myself; could this be happening to me? I was Alice walking through the looking glass! I went in and cleaned up, started a fire to dry out the gear, and kept pinching myself. Lori returned to invite me to dinner with her neighbors. They were having salmon and rice, and I'm sure wanted to see what Lori had dragged home; I don't think they really believed she had done this.

I showered and cleaned up as best I could. On the trail it is nearly impossible to cleanse oneself with just one shower. The outdoor odors so permeate the body that it takes successive washings to get back to "normal." Clothes, and in particular, shoes, take on a permanent odor that no amount of washing can remove. Ultimately, when the hike ended, I destroyed most of my trail clothes.

The neighbors were very sociable, especially when during dinner and conversation it became evident that I wasn't a really smelly serial killer. It seemed ages since I had just sat down in a family atmosphere and enjoyed good conversation, wine and the company of others. On the trail, food is all-encompassing; it becomes an obsession and the joy of eating and social connection fades as the routine of the day makes nourishment a chore, a necessity, rather than something to be enjoyed on its own merits. Lori and her friends brought me back to the pleasantries of earth for an evening.

After dinner, I returned to the cabin. I kept a warming fire going in the stove, dried out my gear, and sat and read a book about moose. I don't recall the title but it had about ninety pages and revealed much about these sensational animals. For example, according to a study, moose are most comfortable when the temperature is a balmy 10°F (-12°C). Their hair is actually hollow, allowing it to capture and hold insulating air molecules. Contrary to the widely held belief, they actually have excellent eyesight, but the field of vision is limited in the vertical plane. Nevertheless, they have a wide field of vision and can practically see their hindquarters while staring straight ahead. I especially noted that the female moose is one of the most protective mothers in nature. Their calves are relatively defenseless and the female moose will aggressively fight to the death to protect her calf. Since I was in the heart of moose country, I added this to the list of dangers on the trail. I was crossing Maine in rutting season and the male moose is notorious for unprovoked attacks during this season. A book by Peter Stark, *Last Breath*, claims that moose kill about six people per year. That's not a significant number when considering the number of humans killed each year by guns, but I was walking through the moose "hood" and figured I would be wise to at least be alert. I had thus far seen a few at a distance and did hope to at least get a good photo at some point.

After a comfortable evening and good sleep, Lori brought me back to the trail. I was slow getting going and almost caused her to be late for work. I offered to give her something for her generosity, which she wouldn't accept. I heard her talking the night before about her involvement with the local food bank and finally got her to take a donation for the food bank. Once again the trail angel, Russ from Baltimore, had me dishing out more money.

Your Move

I had previously saved one of those sanitary paper bands that they place around toilet seats in hotels. I told Kit Kat that I was saving it for a plan I had, so she found me one too. Shortly after leaving Rangeley I came upon the Piazza Rock Lean-to. It's a beautiful shelter sponsored by L.L. Bean employees. It has a privy with a sign on it that reads, "Your Move;" the privy has a built-in cribbage board between the two "seats."

I couldn't help myself; I took out the two paper sanitary wraps and put them around both of the seat lids. I wondered just how many hikers would look at them and wonder if there was an L. L. Bean cleaning crew!

Free Fall

I was about three miles from the Crocker Cirque Camp Ground. It was a warm afternoon and with less than 200 miles to Katahdin, there was vigor in my step and an anticipation that the end was near. From my vantage point, I could see the river down below that I would have to cross; I was moving at a rapid pace. The trail was sloped downhill and made for easy walking. I should have been paying attention, but I was lost in thought and running on automatic. There were lots of exposed roots along this section and there were a number that I refer to as "trip-roots" that come up out of the ground on one side of the trail then go back down into the ground on the other side. A few days previously I had managed to catch my toe on one and stumbled and landed on my side, leaving a badly bruised ego.

As I started to lift my right foot, it caught on a pencil-thin trip-root. With my fast pace and the downhill slope I instantly realized I was in trouble. Typically, in this scenario one of three things happens: the root breaks and you recover and keep going; the root holds and you're able to stop and regain composure; or the root holds and you fall down right there.

My situation was 'none of the above.' What follows happened in milliseconds but seemed to play out in slow motion. My inertia was such that there was no stopping. I started to teeter over and was leaning at the point of no return. Right at that moment the root broke. I started running forward trying to save myself, but my forward speed and angle dictated a crash. Throwing myself sideways in the air, I hoped to land mostly on my pack and let it absorb the blow. Unfortunately, I was careening toward two large rocks on the trail and suddenly realized impact was inevitable. As I made a best effort to land *between* them, I attempted to tuck my arms close to my chest to protect them, but ended up with my right arm folded backwards behind my pack.

For a second I lay there stunned. Going from a calm trail walk to instant terror is shocking, and I was shaken up. Assessing my situation, I found I was laying with my head downhill, my feet uphill and my arm jammed haphazardly between the rock and the pack. I knew my right wrist was bent at unnatural angle and I couldn't feel it. Otherwise, everything seemed okay. I was wedged firmly between the two rocks and attempted to push myself up with my left arm, but couldn't. I was just too heavy with my backpack.

Working with my free left arm, I unclipped the pack belts, and with some effort managed to free myself from the pack and let it slide down the hill over my head. Now, with the forty pounds gone, I was able to complete a one-armed pushup and extricate myself. I rolled over the rock and lay on my back. My right wrist was bent at an odd angle and hurt like hell. I was afraid to try and move it; I just stared at it for a period. I recall thinking that it was only my wrist and if it were broken I'd have to get it looked at, but I could still finish the hike. I was glad it wasn't a leg or ankle. Finally, I mustered up the courage to try and move it and it did move. I then started working it back and forth, assisted by my left hand. It hurt, but it appeared to be okay. I couldn't believe it; looking at it, I would have sworn it was broken but it seemed to be functioning correctly.

I took a break and sat a while to appreciate my good luck. I promised myself to pay more attention and not get careless so close to Mt. Katahdin. I slowed my pace down and was more cautious about roots. Maine had more of these trip-roots than anywhere else on the trail and they needed to be heeded.

Stratton

The walk from Crocker Cirque Camp Ground to Stratton was uneventful. It was only about eight miles, with splendid weather, and no need to hurry. I really enjoyed the walk. My wrist was sore from the previous day's crash but I was feeling fortunate that it was nothing worse than that.

In Stratton I signed up for a room at the hostel, rooming with Yazzie, and then went out to forage for food. I had a mid-day spaghetti dinner and a beer. Life was good.

Stratton was where New York Minute had called me from a few weeks earlier to tell me he was getting off the trail to visit family in New Jersey. He had returned and was just ahead of me somewhere. I figured that if I got out early in the morning and made good time there was a chance I could catch up with him. I knew he was hoping we could summit Mt. Katahdin together. This was wise thinking on his part; Katahdin may be the last five miles of the trail, but as I was to learn, it is the most challenging section of the entire hike.

Figure 35: Maine was just eye candy everywhere.

I planned on leaving the hostel at 06:15 on the shuttle back to the trail. At 06:07 I awakened and realized I only had eight minutes to catch the shuttle! Like an adolescent late for school, I scrambled to throw on my clothes, stuffed my pack, and charged out into the parking lot just as the shuttle was backing out to leave; they stopped and I clambered in.

This day's hike took me over the Bigelow Mountains. The peaks are clear of trees and provide stunning views of north-central Maine. Lakes and mountains provide a panoramic display of everything that makes this region some of the most spectacular outdoors on the Eastern seaboard. The weather was clear, cool and crisp and I was in awe of all that lay before me. The walking was challenging; rocky ascents and descents and the ever-present roots to trip on, but well worth the view.

Bigelow Mountain, also known as Avery Peak, is the last of the tall Bigelows and from it I could see Little Bigelow not too far off to the east. I'd been hiking with Papa Bear and the Preacher Boys on and off during the day and we were all heading for the Little Bigelow Lean-To that evening. We all started down Bigelow Mountain figuring it would be just a few more miles to the lean-to, but Maine has a way of fooling logical thinking. The trail didn't go straight to Little Bigelow. It turned south for a considerable distance (why?), meandered around the valley floor forever, and then *finally* turned back to Little Bigelow and then up along its spine and down the other side. It was near dark when we all finally set up camp at the lean-to. Papa Bear was still suffering the cold weather conditions with summer gear; their cold weather gear was still awaiting them at the Caratunk Post Office. It was going to be a very cold night but there was nothing I could do to help. Papa Bear stayed up most of the night keeping a fire going. He had to be exhausted, but then you do what you have to do on the trail.

In the morning there was a frosty glaze of ice on everything. Thanks to carrying the foam rollup pad, I slept well and was warm enough. It was at this point that I really felt that I was now an accomplished hiker; everything was fine-tuned. I was carrying everything I needed to survive in the deep woods, I was comfortable, and my body was running well. The heart surgeons had repaired me better than new, my muscles were performing as well as they ever had, and I didn't have any pains anywhere! I was having an adventure of a lifetime, and I knew it. I relished every moment, especially when I could sense that it was soon all coming to an end.

Reunion

The seventeen miles from Little Bigelow Lean-to over to Pierce Pond Lean-to was perfect, with rolling hills, forest streams and early autumn weather. In my journal I made a note that it was "nice terrain - for Maine!" Even though I hadn't seen many hikers lately, the lean-to at Pierce Pond was full. I gathered from the conversations that many of the younger hikers were taking blue blazes and skipping sections to make certain they would make Katahdin before it closed for the season.

The lean-to is set right on the shore of the pond and the scenery is definitely out of *National Geographic*. I hung my hammock behind the lean-to and as I was cooking dinner I heard a familiar voice call out, "Hey, K1." It was New York Minute. He was camped a mile or so beyond the lean-to and come back to see if I had caught up to him. He looked so different! When we first met down in Virginia he had a bald head, shaved when he had attended Trail Days in Damascus. It had slowly been growing back, but I hadn't seen him for almost two months; now he had a full head of jet-black hair. I thought he looked much better. We hugged and as I ate, he filled me in on all the latest. He had gone back to New Jersey to visit with his grandmother; she was very ill and he suspected it would be the last time they would be together. He was close to her and it was an emotional trip for him knowing that he might not see her again.

Before he finished the hike and returned home, she *did* pass on. I was so glad he had been able to see her again.

Kennebec Crossing

New York Minute's week off the trail allowed me to catch him. Additionally, he had slowed down his hiking to allow me to catch up. Tomorrow, we would cross the Kennebec River and be in Caratunk. We made plans to meet at the river crossing.

Figure 36: The Kennebec River crossing.

The A.T.C. offers hikers a free canoe shuttle across the Kennebec River ever since an unfortunate hiker drowned attempting to ford the river years earlier. The problem with fording the Kennebec is that an upstream dam occasionally releases water without warning, which can catch unsuspecting hikers midstream and wash them downstream.

The first crossing of the day begins at ten a.m. Even with our arriving early, there were about twenty hikers already queued to cross. I knew most of them; I had hiked with many of them at some point. It was the last time I would see most of them. The crossing was uneventful and I kept looking down to see how deep the river was. It didn't seem very deep. At that time of the year the water was getting frigid so it would have been exhilarating in any case.

Once across, New York Minute and I hitched a ride up to an outdoor center a few miles west of the trail. I needed to re-supply and did not pass up an opportunity to eat at a restaurant. The outdoor center had a restaurant, but no re-supply. We had a late second breakfast and while there, Yazzie joined us. We all caught up on our latest adventures and then parted ways. New York Minute and I had to hitch up the road a few more miles to the local general store for my re-supply. The general store was disappointing from a hiker prospective; they had very little in the way of light, packaged food. It was mostly canned goods and frozen items. I ended up grabbing a few canned goods and we headed back to the trail.

The drivers in Maine were wonderful and contrary to what we expected, we had no trouble getting rides.

Bullwinkle

Late in the day, not long before nightfall, we stopped to set up camp. New York Minute set his tent down near a stream and I hung the hammock immediately adjacent to the trail. The air was cold, so we went to sleep early. Hiker midnight was coming earlier and earlier with the advance of autumn and the shorter days. I fell into a deep sleep almost immediately. About midnight I heard a *thump, thump, thump...* coming down the trail from the east. The night was pitch dark, there was no moon, and the forest cover didn't even let the glimmer of starlight penetrate. I knew it had to be a moose. Deer are not nearly that heavy and judging by the weighty sound, I figured it to be a bull. I held my breath and tried to stay calm. Bull moose are notorious for practicing their battle techniques on small trees and branches. I figured it would be just my luck that I would become a convenient punching bag. The animal slowed almost to a stop right next to my hammock; I could hear him breathing, a heavy labored breath as if he had been hurrying for some time. He sniffed a few times and then gradually picked up his pace and disappeared into the night.

About an hour later I heard another *thump, thump, thump...* coming from the same direction, but this one didn't bother to slow; it seemed in a real hurry. Later still, I heard another animal coming down out of the woods from above our campsite, but this one wasn't on the trail. With much ado it crashed through the underbrush, apparently unconcerned about all the noise. There was now some moonlight, and I peered out through the mosquito netting on the hammock to see a cow moose come down onto the trail and subsequently also head off in the same direction as the two earlier passers-by. It was early in the moose-rutting season and I could only imagine that they were all headed to some sort of moose party. After her passing I was able to get back to sleep.

The mornings were really becoming frosty. On September 21, New York Minute and I broke camp and I left before he did. A mile or so from camp I came to the West Piscataquis River. The grasses along the edge had ice on them and water was bitingly cold. I removed my hiking shoes and put on my Crocs™. I carefully worked my way into the river. The river rocks on the bottom were very slippery and the last thing I wanted to do was plunge into that icy water. I found my way to a small island midstream and then repeated the process on the other side of the island where the water was even deeper, about mid-thigh. The river fords were getting much colder.

Thus far my moose encounters had not been under ideal conditions for photographs. New York Minute and I stopped for lunch on the bank of the East Piscataquis River before crossing it. As we sat there, I could hear the distinct *thud, thud, thud...* of a very large animal and knew instantly that it had to be another moose. I warned New York Minute, who didn't seem aware of the noise. Then on the trail, on the opposite bank, a very large bull moose approached. He had a wonderfully developed full rack. His hair had a bluish tint to it with a tinge of gray hairs at the extremities. He was magnificent! Back when I stayed at Lori's cabin on Lake Mooselookmeguntic, I read that very often they cannot be deviated from where they want to go. We were sitting with our lunch right on the trail, the same trail he was following. He eyed us for a moment and then calmly walked along the bank downstream about 100 feet and then crossed the river just east of us. We both immediately dove for our cameras. The moose crossed the river and then found his way around us, keeping about a hundred-foot radius at all times. Once back on the trail, he continued on his way. New York Minute and I were stunned. It was the perfect encounter; close enough for photos but distant enough to avoid those massive horns. What an impressive beast!

Figure 37: A magnificent Maine moose goes around us.

Later that day we ended up at the Maine 15 road crossing. As we attempted to hitch a ride into Monson, the last town before the 100 Mile Wilderness (160 km), we witnessed numerous trucks and vehicles with large trailers going by with dead moose on them. It was the first day of moose hunting season in Maine. I couldn't help but wonder if one of those marvelous beasts being hauled past us was the very one we'd seen earlier that day.

Shaw's

Shaw's Lodging in Monson, Maine is strategically placed. It is perhaps the most famous hostel on the A.T. since it is the last accommodation before entering the famous 100 Mile Wilderness. The A.T.C. cautions hikers to not underestimate the Wilderness, and to plan a ten-day supply for this section of the hike. My voracious appetite dictated that I would have to carry enough food for an army. In Monson I filled my food bag to its limits and then stuffed even more food in any empty space I had in my pack. In all, I had about fifteen pounds of food. The pack weighed forty-five pounds, more than it had weighed at any point on the Trail. I was ready!

During our zero day in Monson, I visited the library to catch up on my Internet correspondence. The librarian was an engaging woman that was full of information about the region. I gave some more of "Russ's money" as a donation to the library; he was making me a poor man. That night the local watering hole was jammed with hikers. Everyone was in a jovial mood; the end was near and we were all getting to know each other well at this point. We wanted to make the moment last forever, and savor it. Many of us were exchanging contact and email information; some of these friendships would continue after the hike.

The Wilderness

The 100 Mile Wilderness is essentially the last miles of the Appalachian Trail. Contrary to common belief, it does actually have a few dirt roads that cross it, and in an absolute emergency one could be "rescued" on one of them. The reality is that there are no towns close to the crossings and traffic is very light so it could be a long wait. It is best not to rely on any help when hiking the Wilderness section.

I was ready. I had more food than any other time on the hike and I was thrilled to finally be in the Wilderness. This is as wild and wooly as it gets in the east: bears, moose, porcupine, skunk, cold weather, rain, snow, wind, you name it; you'll find it here.

As you enter the 100 Mile Wilderness, there is a sign warning hikers to be prepared and carry enough food for ten days. I had just enough for ten days and New York Minute was carrying something less, figuring it wouldn't really take ten days. This was clearly a case of a pessimist and an optimist hiking together.

Figure 38: The 100 Mile Wilderness warning sign.

New York Minute had been plagued since the beginning of the hike in Georgia with foot problems. His biggest concern going into the Wilderness was his feet; would they make it? Would *he* make it? Oddly, some hikers never have foot problems and others seem to suffer a constant stream of problems. I sense there is a research project there for some aspiring college student who wants to really apply medical knowledge to a true mystery that seems to have no solution for some people.

Our first night in the Wilderness was at the Long Pond Stream Lean-to. With perfect timing, I started having trouble with my headlamp. The wire that connects the battery at the back of the lamp to the front appeared to have an internal break in the wire. If I held it just so, the light would stay on, but if I moved it at all, the lamp would go out. I figured out a way to force the wire into an unnatural position and hold it there with an elastic band and for the most part it would stay on. Occasionally I *did* have to readjust it, but it lasted for the rest of the hike. I was concerned that if I *did* have to do any serious night hiking I could be in trouble.

We did almost fifteen miles our first day out; considering the pack weights, we were satisfied. In all, things were going well but New York Minute was having more foot problems.

On our second night in the Wilderness I looked at his feet. They were bright red and very irritated. I began to question if he wasn't having an allergic reaction to the material in the shoes. We ate our carefully planned meals and hit the sack. I went to sleep concerned about his feet. Was I going to have to carry him out?

On day three of the Wilderness, we did eighteen miles. It rained hard all day and with the trail being a constant obstacle course of rocks and slippery, wet roots, it was tough going. At this pace we were starting to believe we might finish the Wilderness in five days. I was so confident that I ate two evening meals, along with extra desserts. Since New York Minute was traveling light on food I give him a spare Pop Tart, a bag of couscous, and some cookies. I felt like a hiking convenience store.

Day four of the Wilderness was a deluge! The rain was relentless. New York Minute and I stopped for lunch at a shelter along the way and it felt so good to just sit and watch the rain fall without being in it for a few minutes.

It also felt good to eat something hot. I made a pot of couscous and some hot chocolate and savored it as if it were a fine meal in an upscale Manhattan restaurant. After eating something hot and resting for a while, things didn't seem so bad, and we dragged ourselves back into the maelstrom.

The trail resembled the earlier Vermont experience, except Maine has more roots and rock, so instead of knee-deep mud, it was slippery rocks and roots hiding under a layer of water. The wet feet were taking their toll on New York Minute and I could see he was walking with extreme difficulty. Trooper that he is, he didn't complain, but just kept marching on.

In all, we hiked twenty-two miles on day four of the Wilderness. Our goal was the Nahmakanta Stream Campsite. We ended up night hiking for the last few hours. Thank goodness the trail maintainers marked the section well or it would have been impossible. The last few miles prior to the campsite wander around and the trail is not well-defined. At one point, I managed to miss a turn and followed some old markings that were still visible and ended up in the middle of a swamp. The trail had been re-routed but the old markings had not been totally removed. I was perhaps twenty minutes ahead of New York Minute, and while I was wandering around trying to get my bearings, I could see his headlamp through the downpour and the jungle. Rather than backtrack, I decided to take the shortest distance between two points and set off through the underbrush and muck. After much grumbling and tripping I finally made it back to where he was. It was getting late and I was concerned we yet hadn't found the campsite. It had to be within another mile or two, so we soldiered on.

Eventually we spotted a sign directing us down a blue trail to the site. The campsite itself didn't look like it was used much but we were in no mood to argue; it was late, and we were tired and hungry. We quickly set up camp and then sat in the rain to eat dinner. We really didn't care if it was raining as we were soaked to the skin anyway, so we just sat there in the rain as if we were at a nice summer's evening picnic. As soon as we sat down, a deermouse came bounding out of nowhere and ran over to New York Minute's bare foot and then like a world champion trampoline expert, masterfully launched himself right over New York's left shoulder and started running around the camp in large circles. We realized that it was just overjoyed to see us, or should I say, to find a possible food supply. It was absolutely ecstatic! This little critter was Mighty Mouse on steroids. In spite of being exhausted, cold, and soaked to the bone, we both broke into hysterical laughter.

I became concerned that this little guy would be a threat to our packs. We had to take special precautions, hanging them way up high with our bear ropes, hoping our new friend wouldn't be able to figure out where they were. I was also concerned that this energetic fireball would decide to chew into our tents and hammocks just to look around. Fortunately, as it turned out, this was not the case and nothing was damaged.

I had hung my hammock in a hurry and evidentially, carelessly. While I was asleep, about midnight I heard a *ttttwwwwaaaaaaannnnnngggg—GOOOUUUSSSSHH!* I crawled out of the sleeping bag and once outside, realized that my hammock tarp had started to form a pocket of water on it. As the pocket filled, it sagged down, making the pocket bigger, holding more water, which sagged it even more. This continued until it was holding about fifty gallons of water, at which time the lines holding it could no longer sustain the weight and broke, dumping the water. Fortunately for me the water dumped on the ground and not inside the hammock. I tied the broken line and re-hung the tarp and climbed back in and went to sleep. Later, again, *Ttttwwwwaaaaaaannnnngggg— GOOOUUUSSSSHH!* This time it was the other side of the tarp. Once more I crawled out and fixed things. I was shocked that the noise didn't wake New York Minute; that much water being dumped instantly was very noisy, but he never heard a thing. It was the *only* time on the hike that I didn't hang the tarp properly, and see what happened! I kept hoping that maybe the flood washed away the mouse.

It was still raining the next morning, our fifth day in the Wilderness, but our spirits were high and we packed up and hit the trail in a good mood. I suspect that, being close to Katahdin, there wasn't much that could have deterred us at that point. The weather was wet, cold, and dismal. We were hiking through the remnants of Hurricane Kyle.

Amazingly, New York Minute decided to hike in his Crocs™! His feet were just suffering too much. His plan was to hike in the Crocs™ until just before Mt. Katahdin, then he would switch to the hiking shoes for the mountain climb. He was able to hike faster than I could with hiking shoes; I was impressed. He was in constant danger of a twisted ankle or worse but managed to follow through with his plan.

We pushed on and made it to Rainbow Lake, another eighteen-mile day. Under the conditions we were pleased with our progress; we only had another ten miles to go until we would reach Abol Bridge. We decided that from there we would hitch a ride to the town of Millinocket and take a zero day in preparation for our ascent of Mt. Katahdin; we felt we earned it. In any case, I needed to get to Millinocket to pick up my ham radio at the Post Office.

Since I had considerable food left, at Rainbow Spring Campsite I stuffed myself. This solved two problems simultaneously; I removed considerable weight from my pack and I had a feast. It felt so good to eat without limits. I knew we only had ten miles to do the next day, and I could do that without food if necessary.

The next morning, the weather cleared enough so that the rain ceased. It didn't change things on the trail much. The trail was flooded and it was like hiking in a freezing stream; water was flowing everywhere. A few miles from Abol Bridge, on a nice outcropping of flat granite, we stopped and had our last cooked trail lunch. There was no hurry now; we would reach Abol Bridge by very early afternoon and would be back in civilization once again. Our emotions were running high. The end was near, but at the same time there was that nagging sentiment that we didn't want it to end.

Around 2 p.m. I stepped out onto a dirt road and knew it was the one that would lead to Abol Bridge. As was so often the case at roads, there was no indication of which way to go, so I correctly guessed it was to the right, and walked down to the bridge. The bridge itself isn't terribly impressive; it looks like a temporary affair that was installed after a flood. Walking across it afforded a spectacular view of Mt. Katahdin. The summit was perhaps five miles away as the crow flies, but I knew we had at least ten more miles of trail; after all, in the words of Zero-Zero, "the Appalachian Trail is the longest distance between two points!" Shortly New York Minute showed up and we went into the country store at the bridge and picked up a few snacks and found out there was a shuttle coming to pick up "Vigil Auntie" and "Why" and we found out we could get a ride to Millinocket with them... perfect timing.

The shuttle arrived and we all had a long ride into Millinocket. It felt so weird to be sitting in a vehicle, propelling along unassisted. Everything seemed to fly by; it was an odd sensation. Eventually, in the late afternoon, we rolled into downtown Millinocket and were delivered to the Hiker Hostel. We got a room with bunk beds; I took a lower one, New York the upper. Our other roommate turned out to be Boots. Boots, if you will recall, was a hiker I met prior to Pearisburg, VA the previous year. He was there at the Hiker Hostel in Pearisburg when I left the Trail to return for my heart surgery. It never failed to amaze me how many of the same people keep popping up on the trail.

Looking in the mirror I realized I was emaciated. There was absolutely no fat left on my body. I realized that if I had much more trail left I might not have the stamina and body resources left to finish it; I was losing weight at a dangerous rate. That evening I washed my clothes. The hostel had clothes to borrow so hikers could wash everything at once. All they had for trousers was size 8 women's jeans; my six-foot plus body fit into them with room to spare.

New York Minute was suffering sticker shock at the cost of the shuttle and one night at the hostel ($68) and wanted to go right back to the trail the next day, rather than take a zero day. I tend to go with the flow and couldn't find an honest reason to object, so we planned our return. There was also a long-range weather forecast that looked ominous and it was best we got to the summit before really foul weather shut down any attempt at the summit.

I had arranged to have my ham radio equipment shipped to the Millinocket Post Office, so the next morning I picked it up. Everything seemed in good order so I shoved it into the pack along with a turkey sub sandwich for lunch, and on the last day of September, 2008, we made our way back to the trail at Abol Bridge.

We set out in late morning. It was a splendid day and perfect for hiking. Our plan was to get to the campground at the base of the mountain and then overnight there and climb the next morning. It's a pleasant ten-mile walk to the base camp and since ten miles for us was a mere walk in the woods, we took our time. The trail section from Abol Bridge is replete with photo opportunities: water falls, rivers, lakes, and rock formations. New York Minute and I fully enjoyed the warm autumnal afternoon, soaking in the fleeting rays of sunshine that broke through the forest cover. Warmth was becoming a rare commodity on the trail. We stopped at one raging waterfall to take photos and film its thundering fury. The noise was deafening; all this rain had swollen most of the streams and rivers in the region to capacity. Much more rain and I'm afraid they would have been at flood stage. There were several river crossings along the way that were precarious at best: flimsy old logs laying across the fast-flowing, frigid water below. One slip and it would have been a cold, furious bath.

We stopped at a tranquil, sunlit spot along the trail for lunch. That turkey sub that I had packed earlier was calling to me; I couldn't wait to devour it. The setting was perfect: sunshine, warmth, autumn colors, and a nice rock to sit on. I sat down, unfurled my sandwich wrapper and was about to dive in when right next to my head, on a cedar tree trunk, a red squirrel came out of nowhere and started chattering at me at the top of its screechy little voice. New York and I both stopped what we were doing and just looked at this critter in wonder. It was furious, screaming at the top of its lungs and obviously its fury was directed at *me*. It wanted a portion of my turkey sub. No doubt, this little creature had learned about begging from humans; this section of the trail has lots of human traffic.

Red squirrels are much more aggressive than their larger grey or black cousins, and this one showed no fear whatsoever. New York Minute was cracking up; once again I was defending him from a wild animal. Recovering my composure, I yelled at my antagonist, but it just ignored me and continued yelling in my face, maybe only a foot away. No amount of my threatening phased it in the least; it just kept carrying on. It appeared to be getting ready to jump, and I was concerned it would either jump into my face, or worse yet, into my sandwich. Having once baby-sat young squirrels that had fallen out of their nest, I knew that their claws are as sharp as needles. I didn't want to tangle with my current adversary.

I gently grabbed my hiking pole and gave the tree a whack right next to the squirrel, figuring that would spook it and it would scamper away. Nothing doing — it held its ground and continued chastising me. This caused New York Minute to go into such a fit of laughter that I thought he was going to pee his pants. I really whacked the tree again, very close to the squirrel; it merely went around to the other side and continued its tirade. This little guy was an expert. Now I started literally hammering the tree with my hiking pole. If I hit the right side, it went to the left, if I hit the left, it went to the right, determined not to give up. This little guy was playing Whack-A-Mole with me. At this point, I seriously considered giving the squirrel a good blow and sensing this, he finally gave up and retreated up the tree, chattering at me all the way. He then clambered across to a limb where another squirrel awaited, a mate perhaps. I can just imagine the yelling and screaming when he got home: "You wimp, *now* what are we going to have for dinner tonight?" and "*You* promised!"

I went back to eating my sandwich in peace, or at least as much peace as I could find. New York Minute's chortlings over my nearly succumbing to a squirrel were a bit hard to take. With all my heroic stories of bear and rattlesnake encounters, I think he was having difficulty accepting that a squirrel nearly proved my match. Instead of "Grizzly Adams," I nearly ended up, "Squirrelly Adams." Thank goodness the hike was ending; that could have become my new trail name.

After lunch, we packed up and continued on. Baxter State Park surrounds Mt. Katahdin and park rangers manage the Katahdin Stream Campground at the foot of the mountain. Thru-hikers register at the ranger station. The rangers keep a tally sheet on how many thru-hikers show up every year and if I recall correctly, we were near the 500 mark upon our arrival. Of course, technically, I wasn't a thru-hiker since I had taken two years. We informed the rangers we would be climbing in the morning and it appeared the weather conditions would be favorable, although not ideal. There was a good chance it would be cloudy and possibly some rain; this was no big surprise.

Usually during the tourist season the thru-hikers have to go to another campground, The Birches, some distance away. Since it was getting cold and late in the season, the Katahdin Stream Campground was not crowded and we were allowed to camp there. We set up and made ourselves cozy for our last night on the trail.

After I hung my hammock and cooked my evening meal, it was time to try out my ham radio station. I was concerned that something might have gotten damaged traveling around in the mail system, but it appeared to be in good order and looked ready to go. I tossed a wire up in a tree and set the station up on our picnic table. New York Minute had never actually seen me operate the station. I had always tried to be discreet with it and not tarnish the outdoors experience for the other hikers.

New York Minute is also an engineer, so he was genuinely interested in seeing me operate the station. He doesn't know Morse code, so I promised to translate as best I could. I put on the headphones and immediately upon turning on the radio I heard the call letters, "AA9AA, AA9AA K." Since the call letters were sent twice in succession I figured that the station was making a general call to talk to anyone available (a CQ). Gambling this was the case; I called him back. We hooked up and carried on a chat for about twenty minutes. His name was Mike and he was located in Manitowoc, Wisconsin. I explained where I was and what I was doing and he was thrilled. It turned out he was also running a low-power station, not unlike mine, and was amazed at the near-perfect communications despite all these miles. (I didn't recall it at the time, but upon returning home, I realized that Mike and I had previously talked on another occasion. When one talks with thousands of others over many years it is easy to forget some of the conversations.)

The sun was setting and the air was getting bitterly cold. I was shivering and my hands were so cold I was having trouble properly sending the Morse code. I apologized to Mike and cut it short. It was time for bed. I had met my personal goal of making a Morse code contact from each state on the trail. It was now time to finish the hike.

Katahdin

The morning broke sunny and cool. More importantly, the ranger station was giving the all clear to climb, with a warning that the weather could sour later. I decided to "slack pack" and leave my non-essential gear at the station and just carry what I needed for the day. It was liberating to have such a light pack, probably about fifteen pounds; it felt light as a feather! New York

Minute decided he would carry everything. He'd carried it this far he wasn't going to change anything.

At 5,268 feet (1,606 m) Katahdin is the highest peak in Maine. What sets Katahdin apart from most mountains along the A.T. is that, well, it *is* "set apart" from most of the other peaks. Geologists have a term for this — *inselberg*. New Englanders refer to it as a "monadnock." Mt. Monadnock refers to a peak in southern New Hampshire by that name that sits all by itself and very well defines an inselberg. Katahdin doesn't really have anything near it that's approaching its height. Thus it tends to be exposed to any weather that blows through. Unlike Mt. Washington in New Hampshire, and some of the other higher peaks along the A.T., it is basically alone and subject to some stunningly vicious weather. Like Mt. Washington, it is subject to snowfall at any time of the year. This explains the concern on the part of the park rangers; they don't want to have to go out and haul back frozen corpses. For these reason "The Great Peak," as it is known in Penobscot Indian language, the translation of "Katahdin," is usually closed to climbing by October 15th. New York Minute and I were doing our ascent on October 1st.

The first mile of the climb is a nice walk with very little altitude gain. This concerned me. If we didn't gain altitude gradually then we'd have to gain it at all at once, which would imply a very steep ascent. Finally we came to a bridge across the fast-flowing Katahdin Stream and then we started climbing in earnest. The trail was steep and rocky, not unlike the myriad of peaks we had climbed along the way; our bodies were ready for this. Just as we arrived at the top of the tree line, we encountered a couple from Florida, Lee and Rosie. They were stopped on the trail and Rosie was having second thoughts about going any further. She could see some demanding rock formations ahead and didn't feel prepared to take on that sort of terrain. Rosie did the prudent thing and decided to turn back and meet Lee at the bottom. Lee wasn't terribly well-prepared either; he had a light jacket and a water bottle and I don't think he knew what he was getting into. The three of us continued on. Conditions changed quickly and dramatically. The sun disappeared and a thick cloud cover moved in. Actually, we were in the clouds and they rushed by, covering us with cold, wet droplets, forcing the water into any openings in our clothing. Our physical surroundings were also imposing. The trail was now a serious climb over huge boulders, slick and wet and weathered. In places we would follow a perceived route, only to find it would dead-end and we'd turn back and seek the correct route. Visibility was down to about thirty feet and it was tough judging where the blazes would disappear in the mist. In many places, there were no blazes; they were replaced by rock cairns piled high enough as to be seen when snow might otherwise bury them.

Gradually, we worked our way up and up, at times wondering just how far it really was to the summit. Even with the heavy work, our bodies were cooling in the wind-driven mist. The mist was managing to act as a fluid heat sink, sapping our bodies of their life-giving warmth. At about two miles from the summit, Lee made the wise decision to turn back, and shortly thereafter New York Minute stopped to put on his rain and cold-weather gear. I'd already put on my fleece sweatshirt and had my rain poncho on, but the poncho was proving almost useless. On a reasonable rainy day, it affords adequate protection from mild winds, but the winds on Katahdin were fierce and I found myself holding onto the poncho to keep it close to my body. My legs were bare since I really didn't have any rain trousers and I was now regretting that I didn't. There was little I could do about my situation; I wasn't turning back, and would just have to tough it out.

The combination of wind and flapping poncho made the noise deafening! The wind was roaring and conversation became impossible. I had gone on ahead of New York Minute while he put on his severe weather gear. Somewhere along the way, I encountered Hell On Bad Wheels, whom I hadn't seen since Pennsylvania. He had flipped ahead to do the Katahdin summit and still had to go back and do the rest of Maine, but knew he had to get Katahdin done before they closed the park.

To an A.T. outsider the following question may seem a bit stupid, but to thru-hikers that are nearing the end of the hike it makes perfect sense. I asked Hell On Bad Wheels, "Where are you now?" Obviously he was standing right in front of me, but in trail jargon what I was really asking him was how much of the Trail had he finished and if he has skipped sections to jump ahead, where should he be now? The question starts popping up rather regularly by the time the main body of hikers is in New Hampshire. A good percentage of hikers realize they're not going to make the Katahdin closing date and so to finish their hike all in one year they jump ahead to ensure they will do so. Hell On Bad Wheels said that he was back at the Maine border, which made perfect sense to me.

I passed him and impatiently started looking for the signboard at the top that proclaims the Katahdin summit, and the end of the A.T. Finally, after an interminable time and several false images, I could see the outline of the sign.

Gradually, the sign took form and I could make out its details. The sign itself has become perhaps the best-known icon of the Trail. Countless photos of hikers finishing their traverse of the A.T. have recorded emotions that rival that of the end of a war or the winning of a lottery. There are photos of people totally collapsed, others jubilant and celebratory, and yet others looking bewildered. I'd have to say I fell into the last category. I didn't quite know what to make of it. I stood there alone and didn't know whether to laugh or cry. All sorts of emotions raced through my head. Then I took out my brother Tom's Purple Heart Medal, stared at it and thanked him for pushing me to ultimately finish the hike that the two of us should have one day done together.

I put the medal away and eventually Hell On Bad Wheels showed up. He was doing his hike as a fundraiser for a good cause and had thirty signs to hold up to thank various sponsors so I took his photos with each sign so he could give them to the sponsors. This took considerable time and I was starting to shiver. The extremely high winds and near-freezing temperatures were taking their toll on me. During the photo session, New York Minute arrived and he then went through the emotional roller coaster that accompanies finishing the Appalachian Trail.

Figure 39: Terrible weather, but a wonderful finish.

New York Minute then reminded me that another hiker had recently stated that when "He got to the top and was at that sign, his hike was done, it was over, he wasn't going to hike any more." New York Minute tried to make the point to this guy that he was going to have to hike back down, but he didn't want to hear it; as far as he was concerned his "hike was over!" We discussed looking for the body since if he didn't "hike back down, he must be around here somewhere." The laugh helped take my mind off the cold but I was shivering and after a few more photos it was time to leave.

Now that the A.T. was finished we were no longer thru-hikers or long-distance hikers, we were just "section hikers" hiking back to the campground. It was over.

Epilog

Sleeping Around

One night I was sound asleep. As a rule, perhaps half the time, whether out in the woods or in a hostel, I could sleep the entire night without having to get up for a pee break. This particular night nature called about 3 a.m. I awoke and sat up, totally confused. I was indoors and in the very dim light I could make out some windows and bedroom furniture, but nothing looked familiar. My mind raced. I turned and looked into the darkness behind me and gasped; there was a woman in the bed with me! I panicked: how did she get there; was this a result of too many beers? I jumped up with a start, but she didn't move, it was then that it hit me, I was home, and that was my wife, Jane.

I highly advise any wannabe hiker to learn early on to pay close attention to where they are when they go to sleep. Practically every night you'll be sleeping in a different place, and in an emergency you need to know how to evacuate immediately. Each evening, just before going to sleep, I would do a quick check of my surroundings. My hiking pole was typically within reach just outside my exit on the hammock, as were my Crocs™ so I could slip into them for any nighttime bladder relief. My headlamp was always hanging in exactly the same place on the cross-rope and my glasses were placed in the small sack that is sewed onto the cross-rope.

Sleeping indoors at various hostels presented a different set of challenges and preparation. I would study the layout, familiarizing myself with the best exit in case of fire, make a mental note of where everyone else was sleeping so I wouldn't trip on them in the dark, stow my headlamp so I could find it in a hurry, and keep my hiking pole nearby for any unexpected altercation that might come up; fortunately, none ever did.

What Now?

Technology has changed everything in so many ways. In the early days of the trail, any friendships that formed were followed up with a letter, or maybe a telephone call. Today, every new crop of hikers is able to keep in touch with <u>trailjournals.com</u>, email, FaceBook and a host of other methods. I regularly communicate with several of my new friends from the trail and we trade photos and keep up on each other's activities. Some are planning hikes on the other two notable long-distance trails in the west, the Pacific Coast Trail and the Continental Divide Trail. Hikers that complete all three major trails have completed the "Triple Crown" of hiking. I don't plan on doing a Triple Crown; it would just take too much time out of my busy schedule. I have considered doing the Continental Divide Trail by mountain bike and hopefully will find the time and finances to do so.

What Did I Learn?

An adventure such as hiking the Appalachian Trail inevitably teaches you things. I learned, above all else, that regardless of what the popular media has to say, there are a bunch of wonderful, wholesome Americans out there. Time and again I was stunned by the generosity and openness of the people I encountered. What was most amazing is that they were all total strangers, the very people that we so often fear in our everyday lives.

Many of the trail angels that I encountered do not hike and wouldn't know a rattlesnake from a garter snake, but they did know what it takes to be a decent human being and to care about others. I will be forever grateful to those people.

Another thing that I learned was that life doesn't end when you've had heart surgery; in fact, it begins all over again. It was merely a painful bump in the road of life. This is not to trivialize heart surgery; it certainly does change your life, but that is not necessarily a bad thing.

In my case, I was in excellent overall physical condition and my lifestyle was conducive to good health. For many, this may not be the case, but all is not lost. Whatever the change is: smoking cessation, weight loss, a better diet, or exercise, it is a small price to pay for such a wonderful gift — a new life.

My life has also changed in other, more subtle ways. I take time to sleep more, I enjoy my time with friends more and I look for any excuse to goof off. I find myself less concerned with tasks that once seemed of the utmost importance; my priorities have changed.

If only my brother had been able to make the journey with me. In some ways, I suppose he did. At least in spirit and memory, with his Purple Heart Medal, his journey was completed.

As much as the heart surgery changed things, I think in some ways the hike on the Appalachian Trail may have changed me even more. I'm more conscious of the weather, my environment, and what I need to live each day. Until recently, we've had two older vehicles, a mini-van and an old pickup truck. Recently the pickup truck died and it went off to Goodwill. Something in me said "replace the truck," but another inner voice told me that I could live without it. After several months I'm finding the voice is right; I *can* live without it. I plan my days around the weather, the bicycle, and where I have to be and so far, things have worked out just fine.

Maybe I already knew I didn't need the second vehicle, but I think the trail taught me to live with less and make everything serve more than one purpose. Hopefully this book will do the same for you. I'd like to think that the reader would consider positive life changes, be it a hike, bike ride, exercise regimen, improved diet, or some other form of self-improvement. The clock is ticking; don't put it off much longer!

Hiking resources

Appalachian Trail Conservancy
http://www.appalachiantrail.org/

Trail Journals
http://www.trailjournals.com/

Trailplace, A.T. trail resources
http://www.trailplace.com/

Whiteblaze, A.T. trail resources
http://whiteblaze.net/

L. L. Bean
http://www.llbean.com/ 800-441-5713

Eastern Mountain Sports
http://www.ems.com/ 888-463-6367

Quest Outfitters (supplies for homemade gear)
http://www.questoutfitters.com/index.html
800-359-6931   (International) 1-941-923-5006

Hennessey Hammocks™
http://www.hennessyhammock.com/
(International) 1-250-539-2930

Ham radio information

American Radio Relay League	www.arrl.org
Backpack Radios	kd1jv.qrpradio.com
Call letter directory	www.qrz.com
CQ Amateur Radio Magazine	cq-amateur-radio.com
KX1 Backpack Radio	www.elecraft.com
Radio backpacking website	hfpack.com
Yaesu radio equipment	www.yaesu.com

A.T. Ham Radio repeaters
www.fred.net/kathy/at/hamguide.html

NOTE: Web addresses and email addresses have the life span of ripe bananas and may change after this printing. Any search tool should be able to locate changed addresses or check:

threehundredzeroes.com

for updates and photographs used in this book in color.

Other reading material

THRU-HIKERS COMPANION
The Appalachian Long Distance Hikers Assoc.,
http://www.aldha.org/

SKYWALKER - ISBN 1-934144-26-6
Bill Walker, Indigo Pub. Group, 2008,
http://www.skywalkerat.com/

A WALK IN THE WOODS - ISBN 0-7679-0252-1
Bill Bryson, Broadway Books, 1998,

A WALK FOR SUNSHINE - ISBN 0-9679482-2-3
Jeff Alt, Dreams Shared Publications, 2000,

IN BEAUTY MAY SHE WALK - ISBN 1889386626
Leslie Mass, Rock Spring Press, 2005,

THE MOUNTAIN MARCHING MOMAS
http://stores.lulu.com/mamas

NOT WITHOUT PERIL - ISBN 978-1-934028-32-2
Nicholas Howe, AMC Books, 2000,

Made in the USA
Lexington, KY
25 August 2010